W9-CDC-426

Other books by Frances Partridge

A PACIFIST'S WAR
LOVE IN BLOOMSBURY: MEMORIES

Julia

JULIA

A Portrait of Julia Strachey by Herself
&
FRANCES PARTRIDGE

LITTLE, BROWN AND COMPANY · BOSTON · TORONTO

LIBRARY OF CONGRESS CATALOG CARD NO. 83-081067

FIRST AMERICAN EDITION

MV

PRINTED IN THE UNITED STATES OF AMERICA

ACKNOWLEDGEMENTS

My deepest gratitude goes of course to Sir Lawrence Gowing for entrusting me with Julia's papers, and to John Russell (her literary executor) for giving me a free hand to print what I liked from them. John Lehmann has very kindly allowed me to quote at length from *Pioneer City*, one of Julia's contributions to his *New Writing*.

My particular thanks to Barbara Strachey for her invaluable and efficient help in providing letters and photographs illuminating Julia's childhood and adolescence, to Mrs Sally Toynbee for permission to print an extract from her late husband's unpublished diary, and to Dr Margaret Newman for a written memory of Julia's schooldays and some youthful letters.

For photographs I am most grateful to Barbara Ker Seymer, Sir Gilbert Debenham, Mrs Simonette Strachey. For letters I am indebted to Lord Moyne, Robert Kee, Oliver Garnett and the Hon. Laura Ponsonby; and to Heywood and Lady Anne Hill for both photographs and letters.

For permission to print extracts from Philip Toynbee's review I thank Terence Kilmartin and the *Observer*. Professor Quentin Bell and Angelica Garnett have kindly allowed me to quote from the *Diaries of Virginia Woolf*, while Anne Olivier Bell found for me Julia's unpublished Memoir Club paper *The Bathrooms in my Life*.

Others who have given much appreciated information, advice and encouragement are Mr and Mrs Robin Campbell, Gill Coleridge, Lady Mary Dunn, David Farrer, Mr and Mrs Xan Fielding, Mrs Josephine Filmer-Sankey, Rosamond Lehmann, Mrs Colin Mackenzie, Mrs Medas, Lord Milford, Stanley Olson, Mrs Janetta Parladé, Professor James M. Rendel, Dr George Rylands, and David Wolfers.

Finally I would like to thank my publishers for their patience and kindness, and Mrs Topsy Levan for her brilliant and speedy typing.

CONTENTS

ILLUSTRATIONS

Following page 154

THE FAMILY TREE OF THE STRACHEYS AND THE PEARSALL SMITHS

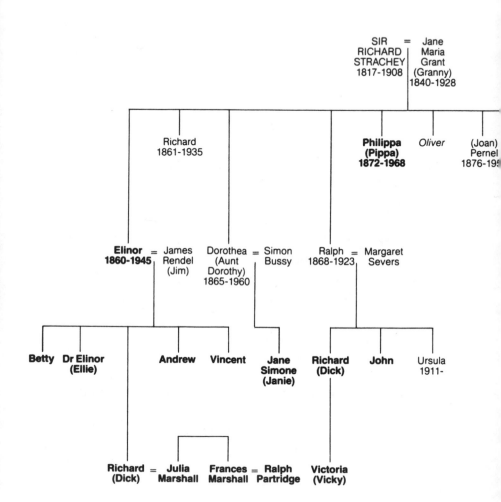

SIR = Jane
RICHARD | Maria
STRACHEY | Grant
1817-1908 | (Granny)
| 1840-1928

Richard
1861-1935

**Philippa
(Pippa)
1872-1968**

Oliver

(Joan)
Pernel
1876-19⁵

**Elinor
1860-1945** = James
Rendel
(Jim)

Dorothea
(Aunt
Dorothy)
1865-1960 = Simon
Bussy

Ralph
1868-1923 = Margaret
Severs

Betty   **Dr Elinor
(Ellie)**

Andrew   **Vincent**

**Jane
Simone
(Janie)**

**Richard
(Dick)**

John

Ursula
1911-

**Richard
(Dick)** = **Julia
Marshall**

**Frances
Marshall** = **Ralph
Partridge**

**Victoria
(Vicky)**

Names appearing in **bold** figure in the book

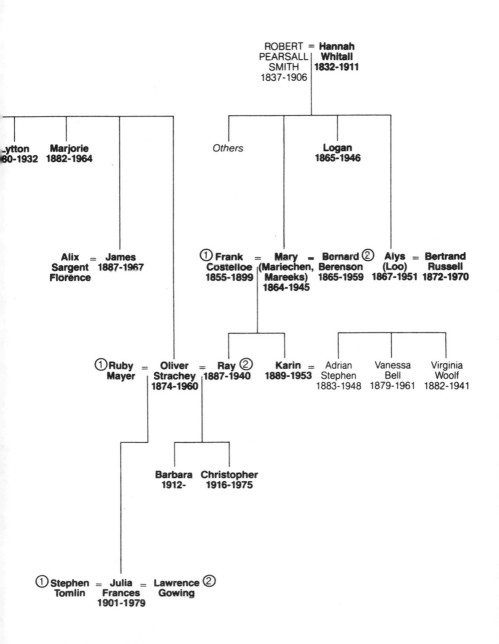

INTRODUCTION

When Julia Strachey died in 1979, after a long life centred on her vocation as a writer, it was many years since anything by her had seen the light. Anything *new*, that is to say; for her two short novels had been reprinted together in one volume by Penguin Books shortly before, when she was unfortunately too ill to appreciate the fact. On their first appearance *Cheerful Weather for the Wedding* (Hogarth Press 1932) and *The Man on the Pier** (John Lehmann 1951, recommended by the Book Society), had both been favourably received by the critics and attracted a number of addicted readers who called for more. But very little more was to come. John Lehmann included some of her stories and sketches in several issues of his *New Writing*, mostly during the forties; others appeared in the *New Statesman* and *New Yorker*.

However, Julia's friends and acquaintances knew that though two marriages and one or two briefly-held jobs occupied her front room, there was always something simmering on the stove of the kitchen behind, some concoction of ideas, images and themes to which much of her daily thoughts and conversation was devoted, and whose savour could be guessed at from the exceptional originality and humour of her letters and conversation.

Why then did she finish nothing else? She would have had no difficulty in finding a publisher. After the appearance of *Cheerful Weather*, the literary editor of the *New Yorker* wrote saying he would publish anything she cared to send him. (It was even said that her book was for a while obligatory reading for his staff.) Characteristically, Julia

---

* A title suggested by a remark of Virginia Woolf's about Henry Lamb, whom she described as "nipped, like a man on a pier". Julia had originally wanted it to be called *An Integrated Man*, and this was the title Penguin used in the reprint.

allowed over a quarter of a century to pass before she sent him anything more. Then, in 1958, he published her brilliant sketch, *Can't You Get Me Out Of Here?*.* I remember Julia's indignation when the proofs arrived with a multitude of alterations aimed at translating her text into New Yorkerese. She fought every single correction, punctuation included, giving her reasons. And she won.

Julia had, I think, a vision of herself as entangled in a web of intransigent practical circumstances created by what she liked to think of as a hostile Cosmos. Getting up in the morning, shopping, being on time—disagreeable molehills to most people—were almost unscalable mountains to her, nor do I believe she fully realised their ubiquity. Her highly critical nature (typical of the Strachey family) persuaded her that she must always aim at the highest standards, that it was in fact immoral not to do so, but when circumstances were too much for her then it was better to throw her hand in, and not aim at all. "Drop it, bad dog," was one of her favourite sayings. And she agreed with Cyril Connolly that a serious writer could only be expected to function properly in ideal circumstances—plenty of money and servants to begin with, stimulating companionship (of new as well as old friends) and a perfect climate in which there were vegetable and animal beauties to be enjoyed. (That is to say she must have blue skies, cats and growing plants.) But she appeared to believe that she was the only aspiring writer who was ever short of these blessings.

Quite late in her life, probably in her sixties, she began to write her memoirs. It was because the news leaked out that a fair amount had already been set on paper with the help of visiting typists and amanuenses that after her death I suggested to her former husband, Lawrence Gowing, that I should look through her papers and see if anything could be salvaged. He at once agreed: there were "only two cases, not very large," he said, so that my consternation was great when he staggered up my stairs carrying two *huge* suitcases, one too thick to go under my bed. On opening them, further dismay! Indeed, my first reaction was to shut them up quickly. But not for long. Inside them a *species* of order reigned, but it was reminiscent of the order of *Alice Through the Looking-Glass*. There were quantities of files, notebooks great and small, and scribbling diaries; there were packets of manu-

* Published in England as *Animalia*.

scripts—many of them typed versions of the same chapter or story with very small differences, others written in various coloured inks (whose significance was not plain) or obliterated by corrections, 'balloons', and cross-references to 'Tall Grey Diary' or 'Shiny Red Notebook', and one and all decorated with labels and more paper-clips than I ever saw in my life, never put on singly but in clusters, like barnacles on a rock. I opened some of the notebooks on whose covers such titles as 'General Cogitations', 'Memos to Self' or 'Thinking Book Chaos' were written in large capitals, and soon found myself impressed by the amount of invention, and the number of attempts at organisation that had gone into them. They were pregnant with interest and stuffed with plans, but plans that often changed in mid-stream—a man might suddenly become a woman, the third person take the place of the first, and real life turn into a play. Yet everywhere I looked my eye caught some original image or acute and comical observation that could only have been Julia's.

I felt as if I had entered a dark mine in which veins of gleaming ore were buried. But I will spare the reader the story of my excavations. Very much as an archaeologist starts scraping away at a prehistoric site, I began to piece fragments together, covering the floor of my flat with heaps of notebooks and fluttering papers as I pondered the rival qualities of different versions. Gradually the first chapters of an auto-biography emerged. Some sections were more thoroughly worked-over than the rest, others needed cutting and editing, and after Julia had passed adolescence there was a temporary break in continuity. But it was clear from her notebooks that she had intended to bring her story up to date, and further research revealed episodes from much later on in her life—dealing with her two marriages, for instance, or her hectic life in London, as well as all-too-few fragments of diaries. Could I perhaps fill the gaps from other sources, such as the innumerable letters she had written to me in the course of a lifelong friendship that began when I was nine and she eight? Could I even illuminate the scene sometimes from the wings, seeing that our paths had often fallen among the same landscapes and figures? Letters and memories might also be provided by other friends.

After much 'cogitation' and weighing-up of the material, I have therefore tried to present, as much as possible in her own words, something between a portrait and a life-story of an exceptionally original human being, someone with acute observation, analytical intelligence and a rare vein of comedy. A friend who has read what follows commented that it should be called *Julia: A Tragedy*. The foundation for this will be glimpsed in the first two chapters, yet since she also had a great gift for enjoyment, and for amusing others and exciting love and admiration, I personally feel 'a tragi-comedy' would be more appropriate. Another friend asked me, "did she herself ever really love anyone?" A difficult question—my answer was, "Infatuations apart, yes—probably two people: her mother and Lawrence."

Supposing that a fortune-teller could actually judge by examining Julia's left and right hands what she had made of her natural abilities, she might perhaps have seconded Virginia Woolf's verdict in her Diary (December 13th, 1924) that she was a "gifted wastrel". Nor was Virginia using the word 'gifted' lightly. When *Cheerful Weather* was submitted to her for publication, she wrote: "I think it astonishingly good—complete and sharp and individual," and accepted it at once. Julia had other undeveloped talents—such as a quick understanding of musical theory which never got far beyond the ragtime stage, a taste for speculation which led her to spend long hours in what she described as 'consecutive thinking', and which left its mark on her writings in some surprisingly acute notes on philosophical issues. Man's relation to the Cosmos was a concept always at the back of her mind. But to make an effort that was in itself boring, even to gain what she earnestly wanted, was impossible to Julia. The most delicious fruit might be left uneaten if difficult to peel. So that, since education involves much boring effort, what her Aunt Alys Russell said of her was in the strictest sense true: she was not educated, though she easily held her own with those who were.

She reserved her energies for things she really loved doing: she read selectively and remembered what she read, she adored animals and could watch them by the hour, but once told me she "respected them too much ever to keep one as a pet"; she was fascinated by human character and subjected her friends to a piercing searchlight; she revelled in the country but craved the stimulation only found in towns. The chief stars in her galaxy were Tchekhov, Henry James, Proust and Groucho Marx; her favourite adjectives of praise were 'stylish', 'scholarly', 'creative' and 'sophisticated'; those of disparagement 'unharmonious'—but also 'wholesome', 'golden-hearted' and 'natural'.

When not otherwise indicated (i.e. (Julia's Diary) or (Julia to F.P.)) the text can be taken as her own autobiographical writing.

My contributions vary in length from chapter to chapter according to need, and are always enclosed in square brackets [   ].

The reader must please remember that the mass of material was immense and repetitive—Julia's letters were quite often ten pages long; a great deal of cutting and editing has been necessary. I make no apology for discarding what was substandard and dispensing with 'dots', which would have been horribly distracting; but I hope I have included all that is first-rate and relevant.

Chapter One

INDIAN BUNGALOW

[Julia Strachey was born in India, in August 1901. Her father, Oliver, was the sixth child and third son of Sir Richard and Lady Strachey (née Grant of Rothiemurchus). After Eton, Oliver went to Balliol, where he acquired among other things an undeserved reputation for homosexuality, as he used to remember with loud guffaws, and was sent around the world—the prescribed cure at that time. Music was his first love, but he never reached a high enough standard to become a professional pianist, so that the job which took him to Allahabad was something of a *pis-aller*. Here he met and married a lovely, young and somewhat flighty German-Swiss girl called Ruby Mayer. Oliver's marriage did not meet with great approval from his parents, but his favourite sister Pippa travelled to India, partly to go on the usual sight-seeing round and partly to visit the little family. She wrote home, "The more I see of Ruby the more fond I become of her. She is *very* pretty indeed and dresses charmingly, and it is a sweet sight to see her with her babe." Oliver, Ruby and Julia visited the Stracheys in London when Julia was about three.]

I remember, when I was four years old, how the Indian sunlight echoed and reflected itself all day long about the white-walled rooms of our small bungalow home on the outskirts of Allahabad. And this despite the Venetian blinds drawn down at all times, from ceiling to floor, over the long French windows. In the middle of the sitting-room stood the phonograph with its huge trumpet horn, attached to which, in a small box, lived the friendly man who seemed always ready to sing the songs I asked him for—except at those moments when my father and mother declared: "No! No, dear! No more songs just now! Later on, maybe." At which I supposed that the amiable gentleman who lived inside this six-inch box was probably eating his lunch at the moment, or having an afternoon nap, and so was unable to oblige.

My father, Oliver Strachey (an older brother of Lytton Strachey the biographer) used to sit at the upright piano in the sitting-room corner, and play Schubert and Bach and Mozart and many others, the very moment he returned from his office in Allahabad at the end of each day. Though at weekends, when he was free, he began to play immediately after he had finished breakfast. I would watch my father's back seated at the piano, and his jumping fingers, as I perched in one of the cretonne-covered armchairs (on to the seats of which I had to be ready to leap at a second's notice, when from time to time the cry rang out in my mother's voice from an adjoining room: "Stand up on the seat of your chair! Quick! Quick! Quick! *And don't jump down again until I tell you!*").

This meant that I would see a snake, which had illicitly entered our bungalow from the garden, go speeding across the rush-matting sitting-room carpet straightened out like an express train, without any of those wavering, side-slipping, coiling movements such as the snakes we see in our English zoos go in for. It would be travelling from the curtained bedroom doorway on one side of the sitting-room, directly and straight as an arrow, to the central arch in the far wall which led out on to the yard at the back. The serpent would travel in a most businesslike and purposeful way, looking neither to right nor to left. He had, I think, simply taken a time-saving short-cut from our front garden straight through our house and out again to the yard at the back, where no doubt he had pressing business. Certainly I never saw one of our snakes linger or dally about, or take the slightest interest in any of the human inhabitants of the bungalow who might chance to be trespassing across his right-of-way to the back-yard. Because of their indifference towards us I was not at all frightened of our snakes at that time.

I remember the tropic glare from the outdoor world flashing and rebounding off all the furniture, especially off the circular Indian-carved trays of solid brass as wide across as open umbrellas, that rested on their short ebony trestle legs, and upon which we, like everyone else in those parts, used to put the afternoon tea-cups and the plates of sandwiches. From time to time this bright tropical light would show up the odd animal 'stray'—a panic-struck lizard, or a black spider, hoping to escape notice by hunching up in the shadow cast by an armchair.

Once I saw revealed, squatting in the centre of the floor of the bedroom shared by my mother and me, a big, portly, indelicately-shaped frog, who with mouth gaping wide open sat there belching and blinking and coughing and trying to haul up a long, wriggling worm's length into its mouth so as to get it down into its stomach once and for all. (Or maybe sick it up again and get rid of the thing in that way—who could tell?)

Anyway, both creatures looked trapped in this situation of dire trouble, and they, I, and everybody else saw that there was no way to rescue them.

In fact at that moment I was a witness, all unaware, at any rate *consciously* unaware of a kind of fable being enacted in the bedroom: an unlucky frog whose eyes had been 'larger than his stomach' as the saying is, in the act of paying the frightful penalty resultant upon blindly following one of the strongest compulsions with which nature had landed him—with which indeed she has landed us all—the compulsion daily to devour (in every sense) another living creature like oneself, with the victim twisting and struggling to escape all the time; while the Universe, brainless and heartless, stands by as the agony proceeds, with total indifference.

But I've gone off the track.

What I had *intended* to convey about my earliest years was simply what a perfect paradise family life in our Indian bungalow had seemed to be! Let me rather then proceed along those lines.

Aged four, I was deeply in love with my mother. And I also adored my father.

My father seemed to me a person in very good heart, in that he was so full of fun, always ready with comic rhymes, riddles, stories and songs; always ready to whirl me around through the air—either high up at shoulder level, or else boatwise—gripped by both my wrists and ankles together, swinging backwards and forwards beneath the bridge made by his long scissor legs as they straddled wide apart on the hearth-rug.

One day I wandered into a vast apartment, or so it seemed to me, next door to the dining-room and normally out of bounds. As I entered I beheld to my surprise, at the far end on a kind of platform, my papa, usually so elegant in his stiff white drill suit and solar topee—standing now, a new colour (a brilliant crayfish pink) in the middle of a sort of

local monsoon, with torrents of water descending in needle sprays upon
his head. I had never seen him in the altogether before—didn't even
take in that that was what it was, and the scene was so unexpected that I
must have stood there gaping, no doubt with the door wide open into
the central dining-room; at any rate I heard shouts from under the
waters telling me to go out again and shut the door.

How could I guess that my Papa—that jovial omnipotent God—was
in reality a frustrated and deeply disappointed man? A man whose
main passion in life was music, but who, having studied for several
years in Vienna with the ambition to be a professional concert pianist,
had finally felt at the end of the day that he simply wasn't good enough.
And so who, having lately fallen in love and got married (and rather
suddenly being made aware that there was a child upon the way and he
with no money to support a family) had of necessity accepted the offer of
the steady, but uncongenial job of Traffic Superintendent with the East
India Railway Company that had been held out to him in the nick of
time.

The offer of the post on the railway had come about in this manner:
ever since that day in the 18th century when a Strachey ancestor had
first accompanied Lord Clive to India as his private secretary, the
Strachey family, in its many branches, had taken a particular interest in
India. Great-uncles, second-cousins-once-removed, their brothers and
their nephews, had spent, and continued to spend, most of their lives
working in various posts on the sub-continent. My grandpapa, Lieute-
nant-General Sir Richard Strachey, though an old man at the time of
my father's marriage and by then already retired, had earlier on spent
thirty hard-working years in India, in a variety of administrative posts
under the British Raj. Amongst others, that of Chairman of the East
India Railway Company. No doubt he had arranged for his son Oliver
(my Papa) to be offered the job of District Traffic Superintendent on
India's Main Northern line, with an office in Allahabad, near to which
stood the little family bungalow of which I write, and in which I lived
the first four years of my life. It was a pity that my father, like the other
younger members of the Strachey family, had already started to rebel
against The Establishment, as we now call it, and so could only feel that
he had had very bad luck indeed in being forced into this dismal
straight-jacket of a job on the railway under the British Raj.

It wasn't so much the work itself that my father disliked—grappling with the railroad's finances, passenger and freight charges, upkeep of the railway buildings, engines and carriages and seeing to the time-tables and the correct running of the trains; nor even the more inter-esting task of coping with the complaints of the native railway employees and smoothing out their personal and family troubles, for they relied, child-like, on a paternal element, and a kind of family-cherishing-protection from their bosses. And he also had a number of rather unexpected problems to deal with—as for instance when an elephant from the nearby jungle strolled out one day to look the station over, and seemingly becoming fascinated by the whole set-up, seated himself comfortably upon the railway line between the platforms, the better to keep an eye upon the station's proceedings, and thereafter obstinately resisted all attempts to dislodge him, either by main force or by guile, thus preventing any trains from entering the station for many days and nights together. Such incidents entertained my Papa and helped to break the monotony of his daily routine.

No, it was not the *work* so much of which he complained. It was the company of his British neighbours. For he had no option but to foregather with a kind of British society—army men and various Civil Servants with their philistine wives—to which he was totally unsuited. Many were the letters he wrote back to his friends in England, and to his family in far-away Lancaster Gate, telling everybody how much he envied his brother Lytton, because he was free, was able to live a civilised life devoted to writing and literature and with no obligations to anyone else. As a confirmed bachelor, with no wife and family to support, Lytton was able to spend his whole time, the lucky devil, cavorting with poets, painters, philosophers, scientists, economists, musicians, and the like; while he, Oliver, was compelled to mingle with people who had never once opened a book in the whole of their lives!

Neither was this envy of Lytton my father's only trouble. It now appears that in our little bungalow—which seemed to me such a haven of paradisaical peace and joy—a series of violent marital storms and tempests were going on all the while, of which my mother—many years later and after I had grown up—gave me a most graphic, not to say fabulous, picture. (My mother's accounts of things were always graphic and fabulous.) Talking about those years, she declared that my father's mistresses had often come to stay at the bungalow, turning her and myself out of our bedroom and forcing us both to sleep outside on the verandah. Also compelling her to serve early morning tea to my father and his visiting mistress, as they lay taking their ease in their bed. Many years later, I also heard the *other* side—my father's version of their quarrels—the tale of all my *mother's* lovers, and how shockingly she behaved over these matters herself. I could not find any common ground of fact at all, I confess, between any of the stories related by my parents. In point of fact, I have never been able, when two quarrelling lovers each tell me their stories separately, to see any coincidental truth between their tales! And as at the time that all of this was apparently going on I was not in a position to perceive any more Reality than a chicken does before it has broken out of its protective shell, the true story of what went wrong in the adult life in that Indian bungalow will never be known.

As I mentioned, I adored my Papa and was deeply in love with my mother.

In the gruelling Indian heat and dazzling light, my mother, an unusually pretty girl of twenty-two or so, went around looking like some kind of a wonderful half-butterfly, half-multi-coloured flower, with her swirling skirts of muslin figured with patterns of immense roses or hibiscus blossoms coloured brilliant pink or cinnamon, and with the dress-hems lavishly befrilled and flounced; while the whole package, so to speak, with my mother folded into the centre, was tied up and drawn very very tight half-way up, to make an elegant insect waist, around which would be twisted pink or blue or apple-green silk sashes, the long ends of which were left floating and rippling out behind, as was then the fashion. Being in love, I was totally involved in every smallest detail of my mother's *charisma*. An important part of my day was spent watching the techniques that she practised in front of the dressing-table looking-glass in the bedroom we shared, and which helped her gain such triumphant results. I would watch wide-eyed and entranced in the early morning—or in the evening if she was going out to dine—as she dressed herself, and performed her toilet, rolling up her long yellow hair into multitudes of shiny 'snail-shells' as we called them, and pinning these all up on to the crest of her upswept 'hair-do' in a gold coronet.

In the daytime, however, my mother's chief glory was her white lace parasol, flounced all over and ornamented with sundry ribbon bows; it bestowed an ethereal air upon her in my eyes, so that I verily considered she resembled the Fairy Queen herself. No less! The Fairy

Queen, I should explain, was the *only* celestial or extra-terrestrial being I had ever heard tell of; for my father, a Militant Atheist if ever there was one, never permitted the words 'God', 'Jesus Christ', 'Virgin Mary' or 'Holy Ghost' to sully his lips. His conscience did not consider it permissible for these corrupt illusions to be so much as *mentioned* in the presence of an innocent child such as myself. Nevertheless, following the tendency shown by the human species to communicate in moments of emotion with some all-powerful, unseen but Gracious Divinities, I would often confide certain strong feelings in my private heart to this same Fairy Queen, sometimes thanking her warmly for delights which she had obviously provided just for me—such as sending a cloud of coloured fireflies to spangle the night-air around my head as I stood on the edge of the verandah at bedtime.

One of my memories of our early life in India was the humiliation caused me by my own attire designed against the heat—cotton pants and vests—and my yearning to join the grown-ups, and emulate the glorious and fashionable *frou-frou* made by their multitudinous lace petticoats ever murmuring in concert with all the other different ruched and frilled under- and over-skirts, whenever my mother or her lady visitors moved about the place. But one afternoon I had a brain-wave. I saw how I, too, could join their sophisticated ranks and become a fashionable lady! Accordingly I went to the lavatory, and tearing off handfuls of crisp paper from the toilet roll I bunched them all around my knees, fixing them beneath my elastic garters to hold them safely in place. I then emerged from the lavatory, and strutted triumphantly round and round the house, touring through all the rooms, raising my knees at each step like a circus pony in order to get full value from the modish crunchy sound as the brittle toilet-roll papers, sticking out every whichway from under my garters (yet hidden from sight under my pinafore) rasped abrasively against each other, and crackled at every movement I made. In this way I was enabled to feel that I had indeed become a fully sophisticated grown-up female at last!

I remember how everyone in the rooms through which I passed stopped dead in their tracks, turned their heads, and stared at me with bulging eyes—the noise of the crackling I made was so great.

I remember my father's face of astonishment in particular. As I passed him by: ". . . What on EARTH—! What in the *world*—? My dear, what *have* you got there? Lift up your pinafore for a moment . . ."

I did so. Revealing all. As he then looked more mystified than ever, I explained matters in a single sentence: "I am a Lady Walking About!"

It dawned on me one morning that my father seemed to be taking a holiday, for I noticed he was staying all day long at home, instead of leaving for the Allahabad Station.

Usually after breakfast he went off to work, wearing his white drill jacket and trousers and his solar topee—more of a helmet than a hat, with its strap running down beneath the chin, and its cloth lining of dark green.

But that morning he remained wrapped in his purple satin dressing-gown, and sitting on the piano stool started playing Bach, Schumann, Schubert, Mozart and all such things, from time to time singing German songs in what he referred to as his 'corn-crake' voice. All his life he never spent his free hours in any other way than this.

My mother told me presently that it was my father's birthday, and that *that* was why he was taking the day off from the office.

Hearing this, "I shall prepare a secret birthday present for my Papa!" I thought. "I will do a splendiferous drawing of some sort for him, as a birthday surprise!" I intended giving him a right royal birthday.

I went off into his bedroom. I looked around. Spotted a large, unused, virgin-white blotting-paper pad lying on the desk there—the very thing! What could give Papa more pleasure than finding a marvellous picture decorating this otherwise quite featureless, humdrum, blank white pad?

I went off and fetched into his bedroom my box of coloured chalks. And now, using as many colours as I could, I proceeded to draw on the great white blotting-paper pad a picture of our bungalow, with its many windows; of our garden outside also, with its tiger-lilies and all the other flowers; and the round stone 'stoep' (a raised circular stone platform at that time found in every Anglo-Indian bungalow garden, upon which deckchairs were placed, so that people could sit up there and chat as the cool of the evening dusk came down, well out of reach of spiders, serpents, lizards, scorpions, and all other tropical creepy-crawly things). So on my blotting-pad drawing I showed this 'stoep' and all around it our little garden's winding paths. Then I drew the long verandah running outside the front of the bungalow, with its numerous parakeets and parrots in their cages hanging from the ceiling. I showed also how these bird-cages were interspersed with all manner of green ferns cascading down from swinging baskets, with brilliant flowers in between. I drew every single one of the cages and baskets which hung along the length of the verandah ceiling.

Next, I drew in all the people who spent their days on our verandah; the journey-men tailors sitting cross-legged, wonderfully turbaned, as they sewed; the chattering Indian cooks; the ayahs in their brilliant coloured saris; the visiting gardeners, and the bashfully giggling working-girls. In fact I drew every single thing I knew was outside the window in my brightly-coloured chalks. To crown all I drew a portrait of my Papa standing indoors looking out of the window at all these interesting things. Then it struck me that it was necessary somehow to make it clear that Papa was indeed *looking* at all these multifarious things. Not simply just *standing* there. But how to do that?

I stopped and thought for a moment. Then inspiration came.

In order to make a clear connection between my father's eyes and all the things in the garden and verandah, I took my chalks and gave him a bunch of immensely long, tubular necks, rising up all together from his shoulders, each neck stretching forth and shooting far out of the window and downwards into the garden, and each neck with his own head on the end of it, with the face and eyes actually touching one or other of the flowers, or a cage of parakeets, or a tailor, or a gossiping ayah out on the verandah. Every inch of the blotting-pad was covered in the end. Then with what pride I stood back and looked at all those long winding necks, and at all the heads with their big staring eyes— each making physical contact so effectually with the world outside!

I finished my drawing. And glowing with good will and not a little pride, to say the least, at the magnificence of my birthday present— which my Papa would be sure to discover later in the day, when he would certainly be overcome with delight and admiration and gratefulness—I gathered up my coloured chalks and ran back into the sitting-room, though without saying a word to anyone about the drawing. It was my wonderful secret—dedicated to Papa.

I went and stood beside the upright piano, where Papa was playing away and singing as usual. I watched his fingers hopping about over the white and black keys. I stared up at his dark olive-skinned face with the sweat pouring down it. He was playing one of the complicated pieces which I have sometimes in much later years heard him refer to as

"sewing-machine music" (Bach, in other words; or other music somewhat in the same style). When Papa became aware of me, his fingers
stopped still on the keys.

"What shall we play now?" he asked. "Would you like a song?"

I nodded.

"What song?"

I named one of my favourites among the popular music-hall songs
that he had taught me. "Hello! Hello! Hello!"

"Very well. *I'll* play. *You* sing," he replied, and off we went:

> —"Hello! *Hello*! HELLO!
> —It's a different girl again!
> Different Eyes!
> Different Nose!
> Different Hair!
> Different Clothes!
> —It's a different girl again!
> —You've tickled the lady's fancy-dress—it's
> A *Different* Girl AGAIN!!!"

"Not 'tickled the lady's fancy-*dress*,' my dear, but 'You've tickled the
lady's fancy,'" my father as usual expostulated, for this is how I always
sang the song. But I was by then unheedingly capering around the
room in full throat, shouting out the song and miming it with wild
gestures. In any case I didn't believe him about tickling a lady's
'fancy'—whatever that might mean. For I knew very well, from
personal experience, the kind of tickling that could well accompany
putting on a 'fancy dress' for a party.

My mother meanwhile had told my Papa that he should go to his
bedroom, get out of his purple satin dressing-gown, and dress himself
respectably, as some visitors were expected for luncheon—and that
very shortly.

I went on prancing around the room singing, "Hello! Hello! Hello!",
so absorbed by my own antics that I was greatly startled a few minutes
later when my father strode back into the room and, coming up to me,
cried out, "You're a very naughty little girl indeed! What's this you've
been doing—scribbling with your chalks absolutely all over my clean
fresh blotting-pad! *You're not allowed into my bedroom to fidget with my things!*
How many times have I told you? Ruby" (my mother's name), "she's

made the most awful mess with her chalks and pencils all over my nice clean blotting-pad!" He turned back to me.

"Never, *never* do such a thing again, I'm extremely vexed with you!" He looked at me indignantly for a second, then swung about and strode out of the sitting-room.

What an unexpected snub! I could hardly believe my ears. How was it possible that he had not been delighted by such an interesting picture, had not been touched either by my thoughtfulness, had not admired my great skill in making him such a wonderful birthday present? And all that trouble I had taken in getting the different long lengths of tubular necks to stream out in every direction from the windows! All wasted.

My mother turned around and asked me reproachfully: "What made you do such a thing? Scribbling all over your father's beautiful clean blotting-pad! How often—"

Then she stopped short, probably seeing my face crumple up in surprise and dismay, and noticing the shock of humiliation causing my cheeks to flame and the tears to roll.

I explained that what I had done to the blotting-pad was in fact Papa's BIRTHDAY PRESENT from me. That I thought he'd be *pleased* to have it on his blotting-pad. I explained to my mother that what I had made was a portrait of Papa himself looking out of the window at all the things in the garden and on the verandah and all at one time.

"Oh, I *see*—you did it especially for a birthday present for Papa! Oh, he didn't know *that*. . . Wait a minute—I'll go and explain . . ." She ran out of the room to tell him.

In a minute or two all had been put right.

My father came back and apologised to me for his mistake.

"Of course if I had known it was a *birthday* present . . . ! But I had *no* idea!" And he thanked me greatly for the magnificent picture I had made for him.

I shall never forget the afternoon when I got my first sight of a cobra.

I was walking with my parents along a path that ran beside railings to the railway station. An old man holding a flute was squatting beside the path. On the ground beside him stood a tall rush-plaited basket with no lid to it. Only a narrow hole at the top. As we neared him the old man raised the flute to his lips and started playing a slow, rhythmical tune upon it. My parents, who recognised that a snake-charming performance was about to begin, came to a halt in front of the old fellow, thinking no doubt that the coming entertainment would delight me.

"Oh look, Ju! Look, look . . . you must see this!"

I looked and saw the neat little head of a serpent rise up with slow elegance from out the aperture at the top of the basket. As it rose ever higher and higher, the serpent started swaying his glittering black length languidly from side to side in time to the flute music.

Had this been all of the performance I should have been well satisfied. But no! This kind of snake (which I had not come across before, and whose name of course was Cobra) had a peculiar—an exceptional—talent. I soon noticed that while the creature was so gracefully swaying from side to side to the rhythm of the flute, something weird and uncanny was happening at the same time. The narrow neat head began puffing itself out sideways—more and more and more. And still the head continued to swell! It was like a nightmare. It swelled. And swelled. And swelled. Changing its shape, changing its size, swelling larger and LARGER, ballooning itself up into the most infernal puffery—it became a black and glittering dinner plate, a grotesque deformity. Meanwhile a baleful hook-and-eye design began to manifest itself, slashed out big and bold across the snake's weirdly transformed head (if head it could still be called, for it had now reached unrecognisable proportions). I had never seen anything like this happen before. And now the monstrous shape began hollowing and caving itself in, in a most uncanny way. Then I noticed with a start how its own former little modest snake face with the small beady eyes was now to be seen perched high up on the very *top* of this new giant face!

I had never before seen a spectacle so wicked and ferocious, so full of evil intent. I recognised Black Magic. A Demon casting straight at us a destructive spell. My heart twisted over and plummeted down into my boots, for I grasped intuitively that this crazed thing was actively menacing me, that all its abnormal contortions were aimed at destroying me!

"There's nothing to be afraid of! It's only dancing!" my mother and father tried to reassure me, looking down and seeing me between them in floods of tears.

Dancing it may have been! But this was plainly a ritual Dance of Death! And what can you do against that?

It was not so much from fear that I wept. My feeling was a sense of bottomless desolation, a kind of Cosmic Despair, at discovering that there existed a being so malignant, a living thing of a ferocity that I had never as yet suspected or could ever have imagined, a creature of such total estrangement from the genial world that I knew.

This was the first moment in my life, I suppose, that I experienced, deep in the marrow of my bones, that truth which, many years later, I was to come across in Shakespeare, where the poet warns:

"The World is not thy friend."

A child of four goes along as it were in blinkers; she cannot of course perceive, and is not interested in, the logical sequences of the real world about her, she is so occupied in dealing with the violence of her own emotions, that she notices nothing of the state of mind or feeling of her elders—unless these feelings are aimed explicitly at her for some purpose. She understands, and most feelingly, the tragedies and adventures of the characters in the mythical or magical tales that are related or read aloud to her. However, of the fact that just such tragedies— fights, triumphs, and despairing defeats are proceeding all the while in full spate between one grown-up and another in the circle that daily surrounds her—of this she is quite unaware.

If I had only known of the dangerous tempests and earthquakes that were at this very moment threatening the whole fabric of our family home, which had always seemed to me to be such a Paradise, and were indeed finally to shatter it utterly! What then?

But I knew nothing of all this. And no doubt that was just as well.

Just as I adored my father and mother, so I trusted them completely. I no more dreamed that they would conspire together secretly to send me away from them to the other side of the world where I could no longer see or talk with them, than I dreamed that they would unexpectedly turn round upon me and cut off my head.

When they actually did so, I did not at first understand that life was over and finished (that's to say life which I recognised as such).

It happened as a result of excellent intentions on their part, I'm sure. (After all, this was long, long before the days when psychologists wrote of the lasting damage that a broken home could do to a young child.) There was a common idea in the English Colonies at that time that when the man of the family had to stay abroad in some Government job, it was important, and for the children's good, to send them back home to England to be educated and live among civilised people and get used to the culture from which the family had sprung. I was certainly not the only little girl to be so treated by any means. But in my own case my departure happened to coincide with the break-up of my parents' marriage. Of which I suspected nothing.

I was five years old when the guillotine fell and it came about that I was despatched all unsuspecting, and without explanation, in a P. & O. liner pointed in the direction of England. I was not required to make the journey alone, of course. From Rome onwards I had as escort the amiable Mabel, a temporary nursemaid hired specially for the last lap of the trip. And as far as Rome itself, I was in the congenial company of my mother herself.

In Rome we halted our journey for several weeks. That was to enable my mother to conclude some 'unfinished business' that she had, of a very personal and private nature. And this business she did sure enough conclude—secretly, in a maternity home run by a company of nursing nuns in one of the Roman suburbs. It was from a bed in that convent nursing-home-cum-hotel that my mother waved her last good-bye to me. Though I had no idea at the time that it was, in fact, the final "Goodbye" of all.

I remember the farewell scene clearly; my mother waving to Mabel and myself and sitting up smiling in her bed. She had the small cot beside her in which lay her newly-born babe (a being to whom I had taken an instant dislike at sight).

So here stood Mabel and myself, gloved, hatted, and coated for the journey back to England, and as we made for the bedroom door my mother kept repeating that it wouldn't be long before she would be following us (together with my so-unpleasing new brother) and rejoining me in England. Mabel and I had arrived upon the threshold and were about to step out into the passage, when my mother called out—addressing me personally—and begged me to give her a solemn promise that I would never, under any circumstances whatever after my arrival in England "eat any bad bacon." "I have heard about a lot of harm coming to people in England from that," she said. I stopped, turned around. And though I believe that at that juncture I had no idea what a rasher of bacon looked like, I gave my solemn promise to this startling and mystifying request. She must have noticed the blank incomprehension on my face, for as I turned back in the doorway and moved into the passage, I heard her explain: "There can be a lot of horrid little things creeping about inside!"

On this we parted—I not dreaming that I had at that very moment lost my beloved mother for ever.

[Oliver was clever, charming, idle and self-indulgent; his chief distinction was gained as an expert in the cipher department of the Foreign Office in both World Wars. But as he will figure a good deal in what follows there is no need to say more about him here. Ruby's case is different, for this chapter contains her first and last personal appearance. Julia seldom talked about her mother during our childhood friendship. Later on she referred to her own rejection by Ruby as a shattering blow from which she never recovered. But never, to me at least, did she paint the attractive portrait of her in words she gives us here.

I must explain that the baby boy, whose arrival in the Roman hospital brings this chapter to a close, was not Oliver's son, nor yet the son of any of Ruby's subsequent three husbands. When grown-up he was told by his mother that his real name was Strachey (as presumably it *legally* was), and sent home to England to present himself to Oliver, who called upon Julia for help.

"My dear, *I* can't deal with this," he said. "You must break it to him that I'm not his father." Julia did so, and tried her best to be kind and helpful to her half-brother. The last news she had of the unfortunate boy came in a letter bearing an imposing crest, which was delivered to her when she was staying with us at Ham Spray.

"I wonder who *this* can be from," she mused happily. Then, on opening it: "Oh—it's from Cardiff Gaol, from my brother. Oh dear! Now what does one send someone in prison? Magazines? Cigarettes?"

Julia says she "lost her beloved mother when she was five", and this is in a real sense true. But several existing letters from Ruby bear witness to meetings between them in the thirties—meetings which Julia described at the time as "acutely embarrassing. I felt she had nothing whatever to do with me." Ruby's letters are dull and rather foolish, though they express obvious affection: "I have never stopped caring for you. I lost you, my only girl. Poor little Julia. You are so beautiful and charming." She writes vindictively and at length about Oliver, claiming that he was cruel (unlikely) and unfaithful (probable). "Then I allowed someone to make love to me—he was the most heavenly handsome creature I've ever seen. Hundreds of men had tried to make love to me." And she describes her current husband as "a very gay lad and a marvellous polo-player".

Oliver once told me that he had met Ruby in a London music-hall many years after their divorce, and felt pleased to see her. "Why, Ruby, you've done very well," he said to her. "You've had five children by four men, haven't you?" "By *five* men, Oliver, but don't tell George."]

Chapter Two

MELBURY ROAD

The Northern winter was coming on when I arrived for the first time in London from India. I was just six years old.

I had been packed off to travel half across the globe, bundled away from my well-loved home in my parents' bungalow, to be boarded out with an old English aunt, in order to be turned into a civilised, hard-working, dowdy English lady like all my other Strachey aunts. That was at any rate the idea. How could anyone have guessed that I was not built of the same material as my Strachey relations in England, but was to turn out to be, as Virginia Woolf was later to dub me, teasingly but to my face, "the black sheep of the family"?

My parents did not accompany me back to England. My father could not at the time leave his Civil Service job under the British Raj. As for my mother, over *her* butterfly movements from one place to another, always accompanied by some handsome, adoring gentleman, it might be well to draw a veil. Meanwhile I was escorted to England and London by Mabel, the young and pretty, good-natured, smiling nursemaid, hired specifically for that journey—and for that journey alone. Mabel duly delivered me, parcel-wise, into the hands of my ancient— and so far unknown—Aunt Elinor Rendel, who lived in a large house close to England's Kensington High Street in a road running out at right angles from it: Melbury Road. We had driven from the station of our London arrival in a four-wheeler cab—a 'fly' as they were then called. When this vehicle arrived in Melbury Road, and stopped in front of a tall wrought-iron gate, Mabel jumped me out on to the pavement and paid off the driver. Then she took my hand, pushed open the gate and led me across a red-tiled courtyard of considerable size. I heard later that the house had belonged to the painter G. F. Watts.

After opening my aunt's front door to Mabel and myself, the

parlourmaid took us across a chequered marble front hall, down a long corridor and on and up the steep stair to the top floor, where she led us to what was called the Old Nursery. Here we were greeted by the Scotch nanny—an ancient crone who had had the care down many long years of my five Rendel cousins, now almost all of them grown up. One only, still in his teens, was at the time I arrived with Mabel away at his public school.

I shall not forget the unaccustomed shock of this institutionalised nursery. Nor the dazzling electric light bulb, unshaded, over-bright, and drawn far too close down to the table-top from the ceiling above— old Nanny's eye-sight being none too good. I had never seen anything like this kind of room before in my life. At home, back in India, I had taken my tea as a matter of course together with my father and mother in our bungalow drawing-room, perched beside them on the sofa, chattering at ease with them as I nibbled a cucumber sandwich and some hot buttered toast. But here, on the great Melbury Road nursery table, high of leg, its top a wide, spreading expanse of desolation, there was only a great block of white English bread all in one piece, and beside it a glass pot straight from the grocer's counter of some sort of black stuff, which I learned later was called bramble jam.

My Aunt Elinor's house was a lordly, towering mansion; to me it seemed strange, weird, abnormal, and quite dismally unlike our gay little Indian bungalow. The yellow foggy London air—the Victorian industrial smog which at that period had not abated—stared in at the windows of her dark, high-ceilinged, silent and empty-seeming rooms, so that they appeared to be illuminated all through by a dark spectral glare—even in the mornings.

I had never before lived in a proper 'house'—a building with several floors to it. The walls of the winding staircase at Melbury Road rose up, up and up, between high cliff-sides lined with what seemed like the wings of large beetles, but which were in reality dark iridescent tiles of deepest peacock-blue—shiny, cold to the touch, inflicting the sensation that one was clambering about at the bottom of the sea. As one floundered one's way upstairs, an Art-Nouveau lizard would manifest itself from time to time, crawling across one of the cold sea-walls. Or it might be a horned toad resting beside an iris; or a salamander peeping around a water-lily. (I was told years later that these decorative tiles had been designed by the artist Walter Crane himself.) However, to me at the age of six the entire building from basement to roof-top seemed to be labouring under some powerful witches' spell. I had come across just such curses in my fairy-story books; and I could only surmise that I had been somehow kidnapped and spirited away in my sleep from my parents by one of those same witches, to be imprisoned for evermore in this Northern Palace of Doom. And I wasn't far wrong at that.

The writer Adrian Stokes has described human beings as being like coral reefs: "We have each," he says, "absorbed organisms and pieced them together. We partake of whom and of what we love, of whom we abhor no less."

My own personal coral reef had been built up till that moment of the clear, strong Indian sunlight, of smiling faces, and human appreciation; of the murmurous chatteration of turbaned Indians, flirting with the giggling native servant girls; of the bold squawks and husky snuffles and sneezes and insolent whistlings of parrots, and the everlasting "squeak, squeak, squeak" of the punkahs fanning our sitting-room air all day long to keep it cool.

Neither were my mother and I silent for long at a time. My mother used tirelessly to tell me stories, teach me rhymes, sing me songs, and discuss her plans for driving out in the carriage in the afternoons to return the calls of her neighbours. Or again she would open her box of paints and her sketch book, and show me the different pictures she had painted of the native families and their children, who all lived together in a kind of encampment called the 'compound', out at the back.

All this would be accompanied by the various songs relayed from the giant trumpet of our sitting-room phonograph. Furthermore, whenever the verandah parrots heard music floating out from within, it would send them into an orgy of hysterical flappings and hoppings as they endeavoured to join in with the music. In the hot scented dusk of the evening, when the journeyman tailors and the daily gardeners and punkah boys had gone home, my father, newly returned from his office in the town, would start playing the piano. But by that time the verandah birds would have fallen asleep, and made no further ripostes. So that in one way or another, in my former home I had been accustomed to a companionable tintinnabulation of variegated sounds and movements all day long, betokening the pullulating congregation of living beings, all very much alive, whatever their race, creed, shape, size of beak, species, colour of wings—or any other feature. How totally different was the eerie upper-class silence, the English inward-turning reserve, and the clammy muffling fog everywhere, that I found in this new civilisation at the house in Melbury Road!

And Aunt Elinor Rendel was no chatterer. Remote, intellectual-looking. Unsmiling and totally unhuggable. The possessor of a hard, high, grating and unlovely voice.

However, during the daytime I existed on the top floor of the tall house in the 'old nursery', and it turned out that I saw my Aunt virtually for only one hour a day, between six o'clock and seven o'clock in the evening. At which time, after having had my hair carefully brushed and combed and my face and hands washed, and a clean starchy white pinafore adorned with pleated butterfly-winged shoulder frills tied on to me by old Nanny, I was escorted downstairs to join my Aunt in her vast drawing-room, with its Burne-Jones paintings, its old leather-bound books, its ruched screens, and its grand piano, in order to have read aloud to me another chapter of some good book she had selected for my edification. Apart from that one evening hour, my life was spent entirely in the upstairs nursery in the company of old Nanny, an unbelievably repressive and grim beldame.

Old Scotch Nanny was granite-faced, even granite-souled. A Presbyterian fanatic. After having been accustomed to the daylong company of my laughing and chattering young mother, who had always made such a fuss of me in our Indian bungalow, and of my Papa who used to play the piano to me and teach me to sing the comic musical songs of the day as long as he was at home, judge of my surprise— indeed amazement—when I found that the old Scottish Nanny at Melbury Road refused, but refused *absolutely*, to talk with me at all! *Ever at all!*

I couldn't understand it, was mystified.

Day followed day, and still she wouldn't speak, or even answer me! Whenever I started, after my natural habit, to chatter away to her, she received each and every remark in dead silence, always wearing on her face a look of barely repressed hostility, something that was as novel to me as was the foggy London air. I shall never understand, and always fear, those people who allow one's remarks to float out upon the air unanswered, who fail to put down the drawbridge, and come out on it to welcome and meet their neighbours half-way.

I was told, many years later, that before unexpectedly hearing of my imminent arrival on the scene, the exhausted old Scotswoman had been greatly looking forward (after a long and strenuous nursery life taking care of my five cousins) to ending her days at long last in deserved comfort, rest, and peace—waited upon hand and foot by the kitchen-maids from the basement below stairs—something which I believe she had been promised. And to sitting beside the nursery fender and giving her full attention at last to her great love—the Bible.

Imagine how disappointed and embittered the tired old woman must have felt on being at the very last moment, and without warning, landed with a stranger, an ignorant child, and what was worse, a hopeless Barbarian, one who not only hadn't the faintest idea of what 'saying your prayers' was, but who had never even *heard* of Jesus Christ, let alone the 'Almighty'!

However, Nanny knew her duty, and set to work at once, first telling me about Heaven and the rest and then trying to teach me the Catechism, word for word. "Thou shalt not commit adultery"; "Thou shalt not covet thy neighbour's wife" and so forth. Our worst moments in these lessons used to come when Nanny would suddenly cry out: "Q! What is thy name?" I nearly jumped out of my skin when she did this the first time. I was well and truly bewildered at this strange query. I knew perfectly well what my name was, so to this cry I would immediately answer, "Julia!" (what else?).

Nanny's rage knew no bounds, for however often she instructed me what to answer I simply could not bring myself to give any less truthful reply.

"ANSWER PROPERLY!" Nanny would thunder. "Again now: Q! *What is thy name?*"

Uncomprehending, I could only feel it my duty to answer yet once more the unvarnished truth: "Julia!"

Only with the greatest reluctance did I finally give her the lying . answer that I had discovered she wanted: namely, "M or N", of all things.

"But my name is *not* M or N!" I would protest.

"Now look ye here Julia—if ye don't answer the Lord's command-ments properly—ye'll go strr-raight and stand in the corner. So now then! Once again! *Q! What is thy name?*"

I would often look out of the nursery window at the dun and foggy atmosphere of our London street, which seemed to have sucked up all the colours and vitality that I assumed the houses, the people and their clothes and carriages would certainly otherwise have revealed, just as they had in the brilliant light of India. In fact I had a feeling of having been cut off not only from my visible surroundings but from just about everything—by the grey blotting-paper curtain of dignified English solemnity—both climatic and emotional—which in this wealthy and cultured house seemed to wrap iced skeleton fingers around my throat and my heart. But it was above all after I had been left alone in my tiny solitary bedroom for the night that I most vividly became aware that the only home I recognised was that old familiar world in which I had lived up till now with my loved and trusted father and mother—a world in which everything was recognisable, solid and real, a world in fact that I had already learned a little bit to be able to calculate upon. It was, as I say, chiefly when left alone in my narrow bedroom in the English night, that I suddenly became aware that the true and solid world had melted entirely, vanished away.

And what was left?

Limbo. "A Durance, a condition," as the Oxford Dictionary defines limbo—"a condition of Neglect and Oblivion, upon the borders of hell." A very exact description of my position at that time in Melbury Road. In the darkness and the nothingness of night, the echoes floating up through my bedroom window from outside betrayed the awful Heights and Spaces out there, of an area that was calmly referred to in the daytime as 'our street'. In the silent blackness of those tear-drenched hours in bed, I would hear the clip-clop, clip-clop of the horses bringing their hansom cabs along the road outside, would hear them emerging little by little from an immense distance, and (after passing our house) retreating again little by little into a further immense distance in the other direction, thus giving me an audible statement of the incalculable remoteness of the vast Unintelligible Beyond lying all around my bedroom and the house.

In the daytime, in the nursery, I spent many hours dictating letters to my mother, through my nurse, anxiously asking her when, just when, she was coming to rejoin me? My mother would answer with long and very affectionate letters, painting lovely pictures in them for my delight; would send heaps of love, kisses and hugs, but never once mentioned the crucial subject of coming back from abroad to be with me once again, or of coming to fetch me right away, which would have been better still. My father also wrote me long letters from where he was still stationed outside Allahabad. And his letters too, were peppered with quite splendid drawings—perhaps of himself dressed up in a frock coat—"as a black beetle"—to receive some visiting dignitary. But here again—no mention of any return to England! No single word referring to the end of my exile, and to my return to our proper family life. It was only many years later, after I was grown up and at long last had left Melbury Road, that my mother wrote me a letter explaining her prolonged absence from me and declaring that my father had positively forbidden her ever to come and see me!

Meanwhile things were going badly with me. I was subject to despairing fits of crying at odd times of the day. Whenever I was discovered by some member of the Rendel family in tears, and asked what I was crying about, I answered with perfect truth that I simply didn't know. I was told many years after that the Rendel family doctor was worried by the fact that I never spoke, during those years at Melbury Road. This wasn't really true. I often talked to Aunt Elinor's daughters and sons—my cousins, who used to come and visit me in the nursery and whom I liked very much.

Betty, the eldest, and by then a grown-up young lady and a student at the Slade School of Art, was my favourite. She was tiny, pale, volatile and emotional. She would come upstairs to the top floor and sit down at the nursery table, and using my paint box would paint pictures at my behest. I led her a dreadful dance, I fear; insisting urgently that she illustrate for me time and time and time again my favourite stories from Hans Andersen—chiefly the sad tale of 'The Little Mermaid', whose fate never failed to convulse me with sorrow, and to fill the whole nursery with tears.

Ellie was 'at college'. She frequently interceded between me and Nanny, taking me out of the 'corner' where I had been sent. She often brought her friend Ray Costelloe to the nursery. The two friends seemed to me as handsome as goddesses, with their standing-out wings of hair, their voluminous tweed skirts reaching to their sensibly-shod feet, their talk of suffrage processions and banners.

Dick was a Captain in the Army, very debonair, with a monocle. He used sometimes to fetch me home from my Kindergarten School in a hansom cab, fascinating me all the way with his sophisticated panache and capital jokes. I remember his younger brother Andrew as being square and stiff, and gorgeously uniformed in pillarbox red laced with gold.

Vincent, the youngest, had just started at Rugby when I arrived. About twelve, he had the most marvellously soulful eyes, which would have done credit to a Ouida heroine, as I noticed when he took his specs off to polish them. Enormous eyes—gentian blue, with bosky fluttering lashes. His line was laconic and disillusioned, out-Rendelling Rendels. He showed me how to melt down tin soldiers in the nursery grate when Nurse was out, and completely glamourised me during the holidays, very kindly promising to marry me when I grew up.

Unable to converse with old Scotch Nanny, I had to make my friends among the people in my fairy story books. When I was not in my day school, I sat in the nursery, in my black ribbed woollen stockings, buttoned boots and pinafore, at a miniature table in the corner, reading through the hours in these magical story books; and writing also, for a photograph taken of me there shows a pencil in my hand, and a notebook open before me, in which I remember writing stories and poems. Nanny sat on the other side of the nursery fire-place, reading her own favourite magic story book. My book was usually *Alice in Wonderland*. Or the poetry and pictures of Edward Lear. Or Hans Andersen's Fairy Tales. But Nanny's book was the same one every day, and was called 'The Bible'. I resisted all pressure put upon me to read cheerful, healthy and normal adventure story books such as *The Swiss Family Robinson* who, when wrecked upon a desert island, could find nothing better to do than industriously darn their torn clothing with needles made from thorns, and threaded through with dry island grasses. Even duller than the Family Robinson I found those persons who galloped around in suits of armour, clashing swords. They were indeed outside the pale; with never an entertaining quip or striking riddle amongst the lot! *What* dullards.

One day my Aunt Elinor took me out into the garden, and I noticed that her expression was more than usually solemn and portentous. As we proceeded along the garden path, she told me that she had something special to tell me, adding the words: "*You must be brave.*" She then announced that my father and mother, out in distant India, had been 'divorced' and that I would never see them both together again. I might see my father—but not my mother. The graveyard tone in which she pronounced the word 'divorced', which was new to me, made it plain that this was something important and she evidently expected the news to be a dreadful shock. I felt embarrassed because I could see the strain all this was for her; she evidently expected me to burst out crying, and I saw that she was geared up to comfort me and staunch my tears. I was embarrassed because she made me aware how far distant we were from each other, how many leagues apart!

I was by then eight years old, had been banished from my parents at the age of five, and already an eternity seemed to have passed since they had cast me off. By that time my daily and nightly weeping-fits were over. I had at last stopped trying to send out all those cries for help in letters dictated to my parents out in India. Truth to tell there was now nothing left to be shocked by. I had well and truly grasped that I had been deserted and betrayed by the two people I loved most, whom I had trusted absolutely, and of whom I had grown to be a part. The catastrophe, and its unintelligible nature, had been already accepted. It had started to fade gradually into the background of my mind. My sense of being alive (happily and normally alive) had really gone for good, leaving a kind of leaden blank in its place, which was so heavy to carry around that I could no longer believe, from that time on, that the place I found myself in was a real world. Certainly it was not *my* world. It was a strangers' world. And I was henceforth outside it, peering from time to time shortsightedly in.

[It is hard to believe that some better solution for Julia's immediate future than Melbury Road could not have been found, but Mrs. Rendel was probably the only one of Oliver's relations who still kept a children's nurse.

A few years after Julia's arrival I got to know the house and its inmates well through the marriage of my sister Judy to the eldest son, Dick. Her picture is remarkably accurate and vivid, as are the portraits of all five Rendel children. The only characters seen with bias are Elinor Rendel herself and Old Scotch Nanny, for the obvious reason that both failed abysmally to take the place of Julia's adored mother. At forty-seven, Julia's Aunt Elinor was the oldest of Lady Strachey's surviving children. A view was held in the family that she was also the cleverest— which is saying a lot. She had a quick, brilliant mind, was well-read in several languages and wrote poetry which she didn't think good enough to publish. Her voice, the first 'Strachey voice' I ever heard, pursued an emphatic, undulant course between treble and contralto, while over-exact pronunciation contributed to the remote and frightening impression she made. Her laugh was sudden and whole-hearted, but she seldom smiled. Her children loved her dearly, and her grandson says that her fierceness was only a façade covering extreme shyness and reserve, as well as kindness; but it is easy to understand that such a character would have seemed the reverse of 'cosy' to the forlorn little stranger from India. My brother-in-law told me that the whole family were touched and charmed by their pretty little cousin, whose desolation and harrowing nightly sobs they tried impotently to assuage.

As for Old Scotch Nanny, she was a character out of Shakespearean comedy. She doted on all her own charges, but Julia must have seemed an unwelcome interloper. A family anecdote may show that she was not entirely grim. When taking the Rendel children, then quite small, on holiday, she had them all clustered around her on Euston platform waiting for their train, when she was heard to exclaim loudly: "Andrrrew me man, whativer arre ye doing? Ye've put yer hand *rrright* up me drawers!"]

Chapter Three

I JOIN THE PEARSALL SMITHS

[By her own reckoning Julia spent about four years at Melbury Road, at the end of which time she had come to terms—*superficially*—with her separation from her now divorced parents. The nightly sobbing stopped and her childish high spirits returned. But a change was thought desirable: it was decreed that she should go to boarding-school, while the choice of an arrangement for the holidays was determined by Oliver's new attachment to Ellie Rendel's great friend, Ray Costelloe, daughter of Mary Berenson.]

Next comes a very different scene.

I am standing in the marble-paved spacious hallway of a large country house where I have never been before—Iffley Court, a summer holiday house rented by the writer Logan Pearsall Smith. It is August, and I am ten years old.

I remember the scene clearly: the big garden door at the end of the hall flung wide open and showing a gleam of river—the Thames, which flowed past the end of the long garden of Iffley Court.

Beside me towered two gigantic and handsome ladies who beamed me a welcome. I saw they were no longer young but in their middle years, because of the pepper-and-salt in their hair, and also a certain rigid stoutness, and loosening of jaw-lines. But I saw also that they were as radiantly healthy, brilliantly blooming and resplendently coloured and fleshed as the summer hollyhocks standing up beside the garden door.

What ladies!

I had not yet been told about the celebrated nineteenth-century American preacher Hannah Whitall Smith, who had left the Quaker sect to which she belonged, come over from America in the late 1870s, and toured around England making a resounding success preaching her highly idiosyncratic interpretation of God's Word amongst the English aristocracy of her day in their Mayfair drawing-rooms. Nor had I heard a word about her three children, grown-up and living now for some years in England, and mixing in cultured, Liberal, and Fabian circles, among people like the Sydney Webbs, Bertrand Russell, Robert Bridges and Graham Wallis.

Hannah Whitall Smith's elder daughter Mary (nicknamed 'Mariechen' by a German governess) had married *en secondes noces* Bernard Berenson ('B.B.'—the historian of Italian art). Her son, Logan Pearsall Smith, was a well-known and scholarly writer; while Alys, the youngest of the trio, had been married for several years to Bertrand Russell (though at the time of my arrival at Iffley Court she had been deserted by Russell a year previously).

It was Alys Russell who stepped forward to take benevolent command of me on my arrival at Iffley Court, and who at once smilingly directed that I was to call her 'Aunty Loo'. This was plainly a very friendly gesture, and warmed me up at once.

"And I am called 'Aunt Mariechen'," announced the second tall and blooming lady, who, I noticed, fluttered and swished her lilac ostrich feather-boa over her draped white lace summer frock; and as she talked she lisped, smiled, and dimpled with fascinating effect, wafting her ringed hands about in the air *à la continentale*.

This was the wife of Bernard Berenson. Every summer she would slip away to England without her husband, from their palace, *I Tatti*, at Settignano above Florence, to spend a little holiday with her brother Logan, in order to see her two grown-up daughters by her first husband, the Irishman Costelloe. For Ray and Karin often visited her during their summer vacations, taking along with them a number of their College friends, and some assorted American cousins.

After I had been presented to the rest of this large house-party, we all trooped off into the dining-room and took our places round an enormous table.

At luncheon I found all the young people—the various cousins and friends of Mary Berenson's two daughters—vociferous and high-spirited in the extreme. As I listened to them all teasing each other, making outrageous allegations, contradicting and doing battle with each other, and laughing all the while, I felt I had been translated indeed! Had been lifted out of the dark ages, out of the foggy brimstone fumes and punishing devils with pitchforks of the old Scottish nursery at Melbury Road; and also out of a little boarding-school I had been sent to, run by a terrifying German headmistress—Miss Grüner. I had been let out from prison into the mellow Pagan airs of this free Olympus, where these jocund, over-life-sized Gods and Goddesses (the Whitall Smiths being all exceptionally tall, handsome, and big-boned) were discovered here at play. I heard laughter, joy, and revelry going on. Things I had not encountered since I had left my Indian home five long years before.

And it so happened that my father, Oliver Strachey, who had only lately retired from India for good, intending to find a new job in England where he belonged, was present now at this house-party at Iffley Court.

There I spent my happiest summer for several years. The young people, and the older ones too, all made a great fuss of me as I was the only child in the party. I, in turn, fell rapturously in love with all these Gods and Goddesses, and the high-spirited manner in which they conducted their life.

It was not long before all of us staying at Iffley Court heard the news that my father Oliver (divorced now from my mother for several years) had become engaged to marry Mary Berenson's elder daughter Ray Costelloe. I greatly liked Ray, who was radiantly handsome and smiling, and whom I had already admired when on occasion she used to come upstairs to pay me visits in my nursery prison at Melbury Road, accompanied by her College friend, Aunt Elinor's daughter Ellie. So Ray was to become my step-mother! I was startled, but glad.

However, I was not to see very much of either my new step-mother or my father after that Iffley Court Summer holiday. I went back again to boarding-school when the September term began and as a matter of fact, after my father's new marriage, I never got very much further than being a kind of visitor, at odd times, in the house in Hampstead which my father and his new wife had bought for themselves after their wedding.

Alys Russell, or Aunt Loo as I shall in future call her, was particularly fond of her niece Ray. She knew well what a busy public life Ray was immersed in—her days chock-a-block with committee meetings and the writing of numerous articles for the newspapers and journals (for Ray worked hard, just like Aunt Loo, for The Cause of Women's Suffrage). Aunt Loo knew also that Ray and Oliver planned to start a new family of children of their own. So one day she wrote a letter to her sister Mary Berenson, in which she voiced the opinion that Ray and Oliver were "obviously always going to neglect Julia," at the same time pointing out that as she herself was feeling desperately lonely (following her recent desertion by her husband Bertrand Russell) she would much enjoy having a child about the house, so that the idea of making a take-over bid for me would seem, one way and another, a capital idea. She would at one stroke relieve Ray and her new husband of a rather awkward cuckoo in the new nest, while at the same time perhaps helping to bring something extra to live for into her own shattered life.

Beyond that letter which Aunt Loo wrote to her sister (and which I only read many years later) I to this day have no idea at all what, if anything, the Whitall and the Pearsall Smiths, and indeed the Strachey family, had had to say upon the subject of how I was to be disposed of. All I know is that Aunt Loo's offer was at once gratefully accepted by my father and Ray. But with just how *much* alacrity history does not relate.

To a child of ten or eleven of course all such plans and plottings made privately by the grown-ups seem to flow right overhead; nor did I have the least idea what was happening.

At any rate, when, after that family summer holiday at Iffley, Logan Pearsall Smith bought himself a handsome country house in Sussex, near Arundel, and went to live in it, taking his sister Alys to keep house for him, I too was trundled along with the pair of them, to take up residence thereafter at Ford Place, as Logan's new house was named.

What this newly-acquired house seemed like to grown-up people at this time I do not know. I can only describe it as seen by myself at twelve years old. Its dark rambling passages hung with what I took to be paintings of ancestors, its panelled rooms and tapestries, its yellow silk drawing-room, its big stone kitchen and sculleries; the rose garden outside the dining-room windows, and beyond the croquet lawn at the back of the house the so-called 'Lovers' Walk' (an avenue bordered by tall trees with strange nearly black leaves, ending at a solemn, lichen-covered, grey stone lady who remained there in all weathers)—to me as a child all this seemed to add up to the archetypal romantic haunted

Manor House that figured in my old-fashioned story books. Those dark passages and big rooms panelled in cedar and oak smelled of ghosts and hinted at evil deeds of past centuries, perpetrated by the sneering ancestors in grand clothes. (Of course I was not to know that these portraits were no ancestors, but had been bought by Uncle Logan at various auctions and antique shops, with the money inherited from the vast Whitall Tatum glass business in America.)

I remember one of them particularly. He hung on the wall of the staircase leading up to the first floor—a wicked figure, life-size, dressed in full regalia of lace collar, satin sash and pink garters—and stared evilly down at me, with one hand on his sword, seeming to be slyly waiting for me to reach that point when I had to brush closely past him in turning the stair corner, as a cat crouches tense and motionless and stares hypnotically at a bird hopping innocently in his direction across the lawn.

The upstairs landing was always dark. The tall Gothic staircase window was built up of tiny crowded panes, the joints between them heavily leaded, the whole enshrouded by thickly lined, looped-up, dark red curtains. A giant walnut tree growing immediately outside caused the light to filter in dim and green on to the stairs and landing, especially in summer time.

There was no electricity at Ford Place. And how pitch dark the big house was at night! For the small circles of orange light shed around by each oil lamp—they were placed at distant intervals along the passages and window-sills, and on the odd tables scattered in the sitting-rooms—gave rise to queer ambiguous shadows behind the tallboys and armchairs, and to a kind of black malevolence in the corners of the rooms.

At lunch, Aunt Loo, Uncle Logan and I used to sit at the same huge round table where later in the day, on Friday nights, ten or so weekend visitors would manage to fit themselves in. I knew that Logan would be radiant as he entertained his friends. Unhappily, at twelve I was not considered old enough to come down to 'late dinner'. I had my glass of milk, and some sardines maybe, on a tray upstairs in my bedroom each night. But I often stole down and peeped through the half-open doors as Katie, the Irish parlourmaid, swept in and out carrying trays into the dining-room, and I intensely enjoyed witnessing the dazzling grown-up scene. I stared at the flickering candlelight and the ladies' shimmering evening dresses, and caught snatches of talk amid the weaving clatter of knives and forks and the rustling of parlourmaids busily cutting bread at the sideboard. I could tell it was the very *ne plus ultra* of sophisticated gossip and dashing intellectual badinage. And the whole performance was led by Uncle Logan! There was wicked laughter and daring jests—how I adored these mischievous sessions! When Uncle Logan was in his glory he appeared to me the wittiest, handsomest and most stimulating man on earth.

Whenever he was at Ford for the weekend, my father would sit looking pretty glum throughout much of these proceedings. (I did not learn till a good deal later in life that my Strachey relatives scorned Logan for being what they considered so trivial, smart and snobbish.) However, my father's new wife Ray, now my step-mother, was more good-natured and better-mannered than he. And although it was all quite disgustingly out of her own line of things, she would in fact sit at the dinner-table and laugh away pleasantly enough, so as not to spoil the fun.

But here, before the visitors had arrived, faced with a lunch of fish-cakes and cauliflower covered in cheese sauce, and with only myself and Aunty Loo for company, you wouldn't have recognised Logan—this stranger who shuffled stiffly into the dining-room to join us, with drooping shoulders and dead face, and who went around the table with the closed, insulated expression of a sleepwalker. Perhaps he was turning over in his mind the phrases he had been engaged in writing in his study all morning? No, I could see he was in 'one of his moods', to put it at its mildest.

During the meal Uncle Logan was almost silent. He ate, and addressed a few practical remarks to his sister about the coming weekend arrangements; but all was done without once raising his eyes from his plate, or changing his expression or the dead tone of his voice between coming into the dining-room and going out of it again. His eyelids, drawn permanently down so that he could see nothing but the food upon his plate, hooded him as the lowered curtain in a theatre hoods the empty stage between performances. At such times Uncle Logan seemed engulfed in a lack of interest in the living world so absolute that I was shocked. Deeply shaken. I suppose it was the first time I had seen someone I knew and admired and talked with every day who was yet afflicted with this particular sickness. Many years later I was told the name of Logan's illness: the doctor pronounced him to be a Manic-Depressive. But at the time of which I'm speaking I had no knowledge that my Uncle was the victim of any illness at all, nor do I believe anyone else was aware of his particular trouble.

As soon as the last spoonful of apple charlotte and the last crumb of biscuit and cheese were finished, Logan rose up stiffly from his chair, and unheedingly letting his crumpled napkin fall to the floor, he would start to shuffle doorwards again as one stunned. You could see he was quite unaware of what he was doing or where he was going.

On the way out of the dining-room, though, there would be a hesitation, a pause at the sideboard. Standing there a moment he would fumble at the fruit bowl among the peaches and figs. His sister would at once jump up and point out to him the ripest and best. Dumbly grasping at them, without the heart (I felt) actually to eat them, he stowed them away for the present blindly in his pocket, as if provisioning himself for his sojourn in some further desert beyond the dining-room.

I would watch his bowed shoulders in his navy serge suit, his handsomely carved ruddy face with the weariness lying over it like a grey powdered dust. Watch him disappearing through the fine panelled Georgian door that the parlourmaid Katie would be holding open for him. I felt deep dismay at witnessing the spectacle of this fallen God.

Aunty Loo disappeared after lunch to grapple with household bills and letter-writing. (It was her custom to send a round-robin letter addressed to all her relations, both in America and over here, every single day.)

Logan had become entombed again somewhere. The green baize service-door to the kitchen quarters was shut now. Silence had fallen on the house. What should I do with myself?

I veered towards the upright piano which stood against the far panelling in the dining-room. Perhaps I would have another go at learning to play my two favourite waltzes: *Songe d'Automne* and *Valse Triste*. I was deeply enamoured of their music, as I was enamoured also of the pictures on their covers. The cover of *Songe d'Automne* showed autumn leaves scattering down over a deserted park, and lying thickest on a bench, while that of *Valse Triste* was quite filled by the enormous face of an Edwardian young lady with huge eyes brimming with tears held close above a luxury fur muff. The face and the tears and the large hat she wore were drawn in the Art Nouveau style. Beautiful! The music of these two waltzes and their cover drawings seemed to suit each other well—as they suited me.

However, as soon as I was settled down at the piano playing *Songe d'Automne*, Aunty Loo came in and gave an exclamation of horror at finding me in such a position on a jolly, windy, sunny day in spring:

"For goodness' sake don't sit grouching there, Ju! On a fine day like this! Darn it—it's really the very devil the way thee spends the whole day mouching about indoors like this. Why doesn't thee get out thy bicycle and go for a ride? *Playing the piano!* Ju, thee knows thee stuffs indoors far, far too much; it's—it's—it's *morbid*! Always either playing the piano or reading a book!"

(The Quaker parlance of their youth in Philadelphia was still always retained by Alys, and much of the time by Logan and Mary.)

Loo came close to me where I sat at the piano; I had stopped playing but my hands were still on the keys. Lowering her voice as people do when they are about to make an embarrassing reference to some practice that is obscene, she murmured:

"Thee doesn't want to grow up all—*thee* knows—all queer—kind of eccentric and *weird* like thy Strachey relations. Like thy Uncle Lytton!" (A specially discreet lowering for his name.) "Or thy Aunt Marjorie Strachey, thee knows; now *does* thee? See what I mean?"

She had startled me. She took for granted that the danger of what she was warning me about was self-evident. But I had no idea what she was talking about. I had always thought of my Strachey Uncles and Aunts as very nice people.

I rose from the piano and made for the dining-room door in a daze. Meanwhile, satisfied (as I could see from her now beaming face) that with her forthright warning she had succeeded in snatching me away from under the wheels of an oncoming train, she seized *Songe d'Automne* off the piano. Folded it, and stowed it away at the back of the music rack.

The garden door was open, and I stepped out into the boisterous flapping and swiping of the March gale.

[Julia refers in only one sentence to being sent to 'a little boarding school . . run by a terrifying German headmistress.' This school had been recommended by my mother, who was a friend of Elinor Rendel's. Its name, 'Brackenhurst', reflects its reputedly healthy position among heather and conifers at Hindhead where my family were living at this time, and I and my elder sister Eleanor were already going to it as day-girls. Boarders had to face bleak bedrooms with walls of varnished planks, and inedible meals of gristly stew or chunks of haddock floating in watery milk.

My mother promised to keep an eye on Julia, and to me her advent was a landmark. It was soon arranged that she should spend every Sunday at our house; we used to drive to fetch her in the pony-trap behind our fat brown cob Molly, I sometimes nervously holding the reins, but the under-gardener, George, a swarthy gypsy, really in charge.

Julia became my first real friend. She was tall for her age but slim as a reed. I see her wearing a dark blue djibbah, with two very thick plaits of light brown hair and a rather crooked parting. Her face was a perfect oval, her wide-set eyes of an unusual sea-blue colour, and her mouth so small that she used to complain that she could only open it vertically when she laughed or smiled. I remember her trying to expand it sideways with my mother's glove-stretchers. We passed happy days, and scarcely ever quarrelled. Our garden was large and contained tall Scotch pines for climbing, as well as an ancient spreading oak, christened 'the Owly Tree' by Julia and full of 'places' which had their own names too. On wet days we camped in the loft over Molly's stable, carrying on long secret conversations flavoured with the scent of hay and harness. We only joined the adults at meal times, sitting side by side at the end of the luncheon table, or (at tea-time) carrying a careful selection of thin sandwiches and iced cake to a window-seat where we pored over picture-books.

Julia was still at Brackenhurst when Oliver married Ray Costelloe; she told me she didn't think of them as parents: "They are more like irresponsible, grown-up cousins."]

Chapter Four

DOING THE FLOWERS WITH AUNTY LOO

"Ju! JU! Joo-oo—Where is thee?"

It was Aunt Loo shrieking along the corridor below. A thundering of determined feet and a rage of whirling skirts and flapping sleeves and jackets heralded the appearance of Alys Russell, rounding the corner from the dining-room.

I could see her through the upstairs banisters which ran along the upper landing. She brandished giant gardening scissors in one freckled hand, and gripped with the other a big Dutch pottery vase filled with the stiff brown corpses of lupins which were falling about inside the vase in all directions.

"HI! Ju!"

Aunt Loo caught sight of me suddenly, standing at the top of the stair and, slamming all the brakes on, nearly tumbled over.

There I was, that morning, on my knees in front of the bookshelves on the first floor landing at Ford Place, investigating Logan's library, when I heard Aunty Loo calling out for me to join her down in the passage below on the ground floor.

"Ju . . . Hi! JU-U-U-U!" came the cry once again. "Come to the flower-room. I am arranging the vases for the visitors' rooms."

So saying she wheeled to the right about, and disappeared again abruptly, ricocheting full-steam-ahead towards the garden vestibule, out of which opened a tiny room large enough only to contain a sink and a draining-board. Shelves were ranged round the walls, and on these stood empty vases of different kinds. More of a cupboard than a room. But situated as it was immediately inside the garden door, it was dignified by the name of the 'flower-room'.

I turned and came down the stairs slowly and—judging from the hanging mirror on the facing staircase-wall—with a Chinese graciousness. At this time I was very struck by Arthur Waley's translations of Chinese poetry, a volume of which I had discovered in Uncle Logan's bookshelves. So I liked to think that as I came down the Ford Place stairs I resembled a Chinese Empress descending from her palace tower.

I got down to the door of the flower-room at last.

There, piled on the draining board, was a big bundle of flowers of all sorts, hastily grabbed, as one could see, from the herbaceous border in the centre of the walled vegetable gardens. Twiggy branches with evergreen leaves from the garden hedges had plainly been torn off at speed whilst rushing back to the house, and were thrown down beside the flowers on the draining-board. Would I help to fill vases with these flowers? Aunt Loo asked. It was for Logan's weekend house-party, some of whose members would be arriving in a few hours' time for Friday evening dinner.

"Why yes—of course."

So we set to, passing the big gardening scissors back and forth between us, I working in my native silence—I seldom opened my mouth in the company of the grown-ups, for I had never received the impression that they would be interested in what I might have to say, while Aunt Loo's thoughts meanwhile exploded boisterously all around her like fireworks as she slaved away.

"Now then! Buck up, Ju! This one for the drawing-room window-sill!"

When we had finished work on that:

"Now one for Molly and Desmond MacCarthy's room. I *hate* doing flowers!"

"But why do you keep on and on doing them?" I enquired.

"People who have country houses *have* to have flowers in vases displayed all over. (Give me that orange gladiolus over there if thee will—thank thee.) *Someone* has to do it. Logan has a saying: 'If the house is on fire—*don't tell me*!!' Well, there it is. Gram* used to say that for a man at the head of a house *that* is the right attitude towards a woman, simply because a man hasn't the gumption to grapple with what happens in the house. So thee sees, the woman of the house must turn to

* Their mother, Hannah Whitall Smith.

in every case—stay on guard, work away. But I *hate* it! Hate 'keeping house'. (What about that Buddleia? No, that purple spike—thank thee—for the staircase window-sill? Beatrice Webb and Sydney will be calling in tomorrow.) There's only one thing I hate more in the world than doing the flowers—and that's eating eel pie. Not that I've had to do *that*, thank Heavens, since we came over from America to live here. As a girl in Philadelphia I used to suffer tortures—we seemed to be having eel pie served up all the time!''

Loo's face fell. The mention of eel pie had reminded her of something that was worrying her.

"It's perfectly *awful*," she said in a lower tone. "I've discovered that Lizzie uses fifty to sixty eggs *every single day* in the cooking when we have visitors! It's the most disgusting extravagance! But Logan wants it that way, thee sees! It's *his* house, and so we've got to have it. That's all! You *have* to please the men with the cookery, as Gram taught me, or they become worse than bears with sore heads. (Take this small white vase for Bob Trevelyan's* bedroom. Laurel leaves will do. And a little verbena—here!).'' She banged the empty vase down in front of me on the narrow table ledge, and jostling out a fistful of herbage ends from underneath all the clutter on the draining-board she flung them, along with some stalky laurel branches, at the vase.

Aunt Loo had safety-pinned a red checked apron on top of the cotton frock with the big blue stripes on it that she had received from cousins still living over in America in their latest 'Mercy Parcel'. (Thus she had nicknamed the monthly boxes of old garments that she had prevailed upon various friends and relations in America to send her regularly by post for her village jumble sales, the money so raised to be spent on 'The Cause', as the Movement for Women's Suffrage used to be called.) It was from these 'Mercy Parcels' that she derived her own wardrobe entirely—whenever she thought of the matter. Which wasn't often. However, the great bulk of old clothes, and other white elephants that she had extracted from her friends and acquaintances, were faithfully put into the jumble sales held on the croquet lawn, and the proceeds duly handed over to one or other of the many charities devoted to the cause of Women's Rights.

"Where's that orange gladiolus gone again? Oh well, these snapdra-

---

* R. C. Trevelyan, poet.

gons will do instead. Off thee goes then with this vase and put it into Bob Trevelyan's bedroom."

When I returned from 'Trevy's' bedroom, having deposited the vase of laurel appositely upon the poet's writing-table, Aunt Loo's reminiscences were still in full spate.

"Gram used always to tease Mariechen about the way B.B. fussed over her clothes, making her go to so many fittings at Worth and Paquin. Gram told her: 'Mariechen, it does seem a dreadful waste of time, and money, and brains and temper too, to turn thee's mortal frame into a dressmaker's block! And most *deteriorating* to the character.'"

Then Mary Berenson would explain that feminine elegance was of the greatest importance to B.B. on account of his artistic eye and his interest in feminine chic. Gram would reply that in that case she mustn't of course oppose him, for the vagaries of the male portion of our race must ever be looked upon as one looks upon earthquakes, or avalanches or other natural disasters: things that cannot be stopped, and that therefore one has simply to stand aside and make way for. At this point Aunt Loo added proudly, aside to me: "My *Bertie** was never like that!"

The dresses that Aunt Loo subtracted from the American mercy parcels for wearing herself would, of course, have been taken over from someone maybe half, or maybe double her size. And it was perhaps to hide the imponderables of the fit of all these frocks of varying sizes that she was in the habit of adding, on top of any frock that she had selected for herself, a number of loose tippets, 'Berthas', tucked capes, frilled jackets, 'Dolmans' and the like. It was August, and today Aunt Loo's assorted jackets were of thin cottony stuffs. On top of all, and always taking pride of place, it was her custom to slip on a white embroidered muslin affair of *broderie anglaise*—whose wide sleeves easily accommodated all the other sleeves crowded within.

This garment had started life as Bertrand Russell's christening robe, so she used to tell ladies who admired the magnificent embroidered butterflies cavorting among honeysuckles—white on white. It had been for a long time treasured in Aunt Loo's bedroom chest of drawers. But latterly it had been made over for her into a jacket to out-jacket all

* Her husband, Bertrand Russell.

jackets, by Miss Keep, our Sussex village sewing-woman. By the look of things it was going to be one of those sturdy heirlooms that last for ever and ever. (I was surprised, many years later, to read in Bertrand Russell's autobiography that he had in fact never *been* christened. Surprised, that is, until I bethought me of the fact that virtually every story one hears related in an autobiography, biography or history, has many different versions to it. Those connected with the acquiring of holy relics most especially perhaps, as in this case.)

As Aunty Loo worked beside me in the minuscule flower-room, she would, as was her way in all conversation, gesticulate widely and with startling energy to impress her points on her listener. So now, as she denounced (by no means for the first time) the soft, luxurious and corrupt style of living insisted upon at Ford Place by her brother Logan (a notable rebel from the Quaker Brethren) she repeatedly threw one handsome well-fleshed arm aloft, clenching the healthy-looking hand with its neatly-trimmed finger-nails whose glowing pinks were flecked over with tiny white speckles, shaking it about in the air most forcefully, and every moment turning about abruptly to carry out some flailing movement with the huge gardening scissors, or turn on the gushing water taps, and bang away again and again with the hammer that was kept on the shelf especially to crush the tough rose stalks, the woody lilac, and other such twigs. At intervals she would whip out her pocket handkerchief to mop up the violent squirts of water that sprayed out all over her dress and her jackets, at the same time hastily scrabbling to catch at the handfuls of falling correspondence—bills, committee-meeting minutes relating to the Women's Suffrage Campaign, and so on, which kept flying out of her gardening apron pocket, while all the while the room rang with her favourite exclamation: "Hell's bells!"

Every so often Loo would dash out through the door leaving the flower-room without explanation, and staying away for perhaps ten minutes or so. On her departure an eerie quiet dropped down over the little room. One felt then as if a crazily-flapping, high-flying wild goose that had been too long confined and crushed into some tiny canary's quarters, had burst open its cage door at last and shot honking away to larger bustling worlds.

I would remain behind alone, dimly weaving about among the mashed stalks and the dank vegetable detritus in my fog of star-dust and my Chinese-Empress limbo—a hundred miles away.

Maybe Aunty Loo had sprinted along to the cottage of our village washerwoman, Mrs Bunting, to hand her a pair of Logan's forgotten woollen pants for washing: or to ask her to come and give a hand with the village women's Monthly Meeting, or the Temperance Band of Hope. However, she would return to the flower-room in the end, and continue the conversation where she had last left off: "As I was telling thee—our Lizzie uses up *sixty mortal* eggs for breakfast alone at weekends when we have visitors! In any case the eggs she gets through in her cooking, daily (even when we are alone here), are numberless. Of course Logan always insists on having corn-fritters on the side-board to go with the bacon and kidneys at breakfast. And then again don't forget all the lunchtime soufflés, as well as the savoury egg dishes for late dinner. Lizzie told me that Canary Pudding alone—for a big party such as we're having this weekend—takes twelve eggs all of itself!"

"It does seem an awful lot of eggs," I used to say wonderingly, "sixty eggs every day!"

"Don't forget all the girls out in the kitchen who have to be fed, though," she reminded me. "Just the same I tell Lizzie she is really *needlessly* extravagant. And when I think what fun Bertie and I used to have *economising together*! I've never enjoyed any occupation so much in my life! Bertie and I turned to, when we were living down at Bagley Wood after our honeymoon, and decided we'd live upon two and sixpence a day—everything all in! And to do it we went to all sorts of lengths! Got up to all sorts of tricks! Our joy in cutting everything down to the barest minimum was intense! And if I had my own way today, thee knows, and wasn't keeping house for Logan, I'd go straight off and live in one room somewhere, with almost no furniture, and feed only on baked beans out of a tin—what rapture!" (One could see it was true—such a radiance lit up Aunt Loo's face when she referred as she often did, to this celestial daydream.) "Yes, Bertie and I both despised the idea of luxurious living to such an extent that . . ." But the water-tap had given a rusty shriek and shot a jet-stream over Loo's skirt, and she broke off to snatch out her handkerchief and mop it up.

"Say, Ju, after thee's finished the one thee's doing now, do this small vase here with some blue Anchusa, for Professor Salvemini's* bed-room—thee knows which it is—the small bachelor's room at the

* Italian historian.

bottom of the servants' stairs. Though why one should call him a *bachelor*! (Pass that duster over from up on the nail there, this handkerchief's sopping wet already)—I say why one should call—(thanks! I guess I'll just spread this wet hanky out to dry on the sill here)—I was just saying how Professor Salvemini, though he's now widowed and single, used to be such a *devoted* husband, and now of course he's a tremendous flirt! Does thee remember—well of course thee wouldn't—*how* we all laughed and laughed when he remarked at dinner here one time: 'Adultery is fun certainly. But you know—it isn't the *whole* of life!' O, how we all ROARED. It was really *perfectly* delicious. 'Adultery is fun. But it isn't the whole of life!' "

This was one of Aunt Loo's most favourite anecdotes. She had been joyously scandalised at the time by anyone using such a casual and matter-of-fact tone when referring to one of the most disgraceful and shocking of life's occupations—sex. But Loo dearly loved a rebel in any shape or form. So that the Professor's remark had excited her in more than one way. And whenever Salvemini's name was mentioned this story invariably came up; and also that other story of his having been in the great earthquake at Naples when his house had collapsed around him, and he had been found in the morning, after the dust had cleared away, hanging from an iron peg high on an upper wall by his collar, wearing only pyjamas and a pair of red bedroom slippers. (I think Aunt Loo must have had rather a crush on Professor Salvemini, judging by her manner whenever she talked about him.)

"And by the way, Ju—try and look more cheerful and jolly when we have visitors, will thee? Thee sits there grouching, looking down thee's long nose, and thee doesn't realise, as thee never notices other people's expressions because thee's short-sighted and *will* NOT wear thy spectacles, how dismal thee looks. Young people should be full of Guts, and Spunk, and Fun!! If thee really can't manage it, I advise thee at the least to make sure to keep the corners of thy mouth always turned upwards—*that* gives a cheerful look. Practise it!"

And as I began to move glumly off towards the door: ("Here! This last vase is for Israel Zangwill* and his wife.") She handed it to me. "So practise keeping the corners of thee's mouth well turned up—in front of visitors at any rate. Try and remember, now! *I* used to practise it I

---

* Jewish writer.

remember, in the underground trains, and in the buses and every-where, when Bertie first left me."

Aunty Loo had taken off her gardening apron and was hanging it on the wall.

"Now I'm just going to see if Cave has moved the two donkeys along to the barn, and cleared the old stable ready for my White-Ribbon Temperance Lecture to the Village Mothers this afternoon." She had opened the door and was half-way into the passage when:

"JU!—HI! Ju! Get out that roll of white wallpaper that is at the back of the schoolroom cupboard, will thee? And some coloured chalks? I'll tell thee what I want thee to do with them when I get back."

When she was gone I felt low. I found this talk of my unsatisfactory facial expression—of my 'looking down the length of my long nose' and my generally debilitating presence in company—wounding.

Funnily enough my eyes had been opened only a week or two back upon this very subject—to the fact that I was a sort of dismal freak that all jolly, decent people must object to. It was Desmond MacCarthy, the drama critic and celebrated social charmer, who opened my eyes for me. He had come into the schoolroom one morning a week or two before, where I was in the company of his three children, who were friends and who were staying at Ford Place—Rachel and her brothers Michael and Dermod. After wandering around the schoolroom a little—I forget precisely what we children were doing, but busy playing some invented game or other—Desmond suddenly turned and ad-dressed me personally:

"Why do you look so *sad* all the time?"

I stopped in my tracks, greatly taken aback. By the suddenness of this accusation, and the expression in his face, I felt that he was attacking me. But for what? For having no *morale* I supposed. (Though I wouldn't at that time have heard of that particular word, I understood at any rate he meant that I was a bad egg of some sort.)

Surprise and humiliation froze me. That this man-of-the-world, this famous expert in personal charm as all agreed ("Affable Hawk" as he used to sign himself in the weekly journals), that he should burst out suddenly with just how wretchedly I showed up in his eyes, in the middle of playing some game or other with his children! Oh dear, oh dear! And what answer could I make?

And now here, in the flower-room, Aunty Loo had been saying

exactly the same thing: "Young people should be full of Guts! and Spunk! and Fun!" And I *wasn't*.

I had of late months been getting inured to my failure to measure up to Aunt Loo's standards of what a child should be. I was never crushed by her criticism, I think, because I recognised that her tastes and ideals were so widely at odds with my own. And that I couldn't respect them. However, after my brush with the fascinating Desmond, I was convinced, at last, that everybody else must indeed see me as Aunty Loo and Desmond did—just a dismal, moth-eaten, seedy kind of a freak, unpleasant and unwholesome for jolly, healthy children to mix with. I was only thankful that Desmond had attached no particular blame to my *nose* as well!

Nevertheless, and apart from my nose, I suspected something would obviously have to be done about my unpleasingly dismal aspect.

The trouble was I had little faith in Aunt Loo's own advised system for creating a cheerful ambience in company, and I instantly wrote off her instructions as to keeping the corners of my mouth firmly pointing upwards by sheer muscle power at all times. Well, I wasn't going to *dream* of practising this robot-style chore, either in the underground, or anywhere else. I received her advice in silence. The fact was that I had observed for too long a time now the desolating, the rigid mask, that this same practice had given to Aunty Loo's own face. I had seen how she did indeed literally 'set' her facial expression officially at breakfast-time (just as she daily set the dining-room mantlepiece clock) to a supposedly bright cheerfulness, thereby making that countenance, on which there was already stamped a most pitiable, barren desolation, into a truly soul-freezing artificially cheery mask. A dutiful mask expressing the same changeless attitude to all things and all comers for the next fifteen daylight hours, right up until that moment when the final good-nights should have been said.

Unfortunately a child of twelve is more observant than understanding. While she will register, maybe unconsciously, the pitiful impress of a personality that rings false in some way, the child won't yet have achieved that imaginative compassion that later on the years of experience can bring, when confronted by some personality who is being pressurised from within, and so twisted a little bit 'out of true' so to speak.

I, at any rate, was too insulated by my own egocentricity and

ignorance to be able to make great allowances for the hidden con-
vulsions that deform us all in some way or another.

When Aunt Loo left the flower-room to discuss with the gardener the
placing in the old stables of the trestle-tables to carry the sandwiches,
cakes and tea-cups for the village mothers' Temperance Tea planned
for the following Monday, it was already mid-morning.

While she was away I rambled off and upstairs to do the rounds of the
passage bookshelves once more, to dig up something further to read
whilst waiting for her to return and continue arranging the flowers.

Chapter Five

DRUNKARD'S INTESTINES

When Aunt Loo returned from the stables she quickly spotted me at the far end of the upstairs landing, on my knees beside the low-running bookshelves, with my head bent over a book of poetry, silently mouthing an old favourite:

> "After the flitting of the bats,
>   When thickest dark did trance the sky,
>   She drew her casement-curtain by,
> And glanced athwart the glooming flats,
>   She only said, 'The night is dreary,
>   He cometh not,' she said;
>   She said . . ."

Aunty Loo was advancing down the passage full-tilt like a frenzied traction-engine, to where I knelt on the carpet beside the bookshelves. I did not move. Went on reading. After a little raised my eyes to where her outstretched arm shook to and fro above my head a large open volume bound in red. The fact was that even through childhood's self-centred insulating fog I had of late become more and more aware of Aunt Loo's general system of setting in motion the events in her busy world—of the clattering paraphernalia with which she operated, of her life-style in fact. I heard, daily, the shrieks and the wrenching from the inner derricks and the cranes of her soul, so to speak; I saw all the ropes, the pegs, the cranks, and giant metal winches with which she engineered the machinery of her daily life. I was learning what it was to live in the house with a 'Public Face' propelled by a demonic energy, directed towards improving the world.

So now I remained cautiously unmoving upon my knees with my open poetry book, my finger keeping hold of the place, waiting to hear myself addressed. I had learnt to be wary these days. Had my Aunt and myself each been equally dynamic in our reactions to each other, I sensed the horrific head-on collisions, the bumps, and the concussions that would have ensued. So I kept my eyes down upon my book for a prudent breathing space, without uttering a word.

Finally I did look up at what was wuthering and flapping in Aunt Loo's hand above my head.

I saw, pictured on the open page of the book she was gripping, something that I could only figure must be bagpipes. Many tangled looping and mysterious tubes were attached to these saggy and battered old bagpipes. It was hard to be certain though at exactly what one *was* looking, for the image continued to undergo gale-force turbulence between Aunty Loo's first finger and thumb.

"I want thee to copy this medical picture of a drunkard's ruined and diseased intestines," she crowed, "in the brightest colours thee possesses. It is for me to use, thee sees, at our Women's White Ribbon Temperance Meeting that we are holding in the old stables this afternoon."

She brought the medical picture down low under my nose for me to inspect, and continued, "Here is the diseased Bag of the Drunkard's Stomach, thee sees! All speckled and spotted over with the poison of Alcohol! And then down here are all the long bowels, coiling and coiling around underneath . . ."

A silent moment, while I stared at the strange spectacle.

Aunt Loo was silent too as we stood and looked.

"I want thee, on thy copy, to colour all the *corrupted* patches in *black* ink mottled over with *purple* and with maybe a peppering of thee's *green* chalks . . . an effect of verdigris and mould together. Anyway, here everything is! All marked out in the diagram. Thee sees?"

"Yes."

"Thee sees these places, these mottled dark patches, where the intestines have rotted away?"

"Yes, I see."

"Well, just faithfully copy it! But remember, everything much magnified. Be sure to make the picture as *large* as thee can make it. Use the plain white back of that unused roll of wallpaper that is kept in the schoolroom cupboard. I want to be able to throw the whole picture over the blackboard I've had Mr. Cave put up in the old coach-house, so as to be able to point out with my wooden pointer in the course of my lecture what the Demon Drink has done to the dipsomaniac's stomach and bowels."

She gave a snort, as it might be cheerily. "Buck up now!" For she saw me beginning dreamily to rehearse the colourful technical operation in my mind, musing upon which might be the most evil colours in my paintbox; picturing what horror I could best make of it all—since that was plainly Aunt Loo's intention.

"Oh, mercy! It's nearly lunchtime!"

I shut up my Tennyson. Started to fit it back again into its place on the shelf, and as I did so I heard:

"I'll leave the picture with thee, then! So thee can get on with it immediately after lunch." So saying, Aunt Loo dumped the medical book on the top of the banister railing behind me.

As she raced away back down the stairs I heard her cry: "I'll give thee tuppence for copying the picture! Thee knows how I believe in paying people properly for their work!" she added with a certain pride. And she was gone.

"Twopence," I mumbled. "Oh, thank you."

I felt snubbed.

Not because I felt the price was too low, but simply because I had been offered money at all. For Aunt Loo's system, always so unexpected and embarrassing, of paying one or two coppers or a threepenny bit for all personal favours done, her rigid principle of treating any favours anyone gave as if they were strictly 'official jobs' which had been ordered by her in the way of business—this attitude I had always found chilling. I felt it was one of her many ways of keeping people at arm's length. Of ducking any intimate emotions.

Personally I expected to do people favours sheerly out of friendliness, with intent to help; but also hoping at the back of my mind to enjoy during the process the interchange of a pleasant feeling of warmth with the person involved. Children very obviously enjoy 'helping' the grown-ups; however, Aunt Loo managed to cut the ground from under my feet every time upon that score, by her brisk forcing of coppers into my hand by way of payment. She intended to show, publicly, that in dealings with *her* no-one was ever going to be the loser. Everyone was to understand clearly how fair-minded she was; how just. Just or unjust, however, Aunt Loo thought nothing of opening a visitor's chest-of-drawers and removing any garments she spotted as likely to be popular on the stalls of her jumble sales and bearing them away for that so worthy purpose without further mention to the owner, or to anyone else. As for instance when my father, working in the same room at the War Office with Desmond MacCarthy during the Second World War, looked up in the middle of one of his code-cracking exercises, and caught sight of Desmond's shirt. "Desmond," said my father, "there's something strangely familiar about that shirt you're wearing to-day . . ." "This shirt?" "That shirt, yes; may I ask where you got it?"

Desmond MacCarthy had looked down vaguely at his shirt, lifting the corner of his jacket. "Oh, I believe this was one that Molly bought for me at a jumble sale. One of Aunty Loo's jumble sales I rather think." "May I look to see if it is marked with any name?" "Why, certainly . . ."

The shirt was marked with a name tape inside the collar, sure enough—my father's name! It had been subtracted out of my father's chest-of-drawers when he visited Ford Place one weekend by Aunt Loo with the highest of ethical motives of course, namely to put it on a stall at one of her jumble sales to be sold for 'The Cause'.

Stories of this kind were legion, and a standing joke in the family, so that this resolute buying-and-selling way-of-life of Aunt Loo's had in fact rather complex roots in her soul.

At that time I hadn't quite tumbled to the fact that this was one of several protective, insulating systems that she had devised for dealing with her fellow creatures without courting the danger of coming into contact with, or even becoming aware of, their feelings at all. That objective must have been very important to her personality for it was a most notable part of her character. There must have been strong pressures deep within her, warning her to keep herself well shielded and immune from possible lacerations and betrayals from her own kind, from which she must surely, at some early and vulnerable age, have endured bitter and lasting wounds.

Such explanations of other people's unpleasing behaviour, such 'understanding', was well outside the scope of a hopeless ignoramus in all such matters—and only twelve years old—such as I was myself. I did not even realise that there was anything to 'understand' and therefore to make allowances *for*, in the chilling manner in which Aunt

Loo kept us all so wretchedly at arm's length. A manner which succeeded most competently in keeping me forever relegated to the position of an alien in her house. The one position—that of an 'alien'—a kind of a cosmic refugee, an unwanted 'changeling' from another planet (as I was already coming to feel myself), this was the one position that it was most necessary for me to be guarded against for the sake of my emotional health.

Aunty Loo had once explained to me how her character came to have taken on its present shape. I remember we were in the waiting-room of some country station at the time, a place where her really searching revelations about life would often come up. (Never shall I forget, for instance, the scene on the crowded platform at Basingstoke, when I was returning to school one time. We were all waiting for the train, when Aunty Loo chose that moment to launch into a lesson, or rather a demonstration, on the mechanics of cohabitation, using her left hand, loosely clenched, as the female reception centre, and the first finger of her right hand held out straight from the otherwise clenched fist, to mime the activities of the male. The while she commented, loud and clear, to the enthralment of the waiting travellers standing around, on the neatness and practical excellence of the whole well-designed job. Although the general principle of the thing, physically speaking, was no news to me at that juncture, I shan't forget my strenuous attempts to indicate to the listening crowd that this robust, gesturing and haranguing lady was a complete stranger—nothing to do with me at all—and that I really wasn't particularly attending to, or interested anyhow, in what she was on about.)

But to return to the explanation Aunt Loo had given me about the development of her own character.

"Thee sees I was quite young," she told me, "a child, when I saw how my older sister Mary fascinated everybody, and was so *wildly* popular with all the young men and indeed with the whole world! She was only fifteen, but *everybody* fell in love with her! Of course she was very beautiful, but then *I* was, *too*! *I* was just as handsome as *she* was." (This was quite true. I judge from the various painters' portraits and photographs of these two teenage girls that there was nothing to choose in the matter of good looks between them.) "But I couldn't be *popular*, and *fascinating* as well, thee sees! It just didn't seem to be my line! So I said to myself: 'Ulus!' " ('Alice' in English), " 'thee can't be fascinating;

so thee must settle for being *good*.' And I decided there and then that if I couldn't be popular, then I would become a Saint instead. And I did!" she finished up frankly.

As a matter of fact I heard Aunt Loo repeat this remark about being a saint more than once, and with the same boisterous bravura with which she struck a number of her attitudes and played a number of her public parts. With some of these she was more at home than with others. One could see for instance that her stance was more uncertain as the Comedy Entertainer than as the Lady Bountiful. For the former role she obviously had certain inhibitions—something to do with forcing herself to appear at ease, happy, or to exhibit the 'human touch'. But I had detected no scruples when, for instance, she pressed ninepence into the hand of our prim parlourmaid Irish Katie, on Katie's afternoon off, and told her to buy herself and Lizzie the cook two seats at the local cinema. The respectable Katie, I remember, had murmured close to my ear with a rueful smile, when once again safely outside the sitting-room door: "The pair of us in the fourpenny seats!! What next! Sure, I wouldn't be seen dead sitting at the cinema in anything under a decent three and threepenny seat! But don't repeat that to Mrs. Russell, will y'now? She means well . . ."

I promised I wouldn't.

I daresay no saint would care to pander to any desire a parlourmaid might entertain of cutting a dash on her afternoon off in the eyes of the local village lads. I was surprised myself at Katie's attitude. But I had no insight yet into class-consciousness, in spite of the fact that I much preferred to spend my time with the servants and the villagers.

I have never come across any other 'saints' and so am rather ignorant of their day-to-day behaviour. But I'm perfectly prepared to believe that it could be a characteristic of a saint to be totally ruthless in his, or her, chosen good cause. As for instance on that day several years later, when I was in my teens and immensely devoted to my own private collection of fairy story books illustrated by Arthur Rackham, Edmund Dulac and such, besides other books with really first-class 19th century woodcuts and steel engravings in them by artists some of whom are in our national picture galleries today. I returned home from my boarding-school one holiday to find the whole prized collection gone. Shelves emptied. Only when invited to explain the appalling mystery did Aunt Loo tell me that, knowing that I was at that age quite 'grown out of that

kind of childish book', she had filched the lot, and sold them all off at
one of her charity jumble sales in my absence, without asking my
permission or so much as referring to the matter. That same collection
of illustrated books would nowadays be worth a fortune by the way,
demonstrating that not only I, but also other people have not at all
'grown out of them', even today.

This kind of behaviour I imagine may very well indeed be the
characteristic of a 'saint'.

From the upstairs landing at Ford there arose a narrow winding
stairway, lit by a skylight. At the top were two doors: one opening out
on to the leaded roof, the other to the 'haunted' attics, about six in
all—immense, rambling, unplastered vaults, without a window among
the lot, situated immediately under the sloping roof of the house. I often
went the rounds of them, my heart in my mouth and a candle held high,
but today I chose the door on to the leads, which overlooked the garden.
The top leaves of the huge old walnut tree grew up even higher than the
roof where I stood. I could have picked them, for they drooped all
around me over the tiled gables. One had to peer between the branches
to get a glimpse of the croquet-lawn below, while off to one side the
farmyard with its wonderful pigsties was revealed as on a map, and I
could plainly see the grassed-over canal which so strangely threaded its
way through the fields, under its crumbling little bridges.

Far below me at the foot of the walnut tree, I spied tea-tables ready
laid, and wicker garden chairs set around them.

Aunt Loo's cry came echoing up through the walnut branches:

"Why Dawsie! Mariechen, just look; see who's come! Here's Dawsie!
Well, Dawsie, thee said thee might be able to drive over, but I
never . . ."

Nobody was directly in my line of vision beside the waiting tea-table
beneath. But from the different voices I realised that Mary Berenson
had already arrived from the small station, Ford Junction, and that
Aunty Loo's closest friends and Familiars, Emily Dawson and Bonty
Amos, had also turned up. All the arrivals were standing in a bunch on
the threshold of the door separating the front garden from the croquet-
lawn.

After brushing the cobwebs out of my hair and dress, I came down from the roof and joined the party on the lawn, to help hand round the cucumber sandwiches and chocolate cake.

It was Ladies' Hour.

This was virtually the only time of the day, as far as I could see, when Aunty Loo's own female companions were permitted to put in an appearance during the course of Logan's cultural weekends. Logan did not attend these tea-parties. Pleading work, he had his tea brought to his study on a tray.

Loo's friends were bosomy hens with spreading hips and feet, tending to be ginger colour all over, more or less, or at any rate varying shades of marmalade with tints of biscuit or toast. All were worshippers and adorers of Aunty Loo. To define them further I would say they were among the professional do-gooders Aunty Loo sometimes picked up at her committee meetings. They were loyally clubbed together under the heading of 'the Girls', or 'Loo's specials'.

And here was I, a spindly, overgrown, leggy twelve-year-old, with dirty bare feet and long tangled hair, taking my place at the tea-table with its white lace cloth. The three ladies all turned to me with benevolent surprise. How did I like my new governess? (A Russian lady who came to teach me daily from Worthing.) How had I made out with Farmer Boniface from up the road, over the row that had ensued when he discovered that his tractor (laid up in the special shed when not in use) had been lavishly decorated with the red and green and pink paint that my cousins, Dick and John Strachey, and I had discovered in tins at the back of the shed?

"Girls!" suddenly cried Aunt Loo, breaking into the conversation abruptly and jumping to her feet. "Thee must see Ju's wonderful picture of the Drunkard's Stomach for my lecture to the Mothers' Temperance Meeting on Monday evening! I won't be a moment fetching it." She dashed into the house, and was soon back again with the great flapping picture on its roll of white wallpaper, explaining to the company the various talking points scattered over it—the foul but vividly-coloured impressions left by Demon Drink on the human entrails.

Shrill cries rose above the sandwiches from all the 'Girls'.

"Why *Ulus*!!" declared Mary Berenson. "Why *Ulus*, what an *appalling* spectacle! It makes me feel I'm going to vomit! Take it away!"

Aunt Mareeks, as I called her for short, spoke in a fainting voice, as with her tiny lace handkerchief held in her dimpled white beringed hand she firmly waved the drunkard's stomach away from the cakes and sandwiches on the tea-table.

"How perfectly dreadful! I never saw such an abominable thing! That's not to say, Julia," Aunt Mareeks turned here to me, "that I don't think it most skilfully and wonderfully done. How ever did thee come to imagine what a drunkard's stomach looked like?"

"Oh, it's quite authentic, ladies," Aunt Loo told them. "I gave Ju a diagram to copy out of Bing's *Friendly Family Doctor*."

"I don't care where it came from," answered Aunt Mareeks. "It's perfectly *disgusting*. I never saw such a sight in my life. Take it away immediately!"

Even when expressing horror and revulsion such as this, Mary Berenson never became crude or over-emphatic, but, as when she was among the beautiful and luxurious formal terraced gardens of her palatial Italian home high above the Arno, a mellow glow, a magical charm, seemed to wrap her ever in its ambience—even as her fluffy feather boas from Paquin and Worth enfolded her Rubensesque shoulders both by evening and day.

Loo's two bosomy hens clucked their kind appreciation of my *chef d'oeuvre*, and in spite of her bleats of dismay Aunt Mareeks herself indulged in some delicious Grand Guignol shivers. Nor was this unusual. She was fond of passing on over cups of coffee and wine-glasses certain bizarre anecdotes (well filled out and furnished in the telling) that she had heard from the lips of some or other of the art historians and cosmopolitan intellectuals who visited her house near Florence, *I Tatti*. When she went into action at such times, her beautiful ageing Titian goddess's face, discreetly veiled in pearly Parisian powder, took on a dreamy and enravished look, while her eyes with their thick lashes narrowed in concentration. One was reminded of a plump. pussy-cat, settling down to business over a good saucerful of creamy milk. For Aunt Mareeks purred her way through society smoothly enough, applauded on all sides by her fascinated audience; and yet it was the kind of purring that ominously aroused awareness of a power-house of energy at work in subterranean regions. Such power-houses were owned and worked by all the 'Whitall Women' (the clan name given by my father to the female descendants of the mighty Hannah Whitall Smith). After marrying one of them himself, he used to tease his wife by wandering around the house humming to himself a parody of a then-popular song:

"It's the Whitall Women!
Those Whitall Women!
They're making (pom)
A Whitall (pom)
Of *me-ee-ee* . . . !
My father brought me up
A
Good-quiet-man!
But oh those Whitall Women
Just *see* what they've done!"

But to return to our tea-party sitting together munching sandwiches in the shifting sun-freckles of our walnut tree: it was not long before Aunt Mareeks was describing to the 'Girls' some scenes that (so she told us) were now taking place at the Russian Court at St. Petersburg, where an amazing kind of werewolf from the Tartar forests, called Rasputin, had settled in and was holding everyone hypnotised under a kind of diabolic spell.

"I wouldn't have believed it," she purred, "except that I had it from one of the Chigi* boys, who had just come back from staying there himself and had witnessed everything! Well, it appears that not only do all the Russian Ministers and the Tsar and Tsarina themselves do everything at Rasputin's bidding, but all the Court ladies are wildly enamoured of this crazed, unwashed illiterate barbarian from the wilds! They'll do any mortal thing he tells them to. At dinner time for instance at the Tsar's table, Chigi described how Rasputin—a horrible-looking monstrosity with his unkempt beard all tangled and caked over with spilt sauces and foods from past banquets—would lean across the dinner table towards one of the Court ladies sitting opposite, stretch out over the silver dishes his filthy greasy hand (for he eats, it seems, only with his fingers, refusing a knife and fork)—this repulsive hand with its long dirt-encrusted claws, like some horrible wild beast's"—here Aunt Mariechen's eyes betrayed a sudden cruel glint, and she stretched out her own manicured hand with a gesture so adroit that bestial black

* An old and aristocratic Sienese family.

hairs seemed to sprout from it and dirty talons appear at the finger-tips. "And he would command the Countess opposite (or the Princess or the Duchess, whoever it might be)"—and here Mareeks' voice fell to a silky murmur—"to *lick* it! And the elegant Grand Duchess would bend her tiaraed head and lick it in front of all the company at the dinner-table. It seems," she continued, "it was a trick he was rather fond of at Court dinner-parties." Cries of shock and amazement from the ginger hens.

Mariechen had not raised her voice at all, but had told her story with stylishly cool detachment. A silence fell on the 'Girls' round the table, as they listened to her scandalous, pornographic tale. The munching ceased. She would not have been able to compel her audience's attention so completely had she not let the spicy odours of lechery, beastliness and sadism percolate through her innocently lisping tones.

Mary Berenson had given her audience a first-class entertainment, and I confess that I had fallen thrillingly under her spell.

Looking back, I see that I was very often aware, at this time, of something in the scene around me that was invisible yet more real than what my eyes showed me or that my ears heard—that a hidden meaning lay somewhere just out of range. I was always alert for mysterious signals, happenings I could not comprehend, veils drawn: all these filled me with a violent curiosity, as if the whole of life was a detective story, so that even as a child I was alert for clues to the real facts beneath those publicly displayed.

[During our holidays from Miss Grüner's school I paid several visits to Julia at Ford Place: the creaking old Elizabethan house was excitingly romantic, as was its rambling garden full of statues and barns, surrounded by high walls of rosy brick, against which grew the figs and peaches Uncle Logan so loved. When in a benign mood he quite enjoyed choosing ripe fruit and presenting them to us. We spent many long hours in the 'haunted' attics, where we were allowed to make any mess we chose, including painting frescoes all over the walls.

My first impression of Aunty Loo was that I had seldom met with such spoiling from an adult, for who else would have encouraged Julia 'nd me to dress up in all her clothes and trail along the dusty road to Littlehampton to pose as grown-up ladies in a tea-shop? Vainly, but not unkindly, she tried to instil a little order into Julia's life, and when Julia once asked her whether I too had not been remiss and untidy, I was much struck because Aunty Loo said politely that I was a visitor and so couldn't be scolded—yes, and I felt guilty too, for I knew that I was almost as absent-minded as Julia. (Travelling to Ford by train, all alone, was a chancy affair, and my suitcase tended to get left at Arundel junction where I had to change. Next time my mother put my toothbrush in a separate packet, but I managed to lose them both.)

Loo was generous in her praise on occasion. "Thee was the belle of the ball, Julia," I remember her saying after a children's party, at which I first met the glamorous Elizabeth Ponsonby, later a star of the Bright Young People. That same night five little girls slept in one large four-poster bed and splashed in the same bath together—a plan conceived by Aunty Loo and meant to enchant us more than I think it did. But she and Julia were like two sieves, one coarse, one fine, which let through particles of quite different size and shape; and just as school-children band together against an unpopular mistress, Julia and I would lie on our beds at night repeating her sayings and doings with gleeful malice. Yet, though Alys Russell was quite unlike most unpopular school-teachers in that she appeared to be armour-plated with insensitivity and a sort of relentless breeziness, it is only fair to balance the account against Julia's amusing but savage caricature by quoting from Loo's letters to her sister Mary Berenson during the Ford Place period:

"I want Julia to feel this is a *settled* home till she goes to school. I honestly think [Ray and Oliver] are neglecting her. However *that* they evidently mean to do always, so I shall cease thinking about it, and look upon myself as her mother."

"I miss the children dreadfully, perhaps more at breakfast than any other time. Their talk is particularly candid and amusing. Yesterday they were saying how *splendid* it would be if there were no grown-ups at all. Julia said, 'I can't see why people call the world unhappy and that sort of stuff.' They had their favourite pudding yesterday."

"The girls hate their Mlle., but I hope they will come round. Eliz. knows much more French than Julia, who is always wool-gathering and won't pay attention. When I chivvy them to bed there are bursts of giggles. Julia has an enchanting laugh which is a joy to hear."

"It is lovely to have Julia back and she is as happy as a Queen. There is a cold wind today so she and Frances are staying indoors to paint their programmes*."

"Today is Black Sunday for Julia. She forgot to put on the clean clothes I put out and left her pinafore in the hay. I'm afraid the child will never form regular habits, but she will have charm and good manners and many other compensating traits."

"I got back from the Ponsonbys in time to see Julia to bed. She seemed *so* glad to see me back, it is touching."

And lastly: "I enclose Julia's composition of yesterday. It shows imagination, Logan and I think. Logan admires Julia very much, and is very fond of her:

What I think of Grown People, by Julia aged 12

I think each person has a different character, but I have tried to pick out their characteristics in general. If one is arguing with them they very often don't stick to the point. Child: Why are children considered inferior? Grown-up (laughing): Well, look at that dress on the floor. See the reason? (Unecesery [sic]. Instead of giving the child a friendly pat and explaining that grown-ups have been educated and had experience.) Grown-ups have a tendency to think children are all 'jolly little mortles' [sic]. Some grown-ups say on a child's tenth birthday, 'Well Mary you will be putting your hair up soon,' and then turn away and laugh to a companion. This doesn't make the 'little person' swell with pride as it is expected to, nor does the 'little person' think it a capital joke. It merely makes them feel foolish and silly and cross. Of course grown-ups are in the right when they say children can't judge; they really are fair. I had to put that in because I criticised them so much."]

* For a play acted to the grown-ups.

Chapter Six

THE EARTHQUAKE

One dreamy sunny summer morning, Aunt Loo, like Jane Harrison, the well-known classical scholar, was having her breakfast on a tray in bed. When I went to say good morning to her on my way down to the dining-room to join those stalwarts who at this hour were already up on their feet—my father, my stepmother, Desmond and Molly MacCarthy and Hope Mirrlees, the poetess who lived with Jane Harrison, I found Aunty Loo's bedroom steeped in sunshine reflected up from the rose garden outside whose four walls were covered in peaches and figs.

Aunty Loo told me she had received a message, through Irish Katie the housemaid, who had brought in her breakfast tray, that Jane Harrison hoped Miss Julia would go in to her for a chat after her breakfast downstairs.

Jane Harrison, who had confided in me earlier in the weekend the particular affection she felt for bears of all sorts, had asked me the evening before if I would allow my greatly-loved companion, Bruno, a gigantic brown teddy-bear, with his wide blue satin neck-bow and eyes that lit up in the dark, to spend the night with her on her bed. I had been surprised at this request, and rather sorry to find a grey-haired lady of such great dignity and scholarly attainments to be still in need of teddy-bears like any child. In my child's crass ignorance it never entered my head that the whole manoeuvre was one of sheer benevolence and friendliness towards me. No doubt she wanted, in her affectionate way, to enter fully into my little world. How perpetually one misjudged the grown-ups through ruthless egotism and lack of experience!

I found Jane Harrison sitting up in bed, her breakfast tray on her knee, and Bruno sitting up beside her. Though I judged this as being strangely infantile on her part, I enjoyed the conversation we had together. It was entirely about bears. Both real living bears and stuffed Teddies. Her interest in this subject was really excessive. After leaving her bedroom, where, by the way, she requested the favour of keeping Bruno for a second night, I went along to the Cedar Room, Aunty Loo's beautifully panelled bedroom, which smelt to me so strongly of incense and sandalwood. In reality it was simply the smell of the cedar wood.

I left my chat with Miss Harrison feeling happy and snug, and vaguely ready for some weekend fun.

After a little conversation with Aunty Loo about Jane Harrison's great love for bears, she put her breakfast tray aside on the bed-side commode and got herself out of bed in her long, fully-flowing, cream flannel nightgown. Going over to the dressing-table she took up a reel of dental floss, kept there for drawing in and out between her teeth, the American alternative, so she had explained, to using a toothpick.

I meanwhile wandered around the room, smelling the perforated Chinese jar containing potpourri, examining her shoe-trees and that sort of thing. It was at such moments as these that I most felt at home, for I always associated keeping company with a lady who was dressing after breakfasting in bed with the happy mornings I had spent in just such a way as a small child with my mother in India. After my mother and I had breakfasted together in bed each morning, we had an hour of terrific fun together, for she would entertain me while she was dressing with anecdotes and songs, fantasies, jokes, and teasing.

Aunty Loo stood with the reel of dental floss in her hand and I heard her saying:

"I always feel so bad—so awfully sorry—that I can never be really fond of thee."

I looked at her questioningly.

"I mean that I can't give thee the love that thee's own mother would have given. It's awful that I can never give thee proper affection."

The words were said in kindness—from the guilt of a kindly heart, but all the same I got the sense of her words with a feeling of shock and horror. I had no idea till that moment that she could never possibly be truly fond of me! I had taken it for granted in fact that she did have a mother's feelings towards me.

Here was an appalling snub, and at such an unexpected moment! And if Aunty Loo did indeed feel she could not love me—why advertise the fact in such a crystal-clear way, I asked myself?

It was one of those moments when suddenly a chasm opens under one's feet, an earthquake, and I saw that I was left standing on the wrong side of it, that my home, so to speak, lay crumbled away in ruins upon the further unreachable part.

I left the room, saying nothing.

I remember wandering along the passages, up and down and round about, with the dim awareness of trying to get back somehow to where I really belonged—only wondering where it could be, and how found?

It had all happened before, earlier on, of course, when I had been sent away from my home in India alone to go to live in England amongst unwilling strangers.

Few people go through life I imagine without at the very least one such experience on the emotional level at any rate. In the Bible this story is referred to as the Expulsion from Paradise.

It was not so very long after my conversation with Aunt Loo in the Cedar Room—the same summer certainly—that the first generalisation about man and his place in the Cosmos took shape in my mind. I refer to my first realisation of Nature's supreme indifference to the Individual.

There had been no previous event on that particular day to herald its coming, though I imagine that it was probably connected with the upsetting remarks Aunt Loo had made during the fatal breakfast in her bedroom. By pointing out to me that she could not ever be fond of me she revealed that I was simply a stranger living at Ford Place among other strangers—the sort of revelation of which I had already had my fill in earlier years. The experience I am about to describe seemed to have been in some way born from a prolonged inspection of the drawing-room furniture around me.

It was another of Logan's weekend parties. After lunch he had taken his guests down to the sea-shore at nearby Clymping. Oysters were to be found upon the sands. A crab tea at the well-known Crab and Lobster tea-rooms was to follow this.

Aunt Loo had cycled off to Lapton, the next village, on some errand or other. The servants had been given the afternoon off. I was left in the house all by myself.

I started roaming about up and down stairs through the dank, echoing, airy shell of the haunted old house. Outside the windows, whenever I stopped at a pane to stare, the walnut trees, the fields, the lawns, the canal and the blue south downs beyond, all stood silent in the windless afternoon, everything waiting. Listening. Hushed and haunted. I felt there was no other word for it.

When I arrived in the middle of the yellow drawing-room I looked questioningly around.

Nothing.

Only the yellow watered-silk curtains.

And the yellow satin-striped Regency chairs, now empty.

Then again the Queen Anne tallboy casting a dense inert shadow across the indifferent grey carpet.

Marble Adam mantelpiece, changeless—just as usual.

I think that I have always been aware of man's predicament—smelt his Cosmic Disaster, in the presence of the numb furniture standing silently in an empty room. Walls, mantelpiece, rigidly unmoving. Curtains, wardrobes—uncannily immense, weightily powerful, menacingly reserved. It is out of such as these that I have often heard a kind of awful reverberating underworld music emanating, sending out to me some poisonous news about the nature of Reality.

It may be that because somebody has chosen to express his private life in symbols in a particular room, one expects to find that the furnishings have themselves taken on—out of sheer sympathy—a warm life of some sort. It is therefore with a freezing shock that one sees that in fact they have *not*.

At any rate, after standing in silence endeavouring to take in the reality of the drawing-room situation for quite a long and concentrated time that afternoon, the non-human, non-livingness of the house penetrated to my understanding and I seemed to perceive its implications.

The reality dawned upon me. 'Why,' I thought—'even if someone that one loved most closely, a most valuable person, far away and out of sight, should happen to undergo a cruel and ghastly accident—slipping over a precipice to be dashed to death on the rocks below or some such catastrophe—even the sea, the sky, Nature (or what later I came to lump under the heading of the Cosmos) would stare at what was happening with indifference. Would lend no helping hand.' I suddenly realised that there existed no permanent line of communication, even between those who deeply loved one another, which would vibrate on such an occasion, and give warnings of the crying need for help. This was the very first time such a thought had struck me.

I felt deeply indignant.

Most certainly there *should* be such a line of communication.

For the first time I sought to size up the relationships, if any, between myself and all the heartless inorganic surrounding matter which so ignominiously submits to the laws that govern it. It was then that I suddenly perceived that some enormous force had all the time been gripping tight hold of me; it was as if a mighty and cold-hearted cosmic nurse had been dangling me (tiny and ignorant as I was), a helpless prisoner in her relentless Titanic lap.

[When, long afterwards, Julia looked back at the incident in Aunt Loo's bedroom, she evidently thought of it as a second rejection, following the pattern of the first by her mother, even though it came 'from the guilt of a kindly heart'. However, it seems possible that the passage of time had wrought a slight distortion or shift of emphasis in Julia's memory, and that Aunt Loo had not meant to be so gratuitously—and uncharacteristically snubbing.

Two jottings from Julia's notebooks are perhaps relevant here. In one she declared: "By the time I was eight I noticed the difference in quality between my own dreams and the outside world." In other words, between what Freud called Phantasy and Reality.

The other (undated) runs: "When Aunty Loo boasted to me that her Quaker faith was one of *acceptance*, I told her that the essence of my morality was to accept some things and reject others." Julia's belief in the importance of being *critical* stayed with her all her life.]

Chapter Seven

BEDALES, OR THE TRAINING OF THE VINE

[Julia added some fictitious characters and incidents to the beginning and end of this account of her schooldays, altered some names, and sent it to John Lehmann, who published it under the title of *Pioneer City* in *New Writing* for Winter 1942–3. As here presented it is purely auto-biographical.

Julia arrived at Bedales in September 1913 when she was just twelve years old, and instantly made friends with another girl called Margaret Leathes,* who has contributed the following note about her:

During her earlier terms Julia was particularly unhappy. She was always in trouble and was given hours of 'extra work'. She invariably lost her hair-ribbons, locker-keys and fountain pen. As an aid to beauty on dancing-class days she sometimes allowed her parting to stray a few millimetres from the centre of her scalp, which was considered 'fast' or 'frivolous'. She hated outdoor games, gym, compulsory runs and cold baths. Apart from English (she excelled at original writing) and a smattering of French, she wasn't good at lessons. Geography and Arithmetic defeated her and she had no memory for dates. Poor Julia lived in an aura of disapproval from the staff. She had very little social conscience and found the 'Bedales spirit' deeply antipathetic—but she loved acting, and was so good at it that she thought for a time of taking it up professionally. Her talent for playing ragtime on the piano was not approved, but her acting was, and so were her clever drawings and paintings. In the holidays I sometimes went to stay with her or she with me, but my parents disapproved of her too—I don't know why, unless it was because she kept powder, and I think rouge, in her navy blue elasticated knickers.

* Afterwards Penrose, and now Newman.

(Julia to Margaret Leathes)

March 8th, 1916. The scene is laid in an old country house. The dining-room walls are partly panelled and partly mouldy through damp. A fine old-fashioned sideboard stands against the further wall. A fire is burning modestly in the grate. Sitting at a writing desk is a young girl, about 15 judging by her youthful contours and delicately formed limbs. Her finely chiselled features wear a slightly discontented look, a faint line between her arched brows is indicative of restlessness—in other words she's bored stiff. The rain beats down with a monotonous roar; if there were a clock in the room it would tick slowly, incessantly and even maddeningly in the silence. Here am I!]

The business of my education fell entirely to my poor Aunt Loo. Between her numerous social works, her committee meetings, her refugee organisations, I saw her doing it. She busied herself preparing my ingredients with the conscientious care of a chemist's assistant, new to the job, making up a prescription for a bottle of medicine.

In the end she chose for me a co-ed school called Bedales. Its prospectus was liberally dotted with such phrases as 'Wise Freedom', 'Home Farm', 'New and more Wholesome attitude', 'Heather and Pines' and so on and so forth. And there was a photograph of one of the handicraft rooms showing the pupils working at trestle tables where were laid out leather blotting-pads, bags and ornamental bookshelves, stamped or carved all over with the grapevine pattern. The prospectus offered the chance of learning how to build a new and better world to each schoolchild.

Clash! Clangle! Clangle! It was the school waking-up bell. Of course. It rang for eternities—and what a torture. Knocking on the head all that one held precious, hacking the roots of our personal lives from under us, leaving us mutilated and abandoned. The dormitory door was open. From my pillow I saw down the narrow passage, saw the sleepy prefect on duty in her dressing-gown. I turned my head and was greeted by the dormitory furniture: cast-iron bedsteads, flimsy stained chests of drawers, all crying aloud, 'I am cheap, unloved and unlovable, but all that you children deserve'. I started to tell the girl next to me how I had dreamt I was given a birthday present of a kitten-plant (three

live tabbies growing from one stem) when Clang! Clang!—the bell for
cold baths began, and the prefect at the door began screeching out our
numbers. Soon my number would be called, and I must abandon what
I was saying; in any case the din of bell-ringing, number-screeching and
feet thumping along the passage to plunge their owners into cold baths
would have drowned my story. Until we were dressed no further
communication was possible, for now all was racket and anxiety. And
then, once disguised in our school uniform (a contraption that made us
look like so many oblong green bolsters instead of human beings), we
were no longer ourselves. No longer individuals. At 8.15 our personal
characters were renounced, school *esprit de corps* took their place. At 8.20
the girls were in the bootroom putting on their outdoor shoes, forming
into groups in the courtyard for the 'early morning run'. But it
happened that I had a blister on my heel and was excused from the run,
so that my time was my own for a quarter of an hour before breakfast.

I took some gramophone records from my locker, and ran—past
tennis courts and playing fields—to the main school building, where, in
my classroom, I was allowed to keep my gramophone. And there I
spent the last ten minutes before breakfast playing a Boston one-step, a
Hesitation valse, and a new dance—a Tango.

Later on that day I was walking along our dormitory passage when
out from a doorway popped a prefect, Joan B., who took me by the
wrist.

Joan was built on singularly broad and simple lines, both in body and
spirit, and with her rotundity and naive enthusiasm always brought to
my mind a sponge pudding, globular, bland and gently steaming.

"Will you come into the cupboard room, please? I want to have a
little talk with you . . ." She smiled: and in her face I recognised with a
start the 'Bedales look'; that is to say she was not looking at me but at an
abstraction on which she was about to shed light. She opened the door
behind her and revealed a room given over entirely to clothes cupboards, each one with a holland curtain stencilled over with the
grapevine pattern. She shut the door softly and proceeded to gaze upon
me for a long while with a kind of happy sadness.

"I happened to pass B2 classroom before breakfast this morning.
Someone was playing a Boston one-step on the gramophone. It was
you, wasn't it?"

"Yes." I looked at my bandaged foot reflectively. "I was let off the run this morning because I have a blister on my heel."

"That is not the point. The point is that you were playing a Boston one-step before breakfast on the gramophone."

"Oh yes," I said happily, and in the heavy silence that followed I hummed a tune, as if remembering something we should both enjoy, and a snatch of words: "Roguish smiles and Peek-a-boo blouses! La-di-dee . . . Every time you kiss me it seems so nice! But you never seem to kiss me in the same way twice! O-O-O-You! YOU'VE got to do it now!" Actually the record I was playing had no words to it, and I had selected the 'Roguish smiles' etc. to hum to her as being of the type of saucy slyness most likely to shock her.

She looked at me. "The trouble is that you don't pull your weight in the boat. Everybody is saying the same thing. Do you think that is very nice to hear? We prefects are here to look after and help you younger ones. And it's jolly rotten for us standing by and watching you make such a foul mess of your life. Because the school is in a sense a sort of lifeboat, you know. Life is a difficult sea, and the Principal and the Vice are trying their very hardest to help us row across you know, and teach us to play our part in the body corporate."

"I don't think the body corporate, whatever it is, minds my playing a Boston one-step in my free time, if I'm alone and nobody else hears it."

"Can't you understand that it's the whole *tone* that's rotten? In a sense it's a good deal *worse* that you should employ yourself in such a way when you are quite alone."

I endeavoured to look amazed.

"Don't you *understand?*"

"Er—not quite . . ."

"But THINK! A Boston one-step BEFORE BREAKFAST! Have you lost all your sense of values? You see," she continued on a lower tone, "they are giving us the benefit of such a new, free way of life, preparing for a beautiful new world, where people can throw off the old constraints and prejudices and revel in light and freedom and loveliness. And they trust us so!" Her voice trembled happily. "And that, you see, is why it seems a little underhand and—well—cheap to do ugly mean things, even if no-one is looking."

Joan's hand was now on the door handle, so that probably the interview was nearing its end. But I knew that first certain formalities would be observed. Which of the two ways in which Bedales was in the habit of finishing up 'little talks' would Joan use? I considered that the first ('I don't think there is much to be got out of continuing this conversation further') would mean that I had won and the pi-jawer had drawn a blank. The second style ('I know that it's not the true YOU speaking' and dismissal with a sweet smile) would mean I had lost and laurels went to the pi-jawer. Again there was not a doubt that before parting I should be advised to play sea-shanties instead of Boston one-steps on my gramophone—'Yo! Ho! Blow the man down!' and probably, 'What shall we do with a drunken sailor?'.

Meanwhile Joan was speaking: "If you must play light music on the gramophone (and Heaven knows I shouldn't want you always to play heavy serious stuff), why not play fine, jolly things? Sea-shanties for instance. 'Yo! Ho! Blow the man down!' is a jolly thing and so is 'What shall we do with a drunken sailor?'."

How angry I felt! I despised those two songs from the bottom of my heart. I answered rudely: "You want to turn me into an old salt or something. But you can't. Instead when I grow up I intend to wear Peek-a-boo blouses and give roguish smiles—to men!"

Tears came into my eyes. When Joan spoke next, after a silence, she sounded happy and gracious: "I don't think this is the *real* you speaking. I have more faith in you (although I'm aware many people have not)." She made for the door, thus closing the interview.

I had lost!

It was only nine-fifteen and I was already worn out! And I remember that the whole day was particularly disagreeable.

In History class, for instance, I made the mistake of doing a drawing of Miss Mackay, our teacher, depicting her as a pelican in top boots. I managed to destroy the drawing in time, but could not avert the exhortation to be frank and share my joke with the rest of the class, so that we could all laugh in comradely fashion together.

"A hearty laugh does everybody good. But we don't appreciate silly furtive giggling at Bedales."

When the class was over Miss Mackay kept me behind for a 'little talk'. It started: "I somehow don't feel you are quite playing the game; and I think a good many others feel as I do," and finished off: "and so here at Bedales we have shaken ourselves free of the narrow shackling prejudices of our grandfathers. We honour all of you with a great *trust* in return for your freedom; but *you*, my child, have a little devil somewhere inside you, who is urging you on to do things which in your heart of hearts you know to be mean. And petty. And cheap. Isn't that so? So now let's see if we can't persuade that little devil that it's really much jollier to be a helpful, useful, fine sort of person in this great beautiful world of ours. And I think you'll find he will agree. He isn't .the *real* you, you know."

I looked in wonder at her humourless, hairy face, pink at the nose tip and eye rims, and at the shrinking neglected body lurking beneath the peacock green gown, which was cut up in the shape of battlements round her neck, as it might be part of the castle towers of her own history lessons—and a new fear came to me: if I stayed long enough among these people, might I not by some unhappy natural law turn out like them, instead of like Aunt Mareeks or Ethel Levey?*

My next 'little talk' was for saying 'Hang' and 'Damn', overheard the day before. The Vice-Principal took over for this, in her cream distempered sitting-room hung with Greuze milkmaids and children biting apples. She had a dignified and pleasant face, and carried herself well in her mackintosh and brown sandshoes, which she wore day and night—in bed and out—so rumour had it. I had a friendly feeling towards this lady; she was so plainly goodhearted, so handsome too, in spite of her black moustache. She placed her hand on my shoulder, and I made sure that now at last was coming a certain 'little talk' I had been dreading, about my discussion of sexual matters with two girl friends in the pine woods behind the home farm the previous Friday.

The 'Vice' went through the whole tale about having broken out into the daylight of a new, glorious, wise and wholesome life, etcetera, not forgetting to mention the sea of life, the rowing boat, the grapevine pattern and the body corporate. When it turned out to be merely 'hang' and 'damn' that were in question I was relieved but surprised that two such ordinary words should be the cause of such ponderous and holy solemnity.

Soon after this I walked across from the main buildings to the girls' block to get tidy for tea.

It was the summer term; but one of those grey hard days when the cricket pitches, the handicraft huts and the red brick school buildings

---

* Star of revues such as *Watch your Step* (1915).

all seemed staring, dead things. We were hot, as cakes are hot. For our world was cut off by a roof of leaden clouds from the living sunlight, and from the freshness and space of the upper airs. This leaden coffin-lid, that protects us here in England so respectably from the more scorching rays of the sun, can give the most unhappy effect to our island. We pride ourselves on having achieved the sober, commonsense light of day, but how deceitful that sensible flat light really is; it is easy to feel that we are all merely living inside a newspaper photograph, showing the dreary measurements of some unknown place. I was feeling something of the sort that afternoon.

And it was then that I saw approaching across the tennis court—the Principal, a tiny figure, a little green fly in a loose sage gown, with hair stacked up carelessly on top of her head. I walked faster. Only think—if the Principal should happen to reach my path just when I did. It might result in a 'little talk'. I flew along.

What was that? She was calling. I had to turn and meet the little lady. Seen from close to, the Principal's piled-up hair was like dried cut grass, with a wavering green velvet ribbon tangled up in its substance. Beneath this stack, the little face stamped over with freckles, with its large wedge stuck on by way of a nose, two round black holes for eyes and sun-toughened skin, reminded one of a sand-man—one of those faces built up roughly on the beach. And inside—what a surprise—a bonfire was alight, for the eyes showed a fiercely burning charcoal glow. Yet there was no sign of a human being looking out, to see one there and give one greeting!

"You are going over to tidy for tea? Come over here and have a little talk with me instead. I think you can spare just a few moments, can't you?"

With tiny pattering steps and fluttering movements she led the way to her private wallflower garden beyond the tennis courts.

"Let us sit together on this nice wall." With a tiny claw the Principal waved me on to the wall and hopped up beside me, underneath the hanging blossom of a laburnum tree.

In the usual few moments' silence that ushered in the 'little talk' the freckled face was turned towards the line of fir trees edging the drive. I wondered at her smiling repose. And yet surely that was *not* a smile? Her burning eyes seemed rather to be watching a vision—of what? (Some sort of dread happening; the burning of Joan of Arc? Someone in a Peek-a-boo blouse dancing the Boston one-step?) Heaven knew what horror. So that it couldn't have been a smile.

She was feeling about for an opening for her 'little talk': "I think you are a person to whom friendship and books, and things of that sort, mean more than cricket or tennis in your spare time?"

"Er-rhmm."

"For you *do* have spare times, don't you? Your 'free times' as we are proud to call them. Times when we can wander wherever we will—take a book down from the library shelves, visit the drawing and painting studios or just lie under the big leafy trees . . . don't we?"

"Er-rhm-hmm."

The Principal pronounced her words with extreme care, and slowly, as to a foreigner. She went on: "Here we are not kept with our noses perpetually ground into our copybooks, as our grandfathers were. We are not supervised by stiff-backed ladies in whalebone corsets—are we?—who tell us every two minutes to sit up straight like ladies! We are not taken to church three times a day, told never to talk to the boys—*are* we?"

"Er—no."

"In fact our boast is that we are all proud, clean, wholesome, jolly comrades on this beautiful, marvellous earth! Here we don't giggle in corners about 'young men' as our grandmothers did. Instead we talk and think of our comrades of the opposite sex loudly! Sensibly! We are frank, we are above board, so that all may hear what we have to say." From here, the Principal rambled on about the striking cleanness, wholesomeness, frankness and jolliness of the love that men and women have for one another.

I was ruminating; the mystery surrounding procreation was impenetrable. Not that we hadn't been instructed in the physical mechanism of the thing from A to Z. At Bedales the youngest child could draw diagrams on the blackboard of its physiological details. But what emotions could possibly accompany this fantastic affair? That was the point that puzzled us all. That was the enigma which we discussed in whispers when walking in the pine woods behind the home farm. The staff at Bedales seemed anxious to give out that the whole process had the character of a super-religious ceremony. When talking of it their faces became portentously solemn, the air would thicken to the consistency of melted chocolate, and I noticed that the phrase 'the body is the temple of the holy spirit' was repeated firmly again and again, with a warning look.

But the Principal was still speaking: "For there need be no furtive secrets about our dear brothers, *need* there? Neither can there be anything to giggle over in the sane, healthy, beautiful kind of love that comes, as you will find yourself when you are older, between a man and a woman—the kind of love which is holily ordained at last to end in the procreation of another wonderful human being—*can* there?"

I heard this last uttered in a particularly triumphant tone, whilst the Principal's eyes stared, smouldering, at the pine trees along the drive. The fact of the matter was that I had been wool-gathering and perfectly lost the thread. The Principal must have said a good many more things, each ending suddenly with '*Don't* we?' or '*Aren't* we?' to be answered by my stolid everlasting 'Erhm-hm' before I at last heard the school bell ringing for high tea.

"You're quite sure there is nothing you would like to ask me?"

"Nothing, thank you."

The Principal jumped down off the wall, brushed a laburnum leaf off her skirts and we went in to tea.

High tea in the dining-hall was certainly a noisy affair. Just as in a railway station it is necessary to tear after the porter who carries one's bags, in order not to lose him, and go bumping amongst groups of people with babies, or dogs on long winding leashes, so it was necessary in that deafening hubbub of voices to keep sight of one's own particular conversation by ignoring or riding roughshod over all the others around one, laughing or contradicting each other, and pursue it through the medley of conflicting sounds. At last a bell rang, and at this signal we all stood up, said grace, and began to file out of the dining-hall.

At this moment I always felt a pang of regret. I enjoyed being in the dining-hall for its own sake. Something about its shape, the statues ringing it round, the great mullioned windows which ran nearly from floor to ceiling at the far end, disclosing a glittering lawn and woods sweeping away into the distance, and then also the unfamiliar echoing of our voices far above us—all these things were exciting and caused life majestically to expand. The architect had designed the hall with a hint—the barest hint it is true—of glory and flourish, but it was enough to raise up the eating of our primitive meals into a mass ritual for which the scene had been feelingly set, so that there grew a kind of pride in the whole affair. And I felt in my heart or my bones that an architect could do more to produce a consciousness of the 'body corporate' in five minutes than any number of 'little talks' could do in five long years.

Being still one of the younger ones, I went with others of the same age up to bed directly after high tea.

I remember, as I undressed, wondering at the unusual silence outside the high windows. No shouting, no patting of tennis-balls, no shuffling of footsteps along the gravel paths. This silence, and a certain deadness in the air of the empty dormitory, seemed to fit the mood which had been lurking all day like a sea-fog on my horizon, and which—now that I was alone in bed—floated forward without let or hindrance, enveloping with its sad greyness the whole scene, my neatly folded clothes on the yellow pitchpine chair beside my bed, the wet soap and flannel on the washstand.

Suddenly, with a crash, from across the drive came a burst of voices singing:

"Halleluiah! Halleluiah! Halleluiah!"

Of course. As I now remembered, the whole upper school was over in the concert hall having a practice for the *Messiah*. I got out of bed, and standing on a chair beside the high window looked out and listened. The school grounds were beneath me, and the whole dead landscape of that afternoon had come to life. The lights were all on, causing the beech trees to blaze with emeralds of every shade, and creating deep shadows everywhere. A soft, warm breeze floated round the corner of the house, stroked my cheek lightly and floated away again.

They had stopped singing. In the silence the cooing of the wood-pigeons echoed sadly among the treetops. Beyond the school buildings the fields and woods lay basking in a magical brilliance; they looked charmed, things seen in a mirror, or in water, as unattainable as remembered woods and fields. I glimpsed for a moment just such a softly burning landscape within myself. And because the long metallic day had left me frozen and desolate—because the contrast was sad—I made my way quickly back into bed, threw the coverings over my face and lay still, trying to forget the world as quickly as might be. And like that I lay, without movement, until the falling night brought the other occupants of the room up to their beds.

So that was the end of my school day. A day like a hundred others.

[After missing Julia's company at Miss Grüner's school for over a year, I persuaded my mother to let me follow her to Bedales in 1915. Here I too made a lifelong friend of Margaret Leathes, but Julia and I were never in the same form, and the year and a half between our ages kept us somewhat apart. I left in 1917 and the other two in 1918.

During her last holidays Julia sometimes stayed in Uncle Logan's Chelsea house. The First World War was not yet over, and from some letters to her friend Elizabeth Ponsonby we learn that "Aunt Loo is going to arrange for me to play the piano a few nights a week at a War Club, where soldiers come to dance with their young ladies." This correspondence is full of girlish gush about actors ("George Robey sent me a ripping photo" and "Nelson Keys wrote saying what a *charming* letter I had sent him!!"). They also contain references to admired or admiring young men, to 'sentimental remarks', 'abominable flirts' and even 'violent kisses', and are slashed with exclamation-marks.]

Chapter Eight

LOVE AT FIRST SIGHT

One Christmas I was told that my Aunt Mareeks had invited me to spend a three-weeks holiday at their villa, *I Tatti*, outside Florence. I had never been to Italy, and I was promised wonders: the art galleries of Florence, Bernard Berenson's beautiful house, built for him by his pet architect Cecil Pinsent, and his marvellous collection of Italian pictures.

With few exceptions, 'pictures' meant to me the illustrations by Arthur Rackham, Edmund Dulac and others, in the big volumes, usually published as Christmas gift-books. These I adored with passion. To sit down and open one of them was to leave behind reality and escape into a Paradise where beautiful young women wearing floating garments and with flowers in their hair spent the hours with their romantic paramours, drifting across midnight skies on the backs of genii, cowering in fear in the heart of forests, or drowning palely in tumultuous moonlit waters.

Before I left for Italy I had chosen two dresses from a batch of designs sent me by Mrs. Berenson's Italian dressmaker, and these were to be made up and ready when I arrived. I had been told that the style of living at *I Tatti* was much more luxurious than that of my philanthropic Aunt Loo, and besides that, there would be festivities in the surrounding villas where other young people were spending the Christmas holidays.

The Berensons' villa was a large white building high up on the hill at Settignano; below it descended a terraced garden furnished with statues, and overlooking the rolling plain through which wound the Arno. On entering the front door I found myself in a marble hallway as big as a church, which stretched away into the interior of the house. The floor was a long glimmering river reflecting archways leading away in many directions; wrought-iron leaves curled up the stairs beneath the banisters, and all was bathed in warmth and stillness, as of a drowsy summer afternoon. Our feet made a hollow clicking sound on the marble, but fell silently on the carpeted staircase, which twisted upwards to the spacious landing off which my bedroom door opened. But hanging on the walls of this elegant landing I saw, to my amazement, the most hideous pictures I had ever beheld—tiny squares and oblongs made of wood and many of them without frames, on which lifeless figures were painted, as if by a child, with stiff limbs and dismayingly plain faces. And all so small! These tiny figures often represented Christ, in which case they were revoltingly gashed, with copious blood flowing from their semicircular wounds and faces miserably contorted with pain. I was horrified as well as disappointed.

I had never seen primitives before.

I was given a large and lofty bedroom, sitting-room and bathroom of my own—a 'suite' in fact—and thus promoted from my old status of schoolchild to that of a respected adult guest. The next morning, and indeed every morning after, instead of the usual soul-shattering struggle with myself to leave my bed and get down to the dining-room in time for breakfast, I was wakened by a dignified ladies'-maid, with the manner of a high priestess, placing a huge tray upon my knees in bed, upon which were a beautifully prepared grapefruit, an *oeuf en cocotte* swimming in cream, and toast and honey. While I was eating my breakfast, this lady revolved round my bedroom with never a sound or a rustle; she glided as if on castors with a graveness plainly expressing a high and holy pride in all her proceedings.

When at last I got up she produced for me to wear a plum-coloured velvet frock trimmed with whiskers of fur round its high neck—one of the creations of the Florentine dressmaker, and an unheard-of get-up for a Bedalian schoolgirl to wear of a morning. In answer to my enquiries as to where my Aunt and the others were, I was told that everyone was still in bed breakfasting; Aunt Mareeks was closeted with the manicurist and masseuse, but she would like me to pay her a visit when they had left her. All this—the silence, the heat, the strong smell of the juicy grapefruit and the honey—blended into a first taste of this new civilisation I had entered, and I marvelled greatly.

Once dressed, I sallied off along the wide corridor, and turning the corner to skirt the front of the house I got my first sight of the Italian landscape lying under the winter sun. Beyond the garden the white chalky roadway wound steeply up among the Settignano hills, while the plain in which Florence stands lay spread out far below, with the silver thread of the Arno zigzagging across it. I saw the snowtopped mountains of Vallombrosa, the radiant Italian heavens shimmering, boundless and brilliant blue, behind tier upon tier of yellow Autumn woods. I felt like a chicken that has just broken and stepped out of its shell, and senses the life surrounding it.

That same evening there was a big tea-party for children and young people, given at the Villa Medici at Fiesole by Lady Sybil Cutting, and I was invited. I was to wear the other dress made for me by the Florentine modiste—my 'party' dress. This was of white chiffon, lace and swansdown, with pink satin ribbons threaded through it, a very low neck and a hooped underskirt. Thus attired I felt I looked more like a giraffe than a human being, for I was one of those adolescents who had outgrown their strength. I consulted my reflection in the mirror with eagerness and trepidation, and thought it looked quite queer. *Tant pis.* This giraffe-like figure was bundled into a voluminous white sheepskin coat (another present from my Aunt), and off we set.

The party was going full swing when we arrived at the Villa Medici and entered the crowded drawing-room, where I found a multitude of children in smart frocks and Eton suits watching a magic lantern show. As I was being taken about and introduced by my kind hostess I noticed a being of unparalleled radiance standing at the back of the audience: a man dressed in fifteenth-century Florentine costume of blue velvet, with a Renaissance pot hat on his curling hair. His face was long and pale and his full-lipped mouth was mockingly amused. Here was plainly no ordinary mortal—in other words I had fallen violently in love with him at first sight.* To my joy this beautiful creature smiled benevolently upon me, and after the performance positively handed me cakes and was solicitous for my comfort.

When the party was over I was helped on with my woolly sheepskin and told that 'Cecil' would drive me home to *I Tatti*. But who *was* 'Cecil'? Imagine my feelings when there stepped into the car with me that very same super-radiant being I have just described. He was in fact Cecil Pinsent, the architect who had designed the Berensons' villa and

---

* A friend who often visited *I Tatti* told me that this was an almost universal reaction of girls to Cecil Pinsent.

was staying at *I Tatti* at the time, busy completing a rococo fountain.

As for the other inhabitants of the villa: Bernard Berenson charmed me by his gusto for life, the beautiful bottle-green suits he wore (always with a fresh pink rose or a camellia in the button-hole). He was a small man with a well-trimmed auburn beard and fine pale hands, a great talker and a great teaser. His kingly presence was well matched by that of Aunt Mareeks, for she was undoubtedly a queen. Although a great beauty in her girlhood, she had become extremely plump in middle age, but—like a splendid peach or tea-rose—she glowed, bloomed and smiled from among her plumes, furs and trailing flounces.

Three persons besides myself were staying in the house at the moment—the architect Cecil, his friend and partner Geoffrey Scott,* and a Swedish girl called Naomi, masseuse and friend to Mrs. Berenson. All used to assemble before lunch and drink sherry in a little boudoir—Mrs. Berenson reclining on a lilac satin settee and radiating enjoyment as if she were eating turkish delight or some rare sweetmeat; Berenson perhaps standing in a bar of sunlight near the door talking of intellectual or artistic matters with the male guest of honour; Cecil with his long legs and arms spread like a daddy-long-legs, and Geoffrey Scott's tall scholarly appearance and cynical monkey's face expressing a certain stiffness as he sat very upright, like an overgrown student, on a tiny eighteenth-century chair, peering mischievously through his black-rimmed glasses.

At home in England I had been all the time with reformers and uplifters, and my school (Bedales) was a 'pioneer' establishment, as we were constantly told, whose religious zeal (or fanaticism) was 'leading us away from the old evil order towards the light'. By contrast, daily life in this house in Italy was something to be much enjoyed by everyone. Everyone was busy, however; Berenson writing all morning, Aunt Mareeks at her myriad 'arrangements', and Cecil, a tall figure among the workmen building the fountain on the terrace, pointing and gesticulating in the sunshine, his long hair ruffled by the wind. At mealtimes the sun streamed in at the long terrace windows and fell on dishes of big sticky *marrons glacés*, crystallised violets and cherries, as well as on the scholars, painters and intellectuals by whom the table was sure to be surrounded. By evening another scintillating galaxy of superior beings would have made its appearance; the candelabras were

* *Author of Portrait of Zélide and other books.*

lit, and below in the wide valley the cold winter mists from the Arno could be seen coiling this way and that, while the red sun sank behind the dark mountains of Vallombrosa.

In the afternoons I was often driven down to Florence and left to wander round the picture-galleries till it was time to be picked up and taken back to the villa for tea. Sometimes as many as five of us would pack in together—Aunt Mareeks in her voluminous furs, Naomi (a straight slender Diana), the two long-limbed architects, and myself in a ludicrous little pudding-basin hat with elastic under the chin, bought for me in London by my saintly Aunt Loo. I remember my first of these excursions, and how the chaste mountain freshness gave way gradually to the cobbles and trams, the shifting, shuffling, grinding, creaking, whip-cracking babel smelling of coffee, garlic and sweat, of Florence. At last we reached the Duomo. I was appalled! I had expected Gothic grey-ness and dreaming spires, and was scandalised by what looked to me like a glorified station lavatory decorated with flamboyant wasp stripes.

And what of the famous galleries?

I enjoyed their vast spaciousness and stillness. I was filled with awe to think that here were amassed the treasures of man's spirit through the ages. It was a complete universe, of which I had not at present the key. Enter it I certainly could not. I gazed at the great dark canvasses filled with draperies, clouds and pillars, peopled by nun-faced women and men with musclebound legs and arms, with numbers of elderly babies and tortured, bleeding Christs. One of the main surprises was the shameless gusto with which, it seemed to me, the artists dwelt on the details of Christ's sufferings, depicting the thorns piercing the soft flesh, the shining red blood and livid, lolling head. Wasn't it indecent, hard, sadistic? With the many scenes of damned souls being prodded by devils or cast out by flames and snakes I got on rather better, for I couldn't help eagerly (but guiltily) searching for the worst and most spectacular torments I could find. While, although the heavenly scenes of rejoicing gave me pleasure, their endless circling together on the grass seemed a dreary and pious form of recreation for the saved, for I had reached an age when my idea of super-human grace was embodied in Ethel Levey doing the high kick in *Watch your Step*. Shocked and oppressed, I went off to the sculptures, and taking a fancy to Michel-angelo's David I sat down beside him and awaited the arrival of my escort. It was Geoffrey Scott who came to fetch me, and the first thing he said was that it was no good looking at David at all, as he was merely a cast.

When Christmas Day came, Cecil asked me what I would like for a present. I told him, and was duly obliged by Edmund Dulac's latest Christmas volume. I was overjoyed—until he looked at it with me and proceeded to explain why in his opinion Dulac was the most repulsive of artists: this, I remember, was because he didn't attempt to put on paper his own personal impression of a subject, nor even to copy any one master, but made a bastard mixture of about seven or eight, added a few second-rate stylish tricks and spread the pages with the resultant medicine. I trusted Cecil's judgment absolutely, so that the result was I had to face up to the ruins of many of the altars I had so fervently worshipped at before I came to *I Tatti*.

The first time a passion for another person had taken possession of me had been at twelve years old. There were no physical expressions at all—that machinery had not started to work; when I thought of what a different thing, or animal, I was turning into it all seemed like a fairy story, something arbitrary and without meaning. But I knew I would some day have those adult organs I saw in females around me and didn't much care about. How *could* this be going to happen to me? I looked forward to savouring the sensation of difference with fierce curiosity. When the time finally came, and I *had* developed these breasts and hips and so forth, I think I felt that I, the experiencer and savourer, was still there making notes about how it felt. And how did it feel? Like a door opening on to my real self, on to a natural growth of generous giving, of loving, and everything that had been banned for me when I was still undeveloped—an extension of soul and accompanying body. Above all it made sense of my emotions: breasts were for giving a child what it should need, and as for bearing children, what could be more miraculously lyrical than uniting with the beloved to produce *more* of a good thing, a repetition of the loved one in a concrete sense. So much was this so that I wondered if I should not have understood it easily if anyone had put it to me in that way when I was quite a young thing.

But to return to the gradual unfolding of the key emotions connected with love and being in love:

At fourteen came the big revelation—Cecil Pinsent, love at first sight, an experience that still remains to me unanalysable and miraculous. Never having seen him before, I realised the instant I clapped eyes on his face that he came from some dimension that was vital to me, just as if I had known him in some other form of living. Still no physical sensations, but now they were surely sleeping, waiting for Cecil's awakening embrace. As he never made his way through the thorn thickets surrounding the castle I drifted out of his orbit and did not fall in love again until I was eighteen.

So it went on all through my adult life. In each case the cosmic emotions, the lyrical emotions, the mysterious musical emotions that are usually produced by nature—the sea, sky, light, smells of living things—each time I fell in love these were withdrawn from the world at large and concentrated, as through a burning-glass, on the man with whom I was in love.

[Julia had been drawn to Mary Berenson ever since their first meeting in England. She saw her as possessing every feminine and seductive quality that poor well-meaning block-busting Aunt Loo so signally lacked. All the more dazzled was she to find her in her own luxurious and civilised setting at *I Tatti*, and the impression left on her by this visit laid the foundations of some lifelong values. Up to this time, when she had been subjected to 'culture' she had tended to react by opposing it. For instance, she used to say that Oliver's attempts to introduce her to Mozart by singing his opera arias accompanied by absurdly airy-fairy gestures had spoiled *Don Giovanni* and *The Marriage of Figaro* for her for good, and made her take passionately to ragtime. Now, at the Berensons', she was confronted by culture appetisingly combined with luxury. Henceforth the concepts of elegance, taste, art and scholarship were to rank high with her, while as for luxury, when asked to describe her ideal life she replied, "Lying on a pink fur rug doing absolutely nothing." However, these new values were often temporarily eclipsed by the excitement of finding herself attractive to a great many more responsive young men than Cecil Pinsent.

At *I Tatti* she also fell in love with the brilliance of Italian light, skies and landscape, and no other country could ever compete in her eyes.]

Chapter Nine

A BACHELOR GIRL

Including Julia's *HARUM-SCARUM LIFE WITH HESTER*

[In 1918 the War and Julia's schooldays both came to an end. What was to become of her? The outline of the next few years can be plotted by reference to letters from those who—while not blood relations—yet felt responsible for her: her step-mother Ray and Aunt Loo.* 'Tragicomic' is the only word to describe their effect. Is one to laugh or cry, and if the latter, for whom should most tears be shed?

From Logan's charming house in St Leonard's Terrace, Chelsea, Julia first ventured forth to Bedford College in 1919, having signed on for what she believed was a course in Psychology. Finding that it was in fact Physiology, she left after one term and entered the Slade School of Art in October of the same year; here she stayed for two years studying Commercial Art, first for six days a week and then three.

"Well, they always say that half a loaf is better than no bread," she remembered Tonks† saying to her; "but *your* drawing is no bread at all!"

The Quaker background of both her substitute mothers did not help them to appreciate Julia's originality and attractiveness, while it made them intolerant of her amazing vagueness. Ray's interests lay mainly in the Women's Suffrage Movement and kindred subjects. Loo seems to have been the kinder of the two, and probably more sympathetic to the fact that Julia (to quote her own words) was by this time "well away with falling in love with young men and young men with me. One I chose was Jack Strachey,‡ with the remote equilibrium and melan-

---

* I am deeply indebted to Julia's half-sister, Barbara Halpern, author of *Remarkable Relations*, for letting me see these.

† Henry, Head of the Slade from 1917 to 1930.

‡ John Francis, son of Sir Charles Strachey, a successful composer of light music, and distant cousin of Julia's.

choly monk's face." For her part Julia often said she liked and respected her step-mother, but couldn't understand her complete lack of interest in clothes and making herself attractive.

All the letters were written to Mary Berenson at *I Tatti*.

In 1919 Alys Russell wrote: "Julia is *immensely* improved in every way and is a real pleasure"; and a year later: "I shall be extravagant and take Julia, and perhaps Elizabeth Ponsonby, to Oxford for a few days at Commem; it's such a unique and heavenly experience in a girl's life."

Whether or not this plan materialised, Julia's early beaux were mostly Oxford undergraduates, and Aunt Loo was certainly responsible for getting up a dance for her and her friends (of whom I was one) at the Adrian Stephens' house in Gordon Square, in June 1920. It came to a tragic and unforgettable conclusion with the death of one of the guests, as Virginia Woolf describes in her Diary. A sitting-out place had been arranged on the projecting roof at the back, with chairs all round, and fairy lights on the low parapet. A young man went across it "perhaps to light a cigarette, stepped over the edge, and fell thirty feet on to flagstones." Adrian Stephen dealt calmly and bravely with the crisis, but the poor fellow (whom no-one appeared to know) died in the ambulance. Virginia goes on, "Aunt Loo bungled everything with her salt American cheerfulness" and "gave her version of the thing 'not in the least a tragedy—a stepmother only and seven other children, and it's over for the poor boy.' No brandy was to be had in any of the three houses." I distinctly remember that Julia and I and other of the young dancers were very much shocked by Loo's attempt to brush the disaster under the carpet.

In 1921 Alys reports: "Julia has left my wing and must muddle along her own way." Fortunately Julia included her own account of what this 'way' was like, in a paper written for the Bloomsbury Memoir Club many years later, entitled *The Bathrooms in my Life*.]

HARUM-SCARUM LIFE WITH HESTER

During my teens, and especially after leaving Bedales, I was more or less established in Logan's luxuriously-run house in St. Leonard's Terrace. The steam from the banana soufflées and American waffles in maple syrup, of which he was so fond, came wafting through the house supplying a climate of good cheer to which I was far from indifferent.

The bathroom arrangements were another matter. For one thing, my Aunt Loo used to come buzzing in at the door like a cockchafer, demanding that I got out before I had well got in. For another, she had painted a thin blue line inside the bath about two inches from the bottom, above which the water must on no account be allowed to rise; so that as a suitable setting for long and profound cogitations Aunt Loo's bathroom was in all literalness a washout. She had a superstitious dread of people who sat still and thought, whether in the bath or elsewhere.

One day, when I was about twenty I think, Aunty Loo appeared before me where I was drowsing on the drawing-room sofa, and made an announcement:

"In a month's time from today, Ju, thee is to become a Modern Woman (I wish I could say an 'educated' one, but that I can't do), living in bachelor digs and earning thy own bread and butter! Here's good luck to thee! I will give thee, to start thee off, an allowance of three pounds a week for board and lodging, and a further twenty-five pounds a year for all extras—clothes, fares, journeys, holidays and so forth. And remember, thee leaves here in a month's time, so thee had better start hunting for somewhere to live, pretty quick." With which she went off to her Jumble Sale, first snatching up and shouldering two of Logan's gold drawing-room chairs which needed re-caning, and her umbrella, and with her trusty string bag on her wrist, ready to swallow up any old carpet slippers or broken inkpots that she might come across in friends' houses en route, which might come in handy for her Sale.

I came to, heaved myself off the sofa, and set off to look for lodgings in the vicinity.

Quite by chance a girl friend of my cousin John Evelyn Strachey's* was also looking for rooms at that moment, as she had just been turned out of her respectable Ladies' Hostel in Pimlico for fast behaviour. We had only met twice, but decided to take a chance and go into lodgings together. We finally found and took possession of two furnished rooms at the top of a house in Wellington Square. My new friend's name was Hester Pellatt, better known later as Hester Chapman, novelist and historian.

In appearance Hester might have been Mata Hari as represented on the films: her figure was luxuriant, her face strikingly pale with a

* Later Minister of Food and Secretary of State for War in Attlee's Government.

retroussé nose, her hair pale gold. In character she was industrious, intellectual, punctual and economical—in fact in every way opposite to me. At twenty-three or so she had a job with the literary agents, Curtis Brown. How delighted she would have been if she could then have been granted a peep into the future, and seen her name printed on the title-page of many successful biographies and novels, for she had not as yet published anything. Hester had abounding vitality and gusto for living, which was expressed in a foaming torrent of jokes, anecdotes, recited poems and mimicry; she had in fact a great comic gift, and I have never laughed so long or so loud or so often as while living with her at Wellington Square. I myself was at this time very demure and repressed, and Hester's ebullience completely dazzled me. I envied her the popularity she had gained by 'keeping the dinner-table in a roar', and it was in emulation of her that I made my first efforts to keep my end up in conversation when in company. Beginning with a few diffident remarks, I soon learned to chatter away like anyone else.

Hester had her bath at night. I had mine in the mornings, after she had gone off to the office.

However late at night Hester got home—after the cinema, evenings of dancing, or dinner parties—she invariably turned on the geyser. She dared not miss, because the dark dye that came off the collars of our cheap rabbit and cat fur-coats had to be scrubbed off in hot steam and with many rinsings. As well as a sense of the comic she had a strong liking for the macabre, and a love of things unwholesome. Something in the ghostly hollow sound of the geyser reverberating in the mezzanine below seemed to set this vein flowing. While the bath filled she would go to her basketwork chair under the hissing green gas jet by which our sitting-room was lit—a seat she specially liked (she confessed to me) because she was aware that the gaslight cast dark triangular shadows over her eye-sockets, producing, so she hoped, the effect of 'La Belle Dame Sans Merci' or 'Nightmare Life in Death'. Seated here she would begin reciting ghoulish poetry in a voice as low, ululating and plangent as that of the geyser itself. I must have heard 'Dolores, our Lady of Pain' and the 'Ballad of Reading Gaol' hundreds of times all told. When she knew by the sound that the bath was full she used to desist, taking up her Elizabeth Arden talcs, creams and almond-scented washing mittens, and go off to it.

When morning came, and it was my turn for a bath, I put another shilling in the meter, but not until eleven or even twelve o'clock, for though I was supposed to be earning my living by drawing advertisements for patent foods, I felt that I could as conveniently draw them after lunch as before. Much earlier I had been sleepily aware from my divan bed in the sitting-room of Hester rushing off to the office—by the hot smell of singeing hair from her curling-tongs if from nothing else.

I suppose most girls have some ideal woman in their minds, whom they hope eventually to resemble. Hester, at that time, kept a fine balance between Dolores our Lady of Pain, and Alice Delysia, the musical comedy star just discovered by Cochran, who was the current rage of London at the Pavilion. So she would emerge from her toilet and leave for the office briskly at eight-thirty, swathed in cheap fur, curling-tonged, her face well whitewashed, and heavily veiled. She possessed a number of gorgeous hats: there was a black hat with a wide velvet brim. (Dolores.) There was a tight helmet trimmed with a Catherine-wheel of flamingo pink feathers. (Delysia.) And there was a gold box fastened to her head with a scarlet veil through which she glimmered with a leprous lustre. (Coleridge's Christabel.)

Hauling myself up on my divan underneath the window I used to watch her go spanking off down the Square, and as she approached the King's Road she would hold up the lorgnette which she wore on a broad black ribbon round her neck, so as to spot the number eleven bus of her choice.

I would have given anything to have looked such a *femme fatale* as Hester, and was disappointed and humiliated by the sight of my own round pink face, lanky virginal figure, and air of obviously being in my green and salad days.

Whilst waiting for my mid-morning bath to fill, I would often seize the chance to sit down at the upright piano I hired by the month and play one of my favourite ragtimes, an occupation which completely intoxicated me; with my coat thrown over my nightgown I fairly made the gas-lamp rattle with the frenzy of my attack. Whenever I couldn't pay the amount due at the end of the month the men would come up and take my beloved piano away, first knocking out some of the banisters of our narrow stairs to allow it to be carried down them. This happened not once but many times; however, within a week or two I always got a new one.

The rest of my day in the Wellington Square flat was mainly devoted to reading *Vogue*, a little metaphysics (on which I was amateurishly keen), and of course my love-letters. Or brooding upon the dramas in my private life—such, for instance, as the nerve-racking night I spent trying to pacify a young man whom I had just told that all was over between us, on Aunty Loo's instructions. He kept referring between sobs to a cardboard box on top of his wardrobe, which he declared contained five expensive pistols, and I felt that I must at all costs prevent him from returning home in such an agitated state of mind. By the time dawn broke he seemed calmer, and we left my flat, to escape from the prying eyes of my landlady, and walked down the King's Road, exhausted from having shed so many buckets of tears, to have breakfast in his rooms at Paulton Square.

It so happened that his father—a stiff-backed colonel—was due to call for him and drive him down to Cornwall. This complicated episode ended by my hiding under the young man's bed, while the colonel, who had somehow got wind of what was up, had arrived at seven a.m. and was banging on the front door, thereby collecting round him a crowd of Chelsea idlers, soon joined by a policeman in a short waterproof cape.

My young man had thoughtfully provided me with a bowl of grapenuts and cream and a spoon to take under the bed, where I was tactfully lying, propped up on my elbows and crunching grapenuts, when the colonel broke his way into the house. I was forced to emerge at last, covered with fluff and having lost my shoes in the fracas, whereupon the colonel greeted me with unexpected politeness (though he couldn't resist delivering a long pi-jaw) and sent me back to Wellington Square in a taxi with a bow.

[In the autumn of 1922 Hester was given three months' holiday, so the Wellington Square flat was vacated and both girls made plans to go and stay in a pensione in Florence.

Aunt Loo wrote to warn the Berensons what was in the air: "Once in Florence [Julia] will have three pounds a week for board money and small expenses, but I don't think myself she will ever get off. She has spent over forty pounds in a month on nothing in particular. She will call on Iris Cutting,* so don't bother. All thee need do is to allow Julia to bring Hester up to tea occasionally."

* Later the Marchesa Origo.

Echoes of the girls' doings reached disapproving ears in London. Both were out for fun with young men—there was no doubt about that. Of the two Hester was the more dashing, even flamboyant, but according to her own account it was the less confident Julia who had most admirers. One of her Italian flirtations gives a clue to the social milieu towards which she was now moving—it was with Eddie Gathorne-Hardy, an Oxford undergraduate who was literary and well-informed as well as a highly amusing and sophisticated companion. He would certainly have been a good guide to the sights of Florence. Their attraction was strong and mutual, although he later opted entirely for his own sex. As for visiting *I Tatti*, which had so impressed her in adolescence, Julia is said to have turned down one invitation on the grounds that she was too busy studying Italian art. From Florence they went to Venice. "Julia has telegraphed asking for her board money to be telegraphed to Cook's at Venice," wrote Aunt Loo in April 1923. "I will send her her April eight pounds—less the price of the telegram."

In February 1924 Ray and Oliver decided to let Julia have a room in their house at 42 Gordon Square, Ray noting that she seemed "very anxious to settle down here for good and shake off Hester. I had very serious personal misgivings. However, after much tossing and turning I decided to give it a really fair, and not a grunching try. I am having the telephone put in the hall so that I shan't hear her inane conversations. Oliver is perfect with her, and they get on like anything, and she herself is so pleased and happy to be sheltered and even kept in control by Oliver that it is touching."

There were hopes of a job for Julia. "She has *finished* about fifty drawings for an advertising agent," wrote Loo in amazement, only to follow in March 1924 with: "Great disappointment. Julia's drawings were turned down for not being commonplace enough. So now she has started at once on posters and *Vogue*, much more her style. She never arises till 1.15 or 1.45, and *will* take baths at 3 a.m." Ray concedes that "she is very industrious", and that "Oliver says she is moving now in increasingly presentable circles. He himself takes a very active part in her social life, and weeds out her bounders rapidly."

By October 1925, Ray was writing: "Julia has decided to go back and live with Hester again. It is a most heavenly relief. I suppose it won't last long." Nor it did. In less than three weeks she was back at Gordon Square, Aunt Loo reported, "with a sort of nervous breakdown. She refuses to return to Hester, and is sleepless and has indigestion. Dr. Ellie [Rendel] says she must have quiet and rest." Ray's version is much the same: "She is clearly rather ill, more depressed and listless than usual. She can't stand Hester's way of life and friends, and wants occupation, home life, care, sympathy. Oliver and I are in despair. We have written to the Bussys,* begging them to take her for the winter."

Next month Julia duly travelled out to Roquebrune on the French Riviera. There is a certain amount of mystery about this episode, to which she herself only refers obliquely in one of her notebooks, which lists the stages of her life: "1.) The child, to 18. 2.) The Young Woman from 18 to the nervous crisis. The real birth of *predicament* and consciousness, on hearing Aunt Dorothy's words." What these words were, and the exact nature of the 'nervous crisis' we shall probably never know. Another note in the same book is rather more explicit. It is headed: "*YOUTH*: Completely deserted by my family, I had only one desire —one real occupation—to find a loved one and get married. Find some family love after all. This made me seem lazy to my step-mother and old Oliver, who thought only of committee meetings and sensual appetites." It is noticeable that all through her life, Julia tended to glamourise the word 'family', as a result, I have no doubt, of her happy memories of childhood days in the Indian bungalow, so abruptly truncated.

This 'one desire' drove her towards the next important step in her life—to marry Stephen Tomlin.

Her choice of a husband was to some degree determined by geography. For the last two years she had been living, off and on, at 42 Gordon Square, in the physical heart of Bloomsbury. On the same side of the square lived her Uncle James Strachey and his wife Alix, Clive Bell, Dadie Rylands, the Davidson brothers, Arthur Waley and the Adrian Stephens, with Leonard and Virginia Woolf near by in Tavistock Square, and (most influential of all) Lytton Strachey and Carrington on visits from Wiltshire. In the spring of 1926 Ralph Partridge and I set up house together at number 41 next door, and my old friendship with Julia (fallen into abeyance but never broken) was quickly renewed. A lot had happened to both of us, but neither had fundamentally changed.

* Oliver's sister Dorothy, her husband the painter Simon Bussy, and their daughter Janie.

In face of the despairing wails of Ray and Loo, it should be said that most, if not all of these new neighbours saw Julia as a lively and amusing young creature, whose conversation was at the opposite extreme from cliché, and who was moreover extremely pretty, with a beautiful, boyish figure and long elegant legs, very graceful and an expert dancer.

It was also true that she had an unfortunate inability ever to arrive on time anywhere, as well as a dislike of the practical side of life which amounted to loathing. These were certainly inconveniences, and they brought many of her jobs to a speedy end.

But she had now embarked on a new profession. "I took advantage of the fact that I was the right shape and appearance for a model girl," she wrote, "and simply went out to fashion shops. Well, it was deadly. I experienced total blankness and boredom." She also gained fashion sense, and her looks were perfectly suited by the mode of the moment, dominated by Mademoiselle Chanel—an Eton crop, chokers of enormous false pearls, and trim little suits with pleated skirts.

As Ray and her two small children stayed mostly in their country cottage, Oliver and Julia were left to keep house together in London. They were not exactly soul-mates, but caused each other—and their visitors—a lot of amusement: they were like two comedians sparring together in a music-hall. "Ray much enjoyed hearing all the complications of Julia's housekeeping," wrote Aunt Loo to Mary Berenson in April 1926. "Oliver takes it very humorously and just dines out when it is too bad. They have a new cook every week." One of these cooks played her part in this knockabout performance—I remember her dumping a dish on the table when Ralph and I were dining there, with the inexplicable remark, "Just because it's a Wednesday, bugger it, the eggs *had* to hop out of the frying-pan!"

Thus Julia was making new friends, forgetting Hester and Elizabeth and leaving the aegis of her two stand-in mothers. It was probably at James Strachey's that she met Stephen Tomlin, always known as 'Tommy', a brilliantly talented, neurotic young sculptor, who dented the hearts or minds, or both, of most people who met him, and who had many friends in Bloomsbury. But the person who was most influential in bringing about the match was certainly Carrington. From their first meeting she had taken a special fancy to Julia, whose imagination, fantastic sense of humour and charming looks entranced her. In her letters she wrote to her as if she was a fairy princess. Lytton and Carrington were both a little in love with Tommy also, and it is very likely that they deliberately fostered the attraction between the pair by inviting them to Ham Spray together.

Not conventionally good-looking, Tommy was short and strongly-built, with the profile of a Roman emperor on a coin, fair hair brushed back from a high forehead, a pale face and intelligent grey eyes.

In October, Ray was writing: "A ray of hope has at last appeared in the Julia situation. She is thinking of marrying at Christmas: the young man is exceedingly nice and I think it would be a mercy. Julia proposes to go to Paris with him in the New Year."

Julia and Tommy in fact spent several months together in his studio in the rue Turgot, Montmartre; while he was working Julia did some modelling for Poiret. It was not an unmixed success, though in June 1927 Aunt Loo wrote: "Julia spent a happy winter with Stephen Tomlin in Paris, but they still cannot make up their minds to marry, and he is now at his tiny cottage in Wilts, while Julia has a room and breakfast in the Gordon Square rabbit-warren. Her landlord, young George Rylands, tells me that she leaves the bath running and the electric lights on, but he hopes she will improve under his lectures. She is vaguely 'writing' and unvaguely hard up. Stephen is afraid his father, the respectable Mr. Justice Tomlin, will hear about Paris and will cut off his modest allowance. She is prettier than ever and goes out every night in a set who rather admire her for her Trial Trip."

Next month, July 1927, "Julia came to tea today and announced her forthcoming marriage, about August 5th in a church (but quietly) to please Judge Tomlin. Stephen is a *very* nice fellow, and she is a lucky girl."

For Alys Russell and Ray Strachey the era of their responsibility for Julia had reached the conventional happy ending. But many years later she told me that marrying Tommy was one of the things of which she was most ashamed. (Where human behaviour was concerned her standards were very high—sometimes too high to be observed.) She was never really in love with Tommy. She was *desperately* lonely.]

Chapter Ten

FIRST MARRIAGE

Including Julia's *CARRINGTON*

[The marriage between Stephen Tomlin and Julia Strachey took place on July 22nd, 1927, very soon after their relations had been informed. Tommy's father the Judge was a clever, rather austere man, while Mrs. (afterwards Lady) Tomlin is vividly portrayed as seen through Julia's eyes and heard through her ears, in Mrs. Thatcham of *Cheerful Weather for the Wedding*. In fact Julia had nothing at all in common with her future parents-in-law, and her introduction to them was symbolic: she tripped on the threshold of their stately London drawing-room, and shot in over the parquet floor face downwards, as though tobogganing. Luckily Oliver and the Judge got on well over their luncheon at the Oriental Club; financial settlements were agreed, and the wedding duly took place in St. Pancras Church.

A good many Bloomsbury friends were present, among them Virginia Woolf, who described the ceremony in a letter to her sister Vanessa:

"A prosaic affair, though the service always fills my eyes with tears. Also the grotesqueness is so great. The Strachey women were of inconceivable drabness on one side, Aunt Loo having also an aroma of hypocrisy about her which makes me vomit; on the other side sat the Judge in frock coat and top hat like a shop-walker. He got locked into his pew, and could not get out except at the last moment to sign the register. He mistook the hinge for the door. Julia was highly self-possessed, and then Angus [Davidson] was glowering behind us. I dare say he takes it to heart, though I repeat for the thousandth time: I cannot see the physical charm of that little woodpecker man.* They dined with us afterwards."

The couple began their married life in Tommy's sturdy, stone-built

* Tommy. Virginia never liked the bust he made of her.

cottage in the Wiltshire village of Swallowcliffe, surrounded by unspoilt country—fine woods, uneven fields, and narrow lanes winding between small grey villages, beside streams fringed with water plants. Ralph and I spent several weekends there, and found Julia distinctly plumper and seemingly contented and absorbed in housekeeping and garden planning. They had acquired a maid called Agnes and a minuscule white kitten. Conversation was always lively, sometimes fantastic (which both enjoyed), sometimes argumentative (dear to Tommy's legal mind). Picnics were taken to Fonthill, or the Wardour woods with their ruined castle. Julia and Tommy were soon greeted as social assets by their neighbours—the Augustus Johns, Henry Lambs, Ashley-Coopers and Hugo Pitmans; later on the Bryan Guinnesses and the attractive and talented Debenham family, one of whom—Audrey—was a great friend of Tommy's sister Helen. Tommy still kept his studio, too, where both stayed when they came up to London.

From now on a large part of Julia's story will be taken over by letters and diaries, mostly Julia's own. Some autobiographical pieces have also been incorporated.]

(Carrington to Lytton Strachey)

September 21st, 1927. Swallowcliffe. I reached the Cliffe about half past two. Tommy was busy drawing out plans of the gates for Lincoln's Inn and Julia making scones in the kitchen. The cottage looks *very* nice inside. Really it's equal to Ham Spray in elegance and comfort, only cleaner and tidier. Julia is in high spirits, and both of them seem very happy. After tea I drove Julia to Tisbury and did some shopping; [her] vagueness about ordering is only equalled by your ignorance! "How many potatoes shall we want?" in a whisper to me. In a commanding imperious voice to the man: "Well, send some potatoes, a good many." Man: "How many pounds? Fourteen, twenty-eight?" "Oh no, not as many as that, about two pounds would be enough, I think." (About ten potatoes.) We laughed so much, and the man could hardly resist smiling. The cooking is really very good. Julia teaches the maid herself with Mrs. Beeton sitting like an immense goddess on the kitchen table presiding. I shall enjoy myself very much as it's exactly the sort of life I most love, talking and painting. Julia seems infinitely better in health. Very energetic and brisked up.

(Julia to F.P.)

March 17th, 1928. Swallowcliffe. We are coming up tomorrow or the day after. Do you think we could have dinner together, Tommy and I and Ralph and you (and will Carrington be up?) and go to a theatre of sorts? Arthur Waley says the Russians are fearfully bad, that Tchekhov's wife is not of the company, and none of the best people are. Ay de mi! Ohé! As some people would say.* The books you sent are lovely—it is a handsome present indeed. All is deep gloom here, struggling with the last drawings of the Lincoln's Inn gates. You must really try to cheer us up when we arrive, but I fear we shall be beyond it by that time—as we certainly are now as a matter of fact. Ohé! Ohé!

(Julia's Diary)

December, 1928. Swallowcliffe. The alarm clock rang out at 6.30 but I felt as though a million weights were dragging me down to the bottom of the sea. So I got into bed again. Despair seized me through my dreams at having broken my vow to get up each morning and earn money for our old age. "Nothing on earth will drag me out of this adorable, delicious, comfortable bed," I said to myself with conviction.

In the afternoon I went for a walk: a feeling of winter lifting off one's head at last. Looking up at the piles of floating clouds saturated by sunlight I was reminded of all my most summery experiences— steam-boats smoking along on the Mediterranean, continental trains, crowds on the esplanades, villas, palm trees; and then, looking down at Wiltshire, there was only a damp ruined-looking village, a bleak old pub (with no-one in it), and a broken-spirited suspicious black cat crouched low on the ivied wall.

The caster is here, tapping away in the studio working at Helen [Tomlin]'s and my heads. I asked him if a meat supper would suit him. "Oh, I told Mr. Tomlin that that is no good for *me*! I asked him to get oysters and champagne for *my* supper!" said he jauntily.

(Julia's Diary)

January 1st, 1929. We hadn't been in bed long before the Swallowcliffe bells began to ring in the New Year—a very feeble chime as they only

---

* A tease aimed at F.P., who had been quoting this phrase from Carlyle's letters.

have three. Tommy went in his pyjamas to the Tisbury side of the house; he said he could hear all manner of chimes from all around. The kedgeree for lunch was like balls of blotting-paper soaked in brine. Tidying the house for the visitors.

(Julia's Diary)

January 10th, 1929. Went to stay with Edith Olivier.* Discussion on Socialism in the evening. Edith wore a suburban georgette dance-frock for dinner, her hair like a negress's on one side and flat the other. The second night, an argument about religion, Tommy telling her his atheistical views and that "the time has really come for people to throw away the crutch of religion." She, being deeply, passionately religious, couldn't take in what it all implied. Went over to Wilton and saw the pictures and statues. Lord Pembroke came to chat to us. Their Michelangelo, Leonardo and Rubens have all been so hung that one is unable to see them at all.

(Julia to F.P.)

February 4th, 1929. Swallowcliffe. A girl called Diana Dampier Wetham (daughter to the famous W. C. Dampier Wet'em) has been having flu in our cottage. Henry Lamb and his Pansy paid us an unexpected call on Friday, came to tea and stayed to supper. And though we enjoyed their company very much *indeed*, when I tell you that it was our Agnes' night out, so that we had to cook an unexpected dinner for four on the spur, as well as a special invalid [sic] supper of fish for Diana upstairs (and also air and make her bed, keep her fire going and practically wash her) while entertaining our guests downstairs at the same time—you may imagine we had our hands quite full that evening. Pansy's sophisticated manner, gurgling voice and dazzling beauty are quite a treat, don't you agree? Well, Cyril Connolly has been and gone. But not a word upon the subject will you get out of me. Such a clever boy! But rather *plain*—don't you think? They *say* he is *most* talented—though somewhat impecunious. They tell me such funny stories about him—I do think people are *beastly* about each other, don't you? I must stop now as your yawns are getting broader and broader. Tommy sends much love.

* Biographer and writer about Wiltshire. Mayor of Wilton for many years.

(Julia's Diary)

February 6th, 1929. Walked up the hill where the foxgloves grow in summer. The village road was a network of gleaming rivers; the little houses so wet in the fading light, and nobody about. The downs were sheathed in an even veil of mist; the landscape reminded me of one of those cheap Japanese fans—no colour, misty distance and black scratchy trees standing about. I thought 'this moment will be no more. It will be over, and never again shall I experience it.' The only sound to be heard was the high "Clink! Clink!" of the blacksmith's anvil. I saw a hot spirt of orange flame flare up inside the forge.

(Julia's Diary)

February 7th, 1929. Fired by hearing about Trollope, I got out of bed at 6.30 when it was still dark, and wrote for an hour and a half. We heard the news that Tommy's father has been put in the House of Lords, and Garrow* seems to think that he will be 'the Hon.' now—whether Tommy and I will also be I don't know.† I went with Tommy on the road to Tisbury. Hearing a sound like a million crickets we looked down and saw a batch of newly hatched chickens. The yellow ones had black rims round their eyes which made them look as though they were made up for the stage—altogether like strutting tragedians. The hazel copse on the side of the hill looked diaphanous in the smoky air and pale sunshine. Every now and again one saw a tree that seemed to have been showered with yellow jewels, or gold tinsel fragments; these were the catkins—the colour of greenish acid drops. The trees seemed to drip with them, reminding one of artificial stage fountains and waterfalls glittering in the limelight, or the fairy story called *The Twelve Princesses*, where the trees had gold and crystal fruit and leaves. I saw a fox chasing another across the field, their long tails streaming behind them.

(Julia's Diary)

Spring, 1929. During the time I was ill in bed at Swallowcliffe, lying locked in the strong struggling embrace of my fever in the white room, the wind in a rage never ceased from flinging itself indignantly down the chimney, and howling hysterically, now high, now low. I came out of

---

* Tommy's elder brother.

† They were delighted to learn that they would.

my fever to find the wind had dropped, the little white room lay silently basking in sunshine. Two sleek fat white doves pattered softly about over the window-sill, like little middle-aged Queens, their bosoms padded out to bursting point, their tiny heads drawn back as if expecting an insult; their coral feet trod warily yet rapidly.

The doctor sent me to London to convalesce. Audrey Debenham asked me to stay at Addison Road (as her parents chanced to be away). Tommy, Audrey and I waited in Audrey's upstairs sitting-room until her twin brother Gilbert made his appearance. He jabbered away as he ate his dinner—intelligent, witty, shy, excitable.

(Julia to F.P.)

Summer, 1929. Smedmore, Corfe Castle. I hope you enjoyed yourselves abroad? Many thanks for the postcard, which is rather an original one, much appreciated. Carrington tells me you have got some more for us—if this should be true please save them up for me and do not send them off until after the 14th, as we have already had the most awful cards sent to us publicly here (at Lady Tomlin's summer villa) by the million! We are coming to London for three nights on the 14th and hope to see something of you then. I suppose I must hurry away to the tennis-court. What a life here! Evening dress and a bedroom as large as a ball-room with private bath and all to match.

[To the interested observer Julia and Tommy had appeared, in the first year or two together, to feel warm affection if not 'love', also pleasure in each other's characters and company. Julia spoke of Tommy more than once as a 'genius'. "I have only known two geniuses," she said when in her seventies, "and I was married to both of them."

It is impossible to be certain when the first cracks in the marriage began to appear, but by early 1930 problems seem to have been acute. The main root of the trouble lay in Tommy's manic-depressive character. When in a depressive bout he drank heavily, and this in turn led to uncontrolled infidelity, followed by agonising guilt. Julia reacted by finding attraction elsewhere. There were two attempts to solve their difficulties by temporary separation. First in the Spring of 1930, and then again in 1931, Julia took refuge with the Bussys at Roquebrune, where she finished writing *Cheerful Weather for the Wedding*.

The following letters from Julia to Tommy, written from France, are strangely out of character, out of key. There is some evidence that she already despaired of the future of the marriage. Was she in some sense acting? Or do they represent the fact that she was never entirely herself with Tommy? Her brilliant, if over-dramatised analysis of his neurotic character and of the final break-up of the marriage will be found in the next chapter, *The Return*.]

(Julia to Tommy)

May 20th, 1930. La Souco, Roquebrune. Darling Piggy. Write and tell me you are glad I am coming back to you so soon now; and that you are feeling happy—a little bit—about it. I miss you, and have missed you you know dearest very much, and have often longed so very much to hug you. I am truly longing to start a joint life with you again, and am very keen to design you some tombstones, statues, even iron gates if required. And will you do another head of me please, piggy, and help me with my story. I was unutterably miserable when I read that you couldn't face Swallowcliffe again. Surely, later on, we could go there —we can have very happy times there again. But what I want to express in this letter is that I do really love you. That I will never leave you unless you want me to, and that I believe we can help each other to be happy now, even though we have been through a miserable period, we shall be so very snug together again.

(Julia to Tommy)

April, 1931. La Souco, Roquebrune. [Her second visit.] I arrived safely yesterday. I have missed you very much and felt so sad at being parted. Dearest piggy, it was so perfectly awful seeing you cry at the boat—but don't let us think about that. I'm just about to write to Gilbert [Debenham] the letter I said I would, saying I don't want to have any correspondence with him. I promise you faithfully I am going to be firm as a rock upon this point. Janie and Dorothy [Bussy] send a great many messages to you. You would hate it out here. The hillside is as bleak and harsh as ever with its staring villas. Really the pink blotting-paper walls of my bedroom, together with the kitchen wardrobe and horrid mosquito-net bed-curtains are as triste as can be. Darling, darling pig, I give you a very big hug.

(Julia to Tommy)

April 6th, 1931. La Souco, Roquebrune. Marjorie [Strachey] has been here for several days. She and Dorothy squawk and squeak at each other like hysterical white mice from morning till late at night. Anything so passionate, or so *shrill*, as their interminable arguments and discussions you have never heard. Janie joins in, very cuttingly and satirically. They all tear their hair and wave their arms about like windmills, and peals of demon laughter fill the air.

I felt rather stunned mentally and emotionally when I first got here. Now things are just beginning to work themselves round in my brain very slowly, like primeval monsters reawakening in the paleolithic jungle. I write all day nearly, and can now no longer bother with forming my letters neatly. Goodbye dearest piggy. Don't drink too much, blow your nose well every night, and write to your piggy.

(Julia to Tommy)

April, 1931. La Souco, Roquebrune. My darling and very dearest of Pigs. I have been in despair since I got your last letter. I imagine you trying to go to sleep, and hating your work, and absolutely wretched at the Studio, and I feel it all too, along with you, in imagination my dearest. I give you a hug and a kiss, darling, so *do* cheer up a little when you receive them in this letter. I want you to write and tell me what you are really feeling; please do not try not to, I beg you. I think of you such a lot dearest, and wish I could comfort you and make you feel more happy. You asked me whether Gilbert had replied to my letter—no, not a word has come from that quarter since I wrote asking him not to communicate. Well goodbye, my darling pig.

(Julia to Tommy)

April 18th, 1931. La Souco, Roquebrune, France. Today I woke up to a shattering roaring and rushing, growing steadily louder as I listened. It is the Mistral, which is upon us in full force. I have just peered out at the sea, it is the most unearthly bright turquoise you ever saw, flecked with white all over, and great congested streaks of deep purple all over that. Janie and Dorothy have both had a kind of flu, and been in bed for days with slight fever. I am struggling with it too I believe. Marjorie is staggering, the way she goes on and on and *on* telling anecdotes and stories and acting every word with a wealth of gesture. She does not make one single remark in an ordinary voice. So we have a Mistral indoors *and* out today, God help us.

(Julia to Tommy)

April, 1931. La Souco, Roquebrune, France. You ask me to tell you a little bit what I am thinking: I am feeling stunned, literally stunned after our awful time in England the last months. I feel sick, anxious, bewildered and absolutely muddled; I can't sleep and feel altogether guilty—terribly guilty and miserable. And remorseful to the uttermost point, which is a hellish feeling indeed. So there you are, darling. I'm in a nervous stew about what I call my physical complexes.* I feel fussed and wretched about them—they have got to be dealt with somehow, but how? It is so terrible arguing about them together—as we used to; that is what I dread on my return to England.

I get up very late—they make me have breakfast in bed—so there is no hope of getting up of course, and I am just dressed in time to write two lines of my story when the lunch bell rings. After lunch sun-bathing, and then of course one goes to sleep afterwards. Tea bell! such horrid teas! Nothing but marmalade and something they call cake, but is really condensed mosquito-netting with currants in it. After tea I *do* write—and most of the afternoon too as a matter of fact. My story is done; I am making a neat copy to send to be typed—it will be ready by the end of the week. I have also written half another story. Goodbye my dearest, dearest little pig. I will write again soon. When you wake up in the night think that I am thinking of you—I will be.

(Julia to Tommy)

April 25th, 1931. I thought I would wait until we had had Rosamond and Wogan [Philipps] to lunch before writing to you, and then all day today I spent in Mentone and Monte Carlo. How are you, dearest pig? I hope to get a letter from you tomorrow or Monday, but I am terribly afraid it will be gloomy. If you only knew, dear pig, how much and how often I wonder what you are feeling, and how I imagine you at the Studio, and how terribly afraid I am all the time that you are feeling sad perhaps. I

* Evidence of those in a position to know makes it seem likely that sex meant very little to Julia—admiration a great deal.

have been struggling with a wretched internal upset for some time now, or it may be the influenza. I had a letter from your mother; I am answering by the same post as this, telling her about the *grippe*, and that I shall stay on a bit to recuperate. Today I walked all along the front at Monte Carlo in brilliant sunshine, and looked down past a forest of cactus to the rocks and sea—which was almost as transparent as at Porto Fino. You never saw anything so *immaculate* as the gardens: there are gigantic palm trees, tall cactus bushes, white cyclamens, and of course the usual magenta, scarlet and purple flowers. The gardener was spraying the wicked-looking emerald velvet grass; and the thickly-powdered and painted faces of the tarts also looked like exotic flowers —camellias and orchids. It was all very nostalgic and depressing somehow—this radiant summer light pouring down over gruesome old Monte, yet I am quite won over by the place at long last I do believe. I very much wondered if you would have hated it all as much as you think. But of course you would. Goodbye dearest, with many hugs.

(Tommy to Julia)

[Undated] I must write to you if only to relieve the horror I am in. I want so terribly to be forgiven, and yet everything I think of saying seems to be making an excuse for myself and I do not believe there is any excuse. I think I am a most horrible cad, and no amount of explanation of why I am one or what it is like to be one can alter or improve the fact. I can't get the beastly business out of my head for a moment and the more I think of it the more nightmarish it seems. It now seems to me that if I had deliberately schemed to wound you and hurt you I could not have arranged it better. O my darling please please believe that though some horrible kink and madness takes hold of me, none of it appeared like this at the time. I only hope to God that, if I have made you unhappy it is not quite as unhappy as I have made myself. If you were here I know you would be perfectly angelic and say don't get in a stew. But I can't help it, it makes it worse your being so kind. Do, for God's sake help. It's really all this drinking. I do so desperately want to make you happy and I do nothing but make you wretched. I will write to Glover.* I feel horribly ashamed.

---

* Edward, M.D., Tommy's psycho-analyst.

[Meanwhile the marriage stumbled on for two more uneasy years. Swallowcliffe was given up, and though Julia and Tommy were sometimes together they were more often apart. At the time of Lytton's mortal illness in 1932, and after his death, they both came to Ham Spray, but Tommy came more often alone, and it was noticeable that Carrington leaned upon him more than she did on Julia at this worst crisis in her life—his very dependence on her and his profound grief for Lytton made him more sympathetic. Julia's great charm for Carrington was the gaiety she inspired, and this was a time when gaiety was impossible. Julia believed sincerely in the need to come to the help of friends in distress, and often valiantly did so, but she was not naturally equipped for the special form of self-abnegation and understanding required. Perhaps she was too self-centred. It would however, be very unjust to call her a fair-weather friend.]

(Julia to F.P.)

*March 13th, 1932.** This is a ghastly and gloomy time for you indeed; please will you let me see you next week and take you out one day. I am going to ring you up on Monday evening and see if you are returned or not. I am staying down at Swallowcliffe till after Easter. I very much want to see you. Fondest love.

CARRINGTON
A Study of a Modern Witch

Carrington was by nature a lover of marvels, a searcher for the emotionally magnificent life; at heart and by vocation she was an impresario, collecting people and their climates, arranging for their exhibition; going to endless trouble in assembling the right properties and accompaniments so that they might display their magic and their microcosm to the best advantage in some great darkened auditorium out of sight. One of her major preoccupations was to counteract the life-frames in which she found people already mounted. She went on tirelessly studying and engineering ways, means and effects, or juggling

* The above letter was written two days after Carrington's suicide. The following character-study of her by Julia was written after her death, but is undated.

with modes of life. She was everywhere, in everyone's house—and once inside, so glowing with sympathetic magnetism and droll ideas for them all that there wasn't a person of her vast acquaintance who did not get the impression that she was their very best friend. There wasn't a lover, or a servant or a cat that did not preen him- or herself on being the most favoured of the lot. For me, in my twenties, she produced powders and perfumes, hats, beads and ribbons; she helped dress me up to go out to parties, and entered into all my most fantastic projects for plays or performances.

She herself had for long spiritually existed in the very teeth of some sort of whirlwind, too near whose path she had chanced to stray, and in whose arms, ice-pinnacled and wuthering, she had built her own nest, living there always in readiness, any instant, to cast herself over the edge altogether and to be done with it all—as indeed she finally did, by shooting herself.

She used to smoke her cigarettes with elbows poised high, like half-unfurled wings, and usually balancing on the edge of her chair, in readiness for all eventualities—an angular elf, turning her face from the daylight in the window, restlessly shaking flies—or whatever they were?—out of her bobbed golden hair.

One noticed her strong impulse to defend herself from all and sundry, by eeling silently out of reach before they had time to approach too close. Perhaps the envelope of deafening guilt, which, as someone remarked, surrounded her like a cloud of loudly buzzing mosquitoes wherever she went, had something to do with the preternatural acuteness of her vision of others. Maybe she felt that her need to reach out towards their essential natures had an acquisitive, greedy and aggressive side to it—I think she even thought of it as 'stealing'. I believe she saw herself as some kind of witch, who would creep out under cover of darkness, call someone's name, run away under the bushes with him, hoard him and nibble him, all the time patting him this way and that with a paw. There was a sort of black magic in her proceedings: first getting hold of the waxen images, then sticking them with pins, then by starlight or rushlight melting them down and refashioning them, perhaps only slightly, but into someone different.

She was a changeling, at once too old and too young. Such people are often artists, or have some queer streak or gift. She wore the progression of youth into age (which is the usual lot of humanity and can be a quite respectable overcoat) like something hired, 'off the peg', thrown on 'all anyhow' and of a most farcically clownish fit.

Carrington had large blue eyes, a thought unnaturally wide open, a thought unnaturally transparent, yet reflecting only the outside light and revealing nothing within, just as a glass door betrays nothing to the enquiring visitor but the light reflected off the sea—something he feels of a 'take-in', considering that it stands ostentatiously wide open, as if inviting him in. From a distance she looked a young creature, innocent and a little awkward, dressed in very odd frocks such as one would see in some quaint old picture-book; but if one came closer and talked to her, one soon saw age scored round her eyes—and something, surely, a bit worse than that—a sort of illness, bodily or mental, which sat oddly on so unspoilt a little face, with its healthy pear-blossom complexion. She had darkly bruised, hollowed, almost battered sockets; and the strange eyes themselves, wide, clear and light as a Northern sky, were not particularly comforting, because of her look of blindness—a statue's blindness, screening her own feelings.

Emotional herself, though she was afraid of others depending on her emotionally, she had an immense richness and range of feeling: was a productive creator, showering jokes, elegancies, and perceptiveness wherever she went, possessing a great gift for 'seeing the point' of another person's wit or style. A lot of her qualities were essentially feminine—her sly teasingness, her lightness of touch, the fact that her whole life was a creation in fire, feeling and style: her lack of general knowledge and education also and the remarkable impression of sunlight she made.

[Julia's relations with Tommy had been becoming all the time more strained and painful to both. In one of her notebooks referring to this time she wrote: "Seeing a loved person absolutely change in personal quality is worse than if they had died. Shakespeare makes Cleopatra say about the dying Antony: 'The crown of the world is melting'. This phrase made Tommy weep violently as he sat beside me in the stalls watching the play."

Subjected to that most agonising form of blackmail—threat of suicide—Julia took refuge with a great friend of hers and Tommy's, Barbara Ker Seymer, a successful photographer, who gave her a nominal job to answer the telephone in her office off Bond Street. Julia had several love-affairs, some quite important, but none providing an ultimate solution.

Her first novel *Cheerful Weather for the Wedding* was published by the Hogarth Press in September 1932, with a dust-jacket designed by Duncan Grant. (Virginia Woolf had asked Carrington to undertake it, when she visited her at Ham Spray on the eve of her suicide, thus proffering her a small interest to go on living, but in vain.) The little book struck an individual and tragi-comic note which was recognised by many critics. When it was reprinted by Penguin Books in 1978 Philip Toynbee described it as "the slightest but the more perfect" of her two novels, and went on to say that "the observer is so sharp-eyed and so delicate-tongued that her book reveals, on one level, the rich absurdity of the participants, on a deeper level the helpless despair which they carry about with them"*]

(Julia to F.P.)

October, 1932. Ker Seymer Photographs. I should love to join you at the Ivy on Thursday. Look out for me therefore—I shall be there. Longing to see you again. You seem to have vanished in a puff of smoke. I am moving furniture and all of a twitter.

(Julia's Diary)

July 18th, 1933. Called on Frances in her nursing-home; afterwards alone, relapsed into a dreary dream with no seeming point in life. Rushed to read a Tchekhov story to bring back a sense of significance, but there was too much stress on the bathos of everything.

(Julia's Diary)

July 21st, 1933. Wogan [Philipps] proposed himself to lunch. We visited his framers in Lamb's Conduit Street—the shop was shut but an old woman let us hunt round for his frames. A tall house, five stories or so. The only light came down the well of the staircase from a single dirty skylight—a dulled and dimmed silver ray lying across the stairs to the basement. Battered bare walls, empty passage, and all in the darkness

* *The Observer.*

except for this long shaft of light, in whose moony phosphorescent glow dust hung in cloudy pillars. The place was dead, shut away like the bottom of a cave. (This is the metaphor that I always feel suits my own life.) When one has for years longed for certain things and always been thwarted and starved of them, after a while interest recedes. The whole transaction of living has grown tedious.

(Julia's Diary)

July 25th, 1933. Lunch alone here as usual. Afternoon: lay on the sofa in the grilling heat and read Turgenev's *Rudin*. At 6.30 flew about preparing the salad for the dinner party, taking seeds out of the tinned guavas, buying soda syphons and cigarettes, telephoning to the Army and Navy Stores who had forgotten my order. Went out and bought some lovely tiger-lilies—Edinburgh-rock pink to match the sitting-room walls, and all speckled with crimson, their luxurious elegance and baroque quality, their fresh crispness which reflected coal blue lights and shadows, their bizarre spidery stamens and corkscrewing petals —in short their sophistication and fragility—were an oasis in the humdrum, boiling, busy afternoon spent as above. Dinner: Virginia and Leonard, Peter Quennell, Aunt Dorothy [Bussy] and Wogan came.* After dinner Virginia talked about her Memoir Club, her 'group', urging us younger ones to have a Memoir Club, at which it seems each member reads out some episode in his life to a group of cronies. But it wouldn't fit into the unstable, passionate lives of my contemporaries, who have to work for their livings. They don't form cliques as Bloomsbury did; through their work they make hundreds of acquaintances. I don't know; it would certainly be very interesting to try and get up such a club. Not half a bad idea.

(F.P.'s Diary)

September 15th, 1933. Ham Spray. Julia has again come to the forefront of our lives. Ralph feels very warmly towards her, and as for me she is the female friend for whom I have felt most affection in my life.

---

* Virginia writes about this dinner in a letter to Quentin Bell: "I prefer Wogan to Quennell. On the other hand Q. has more knives in his brain."

When she stayed here at the end of August she told me about her love affair with Wogan Philipps. At first he was the ardent wooer and Julia held back a little. Then they spent a week at Weymouth together and he was so charming that she fell very much in love with him and he with her. Wogan felt he must tell Rosamond, but Tommy had not been told. He clutches on to Julia as his last hope, in an almost lunatic way and can't bear that his marriage should appear to the world as a failure —this in spite of the fact that he beds with all and sundry, with the exception of Julia for some time past. She longs for a complete parting but dare not take the responsibility, nor let him discover about Wogan. Also Wogan is devoted to Tommy.

(Julia to F.P.)

November, 1933. Ker Seymer Photographs. It was nice of you actually to put pen to paper and write and tell me you had enjoyed my story.* I was enormously pleased—and thank you very much for writing. From what you say I gather you *did* receive the phosphorescent impression I tried to convey in it! Your thinking of it again afterwards pleases me very much; what I want to aim at is hitting the 'heart' (Victorian for 'subconscious') as well as the head. It is so easy to read *about* something, but I want my readers to *experience* the thing I write about in real earnest. I have been reading De Quincey lately, and he certainly has got the knack of hitting below the belt so to speak. I wish I could write like him, Shakespeare and Tchekhov rolled into one—oh! and some of the 9th century Chinese poets thrown in as well, eh? Talking of works of art, your description of the mice was certainly one. Why *won't* you write yourself?

(F.P.'s Diary)

January 31st, 1934. Our Christmas party at Ham Spray consisted of Oliver and Saxon [Sydney Turner] with their puzzles, and the lovers Julia and Wogan. Most of our evenings were lively, some hilarious. Wogan, who perhaps didn't at once get the hang of us and was always rushing headlong into arguments with Oliver, suddenly became quite charming. Julia told me she had decided to leave Tommy, but whenever she tried to broach the subject to him it led to such tears, recrimina-

---

* *Cheerful Weather for the Wedding.*

tions and accusations that she has decided to move quietly when he is out of the house, write him a letter of explanation, and summon friends to his side. Wogan thinks she is very unhappy.

[At last Julia decided that a complete break with Tommy was vital. In February, 1934, Ralph and I were planning a visit to South Portugal, travelling by P. and O. liner to Lisbon; we asked Julia to come with us, and after consulting Tommy's psycho-analyst, Dr. Edward Glover (who put up a non-committal Scottish smoke-screen when Julia asked him whether suicide was to be considered likely) she agreed to come. Oliver and several of Tommy's devoted friends were alerted, and asked to be at hand in case he took the blow badly. In the event none of his supporters had cause for alarm. Meanwhile Portugal proved an excellent antidote to Julia's anxieties and stress: its climate was soothing, and there was so much to entertain her and set her speculating. I see her in a characteristic attitude, standing poised as it were among her reactions, absorbed—whether by the monkey-like pseudo-English chatter of the Malay servants who sat cross-legged outside our cabin doors on the voyage, or by the miming of the Lisbon draper from whom she tried to buy sanitary towels (unheard-of articles in Portugal at the time); or in admiration of the charming little houses painted bright blue, lilac or yellow, the mimosa forests, and huge beaches of hard sand studded with enormous shells. Her favourite excursion was to the old-fashioned run-down spa of Monchique up in the hills, which prompted a story, first designed to be called *I was a Portuguese*, and later published by John Lehmann in *New Writing* for 1940 as *Fragments of a Diary*. Besides this she made a few jottings in her diary.]

(Julia's Diary)

February 13th, 1934. Packing to go with the Partridge birds to Portugal. The morning I decided to come up I was, underneath, in a most uncomfortable state emotionally speaking. The terrible rush, telephoning all over England, and in between calls both instructing Marie (our daily) how to pack and hearing about her bugs and her dream of black rats and her troubles with her Indian husband. Then trying to get hold of money and arrange for it to be sent to Tommy, running to my hairdresser's appointment, all took my mind off my despair. Being in a rush drains off attention from the deeper, earlier levels to the upper, later ones.

(Julia's Diary)

March, 1934. Portugal. Ralph, Frances and I went in a car to Monchique, where there is a famous and ancient hot spring said to have great curative powers. We were shown the *établissement de bains*—a barrack filled with small monastic cells, each containing a big tiled bath full of warm spring water ready to jump into; next the spraying room, and finally the tank where the spring bubbled up. We were now led out and found ourselves walking along a rocky path above the stream, through a thick grove of eucalyptus and mimosa trees. Veils of tiny leaves twinkled in the shadow and sunlight all around us, and the ground was covered in what looked like a pile carpet of green, shivering fluff. In the earthy patches grew hundreds of minute plants with blue or pink flowers. The hillside above us was coated over by heavy pinewoods, as its tough hide coats a rhinoceros.

(Julia's Diary)

March, 1934. Praia da Rocha, Portugal. By our hotel is a waste of sand, the excavation for new villas to be built there. When the weather was bad we stayed indoors and saw out of the windows only these hideous, half-formed villas, sandy roadways and palm trees blowing in the gale. But when it was fine we took our lunch and walked along the cliff tops for an hour to our bathing-place. The flat country, dotted with fig trees and powdered with little white houses, swims in brilliant luminosity and the sky is alive with turquoise light. In the evenings as the sun was setting we would return by the same route, but instead of the colours gradually fading as in England, the landscape grew suddenly paler and brighter and the sea crystal and pink, as if the brilliant landscape was blushing with excitement.

[On her return Julia moved into rented rooms in Weymouth Street. Her separation from Tommy was generally accepted.]

Chapter Eleven

THE RETURN

During the return journey to London I often sat with eyes shut, trying to snatch some sleep. But instead of sleep, Tommy would keep appearing in my imagination, and my four years with him in our Wiltshire cottage occupied my mind. And all the while I felt how unbearable, how mournful, and how ugly it was to be deserting one suffering from an illness of the soul of his particular sort: that someone in his state should be abandoned—suddenly thrown out of the window by the one person that he relied upon.

I kept telling myself that, after all, I *had* managed to hang on for two long frightening—even dangerous—years after the marriage had become unbearable. However I had realised at last that, even if there were indeed now a danger that Tommy might put an end to his life if I left him, I myself would have been in greater and similar danger had I stayed; and I was glad that at least I had managed to telephone to some friends and neighbours of his, explaining my defection, begging them to keep guard over him and help him in any way possible.

Yet, at the same time, I was flooded with a heady relief. Felt a great lightness of heart, happiness at my escape, with (underneath all) a bubbling of excitement and hope for my new future springing up.

Nevertheless Tommy's image kept returning in sorrow.

I had in the past puzzled greatly as to how people could be so taken in by what one of the few who comprehended him had described as "the inspired charade of normality" that Tommy managed to assume.

It had always seemed to me that when he made his appearance in one of the open doorways in a house where friends were gathered together, and paused there silent on the threshold—the stocky unmoving body, apparently carved out of stone, with above it the long, tragic, clever face drained of all colour and expression—it had always seemed to me that people glancing up at him from within the room should have had no difficulty at all in understanding that they were looking at one who stared back at them, with those strangely fixed unfocused eyes, from deep inside some catastrophic personal ice-floe, so to speak, that had long long since overtaken and buried him. They should surely have been able to perceive something of this, *something* of his dread aloneness! But the fact is that people seldom look with attention (if at all) at one another. Or, if most exceptionally they do so, there are always floating, hallucinatory mirages shimmering in between one person and the next, blocking the view.

When I decided to marry Tommy I was making a desperate bid to jump out of a state of 'alienation' which I felt I could no longer endure. And my mode of escape *did* work for a short while; that is to say I found a new point in life in looking after Tommy, and enjoying his distinguished, poetic* and scholarly company. I was, in fact, just on the verge of really making a go of my life—getting to love him physically as well as in more general ways—when he suddenly hurt me cruelly by unconsciously revealing that I wasn't 'real' to him, and that his own psychic catastrophe, which had occurred in the past, still held him in its octopus grip. On he went, collecting scalps, never noticing that I was a person in my own right, his eyes always fixed on far horizons, hoping help would come from them. It destroyed our life together when I realised that I was only a symbol to him. But a symbol of what?

He didn't even try to behave kindly to me; he was too far removed from reality. I could see that I only represented to him a phantasy quite divorced from our life together in our cottage home. Finding myself thus not *in* his life or his heart, I began to get the feeling that I was a mere spectre, floating above the earth in space—in other words just as 'alienated' as before. It was this that made me realise my marriage had failed, and that I must run away from it. This, too, that provided steam for my becoming attracted to other men.

Suddenly I felt myself back in the small kitchen, with its thick walls, of the cottage I was deserting. I remembered how every day Tommy would come out from his studio, where perhaps he had been working, perhaps sitting motionless, simply staring desperately ahead. Perhaps weeping. When he emerged he would stand about, looking out of the

---

* Those who were allowed to read Tommy's poems greatly admired them. David Garnett published a long one, called *The Sluggard's Quadrille, by the Lobster* in the *New Statesman*, and it aroused considerable interest.

kitchen window, but soon stray back into his studio, shutting the door behind him. Later he would come forth again, open the back door and step outside. I would see him through the window, wandering round, up and down the paths which intersected our garden. When darkness fell, he used to sit in our sitting-room with a book in his hands, apparently reading by lamplight, with a dead face. He wept often. Groaned in despair. And at odd times during the day or night, and without looking at or addressing me personally, he would stare ahead into the empty air and articulate his interminable tirades, talking with deep bitterness as if to someone inside himself, endlessly inveighing against all the Ancient Curses, Sins and Primal Glooms of the universe.

How long ago had his heart stopped working? How long since he had felt normal affection? Long long before I had married him—that much I had realised. It was as if the loss of all this, the loss of his heart and of the heart's natural warmth, had left his brain charged with all the extra energy that would otherwise have been taken up by human emotions. Maybe this was the system by virtue of which his brilliance and high talent was enabled to function. Certainly (when he felt up to making the effort at all) Tommy made good use, most remarkable use, of that re-routed energy. For he had one of the most interesting and imaginative minds of his generation. Others had often said so. So I judged also. He was still able in conversation to draw upon all the generous lofty notions, the splendid ideas and ideals, as well as upon the witty and sardonic fancies which he had so surprisingly amassed within himself, and which still made up the most outstanding part of his persona.

Tommy's Muse—his artistic talent—had stayed with him all along. She was, strangely enough, friendly, in fact positively 'in cahoots with' the other familiar who trod upon his heels, that dark and evil Warlock who had taken him over, bedevilled and mesmerised him, holding him under duress now for so many long years. To this black Sorcerer (the cause of all his guilty tears and lamentations) his Muse had no sort of objection. In fact there seemed to have been provided a most lively and fruitful *ménage à trois* in Tommy—the Muse, the Warlock and their Man.

I remembered how those long-drawn hours in the privacy of our cottage were punctuated many times each day by the trilling of the telephone. These often came from an aristocratic female blue-stocking living not far away, a lady who greatly enjoyed being a patroness of the arts, and held a kind of interminable *salon* in her luxurious country house. But also from many others; such as painters, sculptors and writers who had settled in the neighbourhood, most of them famous and monied. Then there were occasional visitors—university dons or philosophers on holiday, who enjoyed visiting their rich patroness and kicking over the traces during the holidays. Telephone calls from these and others conjured Tommy and me to join them for drinks, dinners, luncheons and picnic expeditions. And these invitations, though received by Tommy with direst groans, were nevertheless invariably accepted.

Once established in deck-chairs on the lawn, overlooking the sumptuous garden and drinking cocktails, Tommy would lose no time in going into action. He would set to, as in honour bound (compelled as I could see by some law of ancient sovereignty insisted on by that dark spectral Demon King who was ever at his side)—Tommy would set to and collect all the scalps that it seemed imperative to lay at the feet of his abhorred master. Beneath the whip, he would exert himself to extract from the assembled company the heavy ritual of dues, of total homage that was necessary to maintain the rule of his archaic Magician King. Meanwhile I had become familiar with the sight and sound of those mighty black wings beating upon Tommy, stealthily enfolding him around and around, but invisible to the rest of the company.

The guests sitting relaxed in deck-chairs, toasting each other in the summer sunlight, seemed not to perceive the shocking pallor and mortal sickness on the sculptor's face. He afterwards confessed that what caused him most regret was the fact that, feeling cursed and guilty himself, he determined that the rest of the world should feel the same about themselves; and the happier, the more innocent the person to whom he was talking, the more vitriolic was his ambition to infect them with his sense of doom. To this end, in his famous polemical displays, he was adept in producing statements disguised as objective truths, which were in fact heavily loaded with bitterness and destructive intent. And certainly no-one possessed greater adroitness at running his illegal contraband through the conversational customs, so to speak.

One thing was paramount: Tommy's daemon insisted that not only with their souls but definitely with their *bodies* everyone must him worship. This was the symbol and pledge of allegiance and subjection.

And lo and behold, by the end of any party, everybody pres-

ent—man, woman and child—had fallen in love with him. He had
managed to hook the lot! Without having personally witnessed this
no-one could have believed it possible. But under the lash Tommy
worked hard; those persons who hadn't been well and truly 'laid' by
him on previous occasions, and had their scalps duly collected, must be
laid *now* at this party. Naturally these amorous guerrilla attacks took
place out of sight—though only just. Maybe round a twisted corner of
the terrace. Maybe indoors, up in the bathroom for instance. Those for
whom there was positively no time on any given occasion were simply
stowed away senseless, in the game-bag, already partially de-feathered,
trussed up, and almost oven-ready for some future occasion. (In my
bitterness I made use of all such crude similes and metaphors, not in
unfeeling ribaldry, but under the influence of nightmare, where such
images are no matter for laughing.)

When the party was finally over Tommy and I would return along
the Wiltshire lanes to our cottage, and only next morning did we have to
face the most ruinous part of it all. All through the following day:
recantation; contrition; repentance. And again the long long hours of
shriving. Of maceration in sackcloth and ashes. And all poured forth in
scalding cataracts in which he would plunge about endeavouring to
destroy himself.

This was the worst part of our life together, for me.

If only, oh if only Tommy could have been content with the actual
sins he had committed. If only he would have done without this
aftermath of tortured guilt! Then, ah then, there would have been a
little time left over for companionship with me. And yet I was aware in
my secret heart that I only truly felt at home with just such spectres and
revenants as my husband. I had always made a bee-line for refugees
and exiles hailing from the same far-off and despoiled kingdom from
which I, too, had long ago been driven. They were my own people. I
understood them, how their hearts and minds worked, having all my
life known what it was to have been forced to scratch up, with bleeding
fingers, some sort of a living upon alien territory. Refugees recognise
each other, I reflected. Ghosts of their former selves, you can see them
striving to hide away their deformities and appear to be like other
people.

My journey was nearly over. Passengers were standing up, then
bending over to collect their parcels and overcoats. But as I walked

across the platform towards the Exit I realised that in a wider sense the return had only just begun. I had not even begun to grapple with the practical, nor yet the nervous and emotional framework which was to support my resurrection.

It was nearly midnight when I fitted my key into the front door of the small house in Weymouth Street, London, where I had newly rented rooms.

The long street was empty and deserted. Even at night one could barely hear the murmur of the late returning traffic on the Marylebone Road. When I had been here in the afternoon supervising the removal-van men, the shop-window of the Italian Delicatessen next door had glittered with a display of Mediterranean good living. From a silver bar fixed near the ceiling hung regional sausages, marbled and mosaic, in abundant variety. Below them in two long rows on the counter stood small white trays of dressed salads—marinated pimentos, anchovies, purple aubergines artfully sliced, half-eggs with yellow centres swimming in lubricious mayonnaise, chopped fennel, walnuts . . . everything sprinkled lavishly with herbs, chives, mint, chopped parsley. Refreshing even to look at! It seemed as if the shop were tenderly offering all its delicacies to welcome me to my new home.

But that had been in the afternoon. Now, at a quarter to midnight, I saw that the place had undergone a complete change of heart. Only cold rays from the street lights outside pierced the plate-glass window, and lay wan and dim across the empty counters. All the tempting trays were gone.

I stepped into the hall, shutting the front door behind me, found the light switch and turned it on. No light came. There was no-one else at present living in the building—that I knew; but I had come to Weymouth Street with the express intention of making a new home for myself, and now was the time to start digging its foundations. "Go upstairs to your new flat," I told myself, "find the packing case in which the van-men dumped your sheets and blankets; put them on the divan-bed and get yourself off quickly to sleep. Tomorrow will be Resurrection Day!"

At that instant it suddenly occurred to me that I had forgotten to arrange for an electrician to come round and connect things up. Good grief! I should have to make up the bed and do everything else in the dark. I hadn't even got matches. *Resurrection* indeed!

How, for example, had the Great Expert in Resurrection himself made out after arising from the Tomb? I began to ruminate—to try and recollect Holy Writ, though my knowledge of the subject was not of the best; I could only call to witness the famous pictures that I had seen, dealing with His life. Doubtless Jesus was presented with cooked meals wherever he went; and I had never seen a picture of him helping to wash up or anything like that, so that it was no use my looking to him as an example of how best to sort out my pots, pans and blankets. Ah well, he had never been brought up to any of all that, of course. But then neither had I been instructed how to do housework or cook. Why, I wondered, had not those old Aunts and Pretence Aunts whom my father had sent me to live with during my growing-up years—why had they not taught me such useful arts?

Those old ladies all had hordes of servants—I remembered them well because I had preferred their company to that of the so-called aunts themselves. But the trouble was that until I reached my teens I had imagined that hot meals were conjured out of the air. I remembered the talk to visiting friends about 'Cook', and how extravagant she was with eggs. A Cook was something out of a pantomime, so I gathered; and as for the maids, with their long streaming tails of white linen fixed to their caps, and their talk diversified by sudden explosions of maniacal giggling, their jokes and mimicry (so much enjoyed when I was with them behind the green baize door, or in pantry or scullery)—I had taken them as if they were some sort of characters from the *Commedia del Arte*.

However, I knew that these reflections were getting me nowhere. I was simply indulging in them so as to stave off the moment for recreating my world from chaos, the jungle of piled-up furniture, books and face-flannels awaiting me on the first floor. I ran upstairs, opened the door and went in. The light from the street lamp outside revealed forests of wooden legs sticking out at all angles, standard lamps separated from their shades, empty bookcases, and a host of mysteriously-shaped objects.

Blindly I dived into this forest, a human cockchafer, searching for the packing-case with the bedclothes in it. Somehow at last I found it, dragged out my bedding and flung it over the divan.

In bed at last, with my head on the pillow, I again surveyed the great mound of uncouth shapes in the centre of the room.

'The universe is going to end up in just this sort of way,' I thought; 'in higgledy-piggledy confusion.' I had read how all the tiny particles that at present dutifully build up into things with meaningful shapes and clear-cut purposes are even now busily disintegrating as energy runs out of them. It seems that our universe is steadily falling apart, and the very atoms are rebelling against our system here, small blame to them! Off they fly—the wild things—cavorting crazily in their disruptive dance. What do *they* care about law and order or the Conservation of Energy?

"Down with Statistical Uniformity!" is their cry. "Chance is the leader we follow! So forward to total disruption, and UP ENTROPY! What's that you're mumbling, Professor—or Archbishop or whatever you call yourself? Oh, never mind the *Origin* of everything—on that subject, least said, soonest mended!"

Chapter Twelve

THE HECTIC THIRTIES

[Since the small house she had rented in Weymouth Street was too large and too expensive for Julia on her own, Ralph and I arranged to take part of it off her hands, as a *pied-à-terre* for ourselves when we came to London. We took with us our faithful Marie, who had looked after us in Gordon Square, after formerly working for various people on the fringes of a world we knew. Dorothy Warren (of the Warren Galleries), Philip Morrell* and the Johns figured in her anecdotes, which were racy, to say the least. Possibly because Ralph and I were not married when she first came to us, she took to addressing us as 'Mister Ralph' and 'Miss Frances'—an old retainer touch which was expanded to include 'Miss Julia', and I rather think 'Mr. Augustus'. "Have you ever noticed," she once said to me, "that Miss Julia's hands seem to have a life of their own?" Julia's relations with Marie, as shown in the following letters to me, illustrate in miniature the pattern taken by many of her friendships and love-affairs. They began with delighted exploration of the new personality—the 'honeymoon period'—but criticism soon followed, and sometimes proved fatal to the relationship. This is a fairly common phenomenon; what was exceptional in Julia was her way of objectivising her feelings—treating them' as true observations of reality, even though they so rapidly contradicted themselves.

"I always thought X was a fearful bore," she said to me once. "What on earth can have happened to him? When he came to dinner last night he was absolutely *brilliant*. Marvellous! Witty!"

But next week it was: "You remember what I told you about X's brilliance? Well, whatever it was, it has *completely* disappeared. Last Monday, when I dined with him, he was a dull dog indeed!" Note that there was no question of poor X having good days and bad days, or of

* Husband of Lady Ottoline.

Julia having moods of sympathy and antipathy towards him. She was quite confident in her own arbitration. As she had truly written in reference to Aunt Loo's theory of 'acceptance', she would never let her critical faculties lapse. While this contributed to the spice and sparkle of her talk, it also made her formidable. She would allow no 'warts'—no freckles even—to go unnoticed. A great friend who had once shocked her by approving blood sports was never, all her life, quite forgiven.

So it was with her many admirers. She was very impressionable— a *cognoscente* (as she herself liked to put it) of male beauty; but few of the young, attractive and intelligent men who captured her interest during the years between her two marriages were able to hold it for long. Nor could any of these love affairs be said to have had a happy ending.

However, during these interim years she flung herself into social life, both bohemian and aristocratic, country house parties and dinners alike, accepting nearly all invitations, and going wherever she was asked. The people whose company gave her most pleasure were often painters like Henry Lamb (who did several portraits of her), Stanley Spencer and Adrian Daintrey. Indeed she had many happy times, but on the whole she was restless. "I don't think I *can* come to you for Whitsun," she wrote to Bryan Guinness in April 1934. "I have had a letter from Henry inveighing against flippant ladies who stroll in and out of sittings as the fancy takes them."

Julia wrote no set piece referring to any part of this period; perhaps her social life kept her too busy; but her urge to write took the form of intermittent jottings in a notebook always referred-to as 'The Coverless Diary' or 'Diary of the Thirties', written partly in almost indecipherable pencil, and all of it spontaneous. I have quoted from it freely. Otherwise, this period is documented from Julia's letters and also by an extract from the Diary of Philip Toynbee describing a month he and Julia spent in the country together, for permission to use which I am extremely grateful to Mrs. Sally Toynbee.]

(Julia to Ralph Partridge)

March, 1934. I haven't ever told you how grateful I was for the Portugal trip, or even thanked you at all; but I do so now—merely giving voice in one feeble letter to the feelings I have had so strongly all the last three weeks. I enjoyed it, it was fascinating, and I loved being with you and Frances; and I shall be undyingly grateful to you for being so uniformly *sweet* to me all the time. Now that the ground has given way under my feet so to speak, and I am plunged into God knows what seas and marshes, you have both made all the difference in the world to me.

I have been whirled all over the place since I got back, and I feel if I don't sit alone in a dark hole and pull myself together I shall disintegrate for good and all. I went to see Tom, the solicitor. He advises 'cutting the knot definitely by divorce'. I couldn't help but agree with him, but I gave absolutely nothing away.

Meanwhile Tommy is apparently still unable to face that the separation is a final one. He begged Oliver not to consider it as final. Well, if it helps him he had better feel this for a few months, by which time he will be able to face it more easily, I imagine.

(Julia to Bryan Guinness)

March, 1934. We are back again from Portugal, and I am hoping to see you again some day. I dare say you will have heard my news by this time. I am separated from Tommy and living in future entirely on my own. I am not leaving Tommy to go to another man; but merely because we were so wretchedly unhappy together. These last three years it has been touch and go as to our separating, all the time, and in fact three unsuccessful attempts have been made. Now it is really done for good and all. I hope you have not thought it unfriendly never to have talked about myself more. Tommy couldn't bear anyone knowing about our difficulties.

(Julia's Diary)

April 1st, 1934. Easter with the Pitmans at Odstock. Hugo fished, Reine and I walked on the downs discussing jealousy. David and Rachel Cecil, Henry and Pansy [Lamb] to dinner. My walk with Reine was lovely. Summer sunlight flooded the fields, the downs and woods, rather hazily. We sat on a bank on the edge of a pinewood and looked down at Wiltshire. On Saturday an attempted picnic with the [Augustus] Johns. We arrived at Fryern at 12 o'clock with hampers all ready, and found Vivien [John], Baba and Igor [Anrep] sitting writing 'romantic letters' in the sun. Augustus, Caspar and Edwin had gone to the pub and 'would be back at 12'. We waited till 1.30, when Caspar rang up asking, "What are the plans?" "Why don't you come *back*?" shouts Vivien, and we are told to go ahead and meet them at the

Blandford crossroads where of course there is no sign of them, so we ate
our sandwiches and hurried home.

That night we dined at Fryern. Dodo* at one end of the long table; I
sat between Edwin and Igor. No-one had anything to say but Edwin
and myself, who hummed together in a whisper—the regulation Edwin
flirtatious style. I told him I was working in Bond Street. "But I
remember the very sound of the word is an abomination to you. You
said so one Christmas when I was staying here."

"Why rake up the past? What is past is done with. Why can't you
take me as you find me?"

"What! Do you mean to say you wipe the slate of life clean every
day?"

"The slate of life I know nothing of. But let us go and dance," said
Edwin. As we danced he said, "You are a very thrilling person. That's
an expression I never used before. You make my breath go shorter and
then I lose my sense of propriety." Etcetera, etcetera.

(Julia's Diary)

May 1st, 1934. I was writing letters at Barbara Key Seymer's flat. Bunny
Garnett had arrived to see Barbara, and now there was a ring at the
door-bell and Peter Spencer appeared, asking for dinner. The remains
of my tongue and bread and pickles and chives were brought, a bottle of
red wine opened, and we all sat round while he ate. Conversation about
the peerage. (Peter has not long been a Lord.)† Bunny described going
to the House of Lords, and stepping over a dead Bishop's gaitered legs.
Peter began explaining the degrees of the aristocracy, and telling us the
difference between a Baron, a Viscount and an Earl, taking for names
the articles of food on the kitchen table in front of him: "Lord Sugar, the
Earl of Chives, Viscount Chutney, Lady Decanter," and so on. He was
bewailing having no robes to take his seat in. We suggested hiring from
Clarksons; but he said if there was a rush Clarksons started palming off
old-world styles when the up-to-date ones had all been snapped up. "I
expect I shall be dressed up in chain armour or have a Grecian chlamys
thrown round my shoulders," he says gloomily. Bunny told us how he
and his son Richard—then about seven years old and at Bertie
Russell's school—had been looking at a statue of Lord Beaconsfield.

* Dorelia John.
† Lord Churchill.

Richard said: "I only know one peer as a matter of fact—the Vizzcount Amberley,* and he happens to be one of my closest friends." Then Peter described the frogs he saw floating in the canal, and how they swelled to enormous proportions after little boys pricked them. Olga Lynn looked like a pricked frog, he said, after Lord Berners' lunch party, when they had been given blinnies and cream, creamed lobster, creamed chicken, and billows of cream on the pudding.

(Julia to F.P.)

May 7th, 1934. I *did* so enjoy seeing you both on Saturday. It was a great treat for me to have got away down and had a chat with you; and I feel so much better for it in spite of the guilt entailed. However I discovered that Barbara had soon cheered up on the Saturday, and by teatime was wreathed round with Queens and supporters of all sorts, including the prime favourite—Lord Churchill. When I arrived on Sunday she was descried through a thick fog of tobacco smoke sitting on the knees of four Queens at once, like a mother bird sitting on eggs in a nest, so to say. I had a crashing evening last night. John Banting invited his friend the 'genius hatter' back to Maddox Street, also Bryan Howard, Lord Churchill, Barbara and me, and by the light of two stump candles, completely in the nude, he flung himself all over everything in a frenzied mating dance aimed at the genius.

(Julia to F.P.)

June 21st, 1934. Weymouth Street. Today is a bad day for me, my dear. Wogan and I have finally decided to call it all off, and that as a love affair it has no more possibilities. Though actually it is a nervous strain trying to keep on with it, it has been so nearly a possible source of happiness that one does feel sad at shutting the door on it all for the last time. When I sit down and think of all the boiling feelings we *did* have for each other, which were simply strangulated from the start, it does make me feel hopeless about the chances of success in love ever. It has been a horrid two days. Wogan and I both say that the *other* one ruined the affair by holding back and being cold right from the start. We seem to have misunderstood every word each other said all along the line, taken everything the wrong way and done just the fatal thing each time in consequence—a horrid vista to peer down.

* Bertrand Russell's eldest son, the same age as Richard.

I am being motored down to stay with Hester on Saturday, feel I should like the crazy distraction that descends on one at Spyway.* Apparently she is intending to separate from Nigel.† She confided this in Anne Barnes, who told Dadie [Rylands], who told Rosamond at May Week, who told Wogan, who told me, who told you, who told Ralph, who told—? history doesn't relate.

(Julia's Diary)

Summer, 1934. Lunched with Henry [Lamb] at Bryce and afterwards went to the National Gallery. Henry was looking his best; his face stood out among the others—finely carved, alive with nervous energy, pale and meticulously modelled, with his hair just showing under his dark slouch hat and looking like the apprehensively-ruffled feathers of a bird, just as it feels a draught strike it. He made other people look like hogs, with their coarsely-coloured chaps and snouts.

At the Gallery we saw among other things a wonderful life-size portrait of a lady by Sir T. Lawrence. Henry pointed out that he could tell it had been painted when Lawrence was quite young—twenty or so—by the way the hands were too highly focused for the rest of the picture. It was true; they were much more solid and real, where the rest of the portrait was more lyrical and poetical, a degree further from life. Then he explained how one could tell at once that El Greco was homosexual, by the 'unction' with which the naked young men in *Laocoon* were painted. As he said they looked *very* naked, and gave one a shock as a real naked man does, as opposed to the other nudes we looked at. Afterwards Henry treated me to ices at Gunters. There's something very Edwardian about Gunter's tea room—the glass roof, perhaps, shedding a conservatory radiance over the expensively-dressed old ladies and innocent-looking children, the naive young women covered in curls, and the pet dogs. At a table near us sat a regular Renoir party: a stout white-haired matron in a flowered frock, two little girls in wide straw hats wreathed in daisies, and a man like a doll in a frockcoat with a black moustache. Henry uses marvellous distortions of words—for instance: Frances Penrose's 'volumptious bosoms'; Peter Quennell's 'Quennelerousness'; 'after the long straw it's

---

* A prep. school Hester was running in Dorset.
† Chapman, her husband.

the last struggle that breaks'; 'he's very bad when he's out of his water'. He shrinks from the sensation of the actual, hence his passion for immediately transmitting phenomena into schemes or mental pictures, quickly putting them at a distance at any price, often at the expense of accuracy and truth. He dreads the violence of his own reactions, hates accepted excuses for superiority and organised defences—e.g. fashion in any form, which he calls 'paws up'. ('If *I* put my paws up, *You*'ll give me a lump of sugar'.) Augustus's panache likewise comes in for severity: apparently he came in last night and talked about his scheme for voyaging round the world. When he got up to go, in his flowing overcoat and scarf flung over his shoulders, he threw out his arm with a generous gesture and bid everyone a hearty goodbye.

"Are you starting out already?" asked Henry, startled.

"No, not yet; in the Autumn," barks Augustus, whose theatrical leave-taking reminded Henry of some grizzled Viking chief bidding farewell to his good comrades on the beach.

(Julia to Bryan Guinness)

August 9, 1934. With the Lambs at Coombe Bissett. The breezes are moaning round the house and sighing in the chimney. We went to bathe yesterday, and can you imagine my horror on emerging from the river to find *leeches* feeding upon me. I tried to wrest them from me but they wouldn't budge. Yesterday a strange-looking farmer type descended upon Henry and begged for drawing and painting lessons during his fortnight's visit to the neighbourhood. Finally Henry agreed, and it then turned out to be none other than H. M. Bateman the famous comic artist. So he had his first lesson today.

(Julia to Bryan Guinness)

August 14, 1934. West Bradenham, Norfolk. Immediately after I'd written [from the Lambs], Pansy cheered us up completely and said she had been feeling furious with the cook about something. We had a terrific week of children—the whole outlook seemed to resolve itself into children's faces covered with tomato pulp and blobs of marmalade. Jungles of food, to use Henry's own expression, lay knee-deep all over the floors. I don't know why, I am feeling horribly liverish, as weak as a kitten.

(Julia to Bryan Guinness)

August, 1934. Weymouth Street. May I really come on Thursday evening to stay? I would love to come if I may, and you won't mind if I am still yellow in the face with my liver? I remember you said on the telephone that you would treat an invalid kindly—please do. I have written a poem! What do you think of that? And about you, too. Also about me. It is called 'Lines to a Young Man who plays chess while he plants forget-me-nots'. But perhaps you don't like the title? It is really quite complimentary and poetical when you come to take its meaning; which is rather a laborious process, as when I write poetry I *write* poetry—symbology, cosmogony, botany, zoology, nothing is left out, I can tell you.

[That summer Julia went on a round of visits in Ireland—first to the Longfords at Pakenham Hall, then to Bryan Guinness at Knockmaroon, near Dublin, where she was joined by Ralph and myself, and Raymond Mortimer.]

(Julia to Bryan Guinness)

September, 1934. Pakenham Hall. How is the brewery? I am longing to see it. Will one be permitted to be shown over? We are so looking forward to coming across to stay with you. Henry quotes you as being the only person Edward and Christine [Longford] have liked. John Betjeman is here, without Penelope. Henry is waging war direct on Betj and Betj is mustering his opposing forces in really gallant style. The Lamb party have not made themselves very popular, and are now left in sole possession of the Castle, having driven everyone else away; we have put up the drawbridge and let down the portcullis, and settled down for a nice homey visit.

(Julia to F.P.)

September 21st, 1934. Knockmaroon, Co. Dublin. I can't tell you how pleased I was to get a letter from you yesterday. I have been stranded in foreign parts now it seems for an eternity, and it was such a relief hearing that you and Ralph are coming here. I am feeling completely changed since we last met—a case of 'Full fathom five thy Julia lies, of her bones are ashtrays made, these are hors d'oeuvres that were her eyes, nothing of her but has suffered a house-party change.' I am so longing for you to arrive, and am staying on next week borne up by the thought. Your poems enclosed were wonderful, I loved them both and am very glad to have such a nice one about my admired Dr. Glover. My stay at the Longfords' Irish castle was extraordinary, not very nice really. I will tell you all about it when we meet, as my house-party ashtray bones won't permit me pulling myself together enough to write a coherent account of anything, alas and alack! Here we have Roy [Harrod], Mrs. Henry Yorke,* Lady Anne Cameron, and Lambs: when you arrive there will be Pansy's beautiful blonde sister, Mary Pakenham, and I hope delightful Peter Hesketh.† As to love and so on, Henry is giving me great trouble in that direction. Oh God! the car is here; I have to fly in order to see the pictures in Dublin.

(Julia to Ralph Partridge)

October 9th, 1934. Weymouth Street. Do you see in the paper that Tony Powell is engaged to Pansy's sister Violet? We saw the whole thing going on under our noses at Pakenham Hall in Ireland.

I have seen no-one but the Boss.‡ She was all amiability. Apparently Hester has been staying with her. Bunny, who is still lodging with Barbara at King's Road, was frightened into fits by coming down to breakfast one morning, and finding Hester seated alone in the kitchen munching an apple, dressed in a lilac swansdown dressing-gown, with her face covered with medicinal beauty paste, and her hair filled with 'iron girders' to quote Barbara. This was the first he'd seen of her. When she munches an apple, you know, there's a sound as of twenty horses crunching oats. I can't think why I'm being so catty.

(Julia to Ralph Partridge)

[Undated] I want to write and thank you again for your perfectly lovely present to me.§ I can't tell you how amazingly charming I think

---

  * Wife of Henry Green, the novelist.
  † Architect, whom Julia had taken a fancy to.
  ‡ Nickname for Barbara Ker Seymer.
  § Ralph gave her a present of a French model dress, to be chosen by her. Her letter shows she appreciated the special kindness of the gift in view of his own total lack of interest in such things.

it—I can't get over it at all. I am so excited and enraptured at the idea of choosing it, and better still, wearing it. What is so sweet is that you should give me what *I* like best—whilst I know you yourself feel there is nothing in a 'French model'. It must seem crazy to you, the whole conception, and yet you give me this handsome present! How unlike some people's present-giving that is. Well, you are an angel. Since I left you I have had my nose to the grindstone writing this story for the *Nation*. It is sent off at last, however, and tomorrow I am going to begin my search. Hurray. Give my fond love to Frances.

(Julia to Ralph Partridge)

[Undated] The clothes have come back. They are lovely—*exactly* what I wanted. Just ordinary day clothes, black—but ah! to the eye of the expert—oh là! là! Could you and Frances come to dinner on Wednesday night? I am asking a practical blond to meet you. John Banting is back, and has been at the office. He says he went straight to Eddie's [Gathorne-Hardy] flat, as Eddie had asked him to stay. He found it ceiling high with old bottles, cobwebs spun between them, old basins full of punch cup with moss three inches high floating on the surface, coal black sheets on the beds, all gas and electricity cut off, so no hot water for baths, no food, no anything, only raw toadstools, moss and spiders as hors d'oeuvres.

(Julia's Diary)

November 3rd, 1934. Henry John to tea. He conducted the whole conversation—which was almost entirely metaphysical—sitting in profile, and only looked at me three times during the whole session, which lasted from 4.30 until 7. What lies behind this habit? Is it, as with Ivor Novello and Owen Nares, to display his profile, which is beautiful, the shape of his head as in a Renaissance painting. It would be pleasant to indulge my daydreams about him, inhibit my critical faculties and concentrate only on—say—his profile, forgetting that his full face is disappointing and makes a certain impression of insensitiveness.

(Julia's Diary)

November, 1934. There was Peter Hesketh fumbling about with the bowler hats in the hall at Violet Powell's wedding cocktail party. He was just going as I was entering, not even waiting to see if I should turn up or not. This should take me down a good peg by rights. He looked somewhat mediocre and I was unpleasantly surprised. The short conversation we had together went by as a waterfall goes by—one cannot understand what the shape of the water is as it flashes past, it goes with such a rush. I felt as if I were being translated into another dimension, just as at Biddesden when we first met. What was it that produced that bewildering effect on me?—like talking to a visitor from Mars.

(Julia to F.P.)

December, 1934. Marie* has been in the first water lately—I have absolutely lost my heart to her now. And what copy she provides, really wonderful! Today she said: "Sometimes Mr. Ralph looks so like Mr. Philip Warren! Of course all college men have got the same sort of sparkle, haven't they?" And yesterday: "Here's a letter for you from Miss Frances, please *do* let me know after you've read it how she is. I'm very anxious to know how she's getting on; I'm *like* that, you know, Miss Julia."

(Julia to F.P.)

January 6th, 1935. West Bradenham, Norfolk. I *am* glad, so frightfully glad and pleased to hear that all is going well, and look forward with most eager impatience to—July? or whenever it is when we may expect to welcome a baby partridge among us. Christmas at Forthampton (old Mr. and Mrs. Yorke's† house) was interesting. There was just the old birds and the two young birds‡ and Adrian Daintrey and myself. It is a huge place, and a lot of it built in the 14th century—the living-room, for example, looks much like the concert hall at Bedales; there are endless winding corridors, all centrally heated, and by far the best cook I've ever come across. My dear, the food was heavenly beyond words. Old Mrs. Yorke is a dowdy, huntin' character, very bright, telling racy stories all the time. Adrian was simply delightful, he is first-rate company; Henry and Dig were as usual, he incomprehensible, and she very nice. We went to a grand dinner-party from there at the house of a certain Lady Mary Strickland; there were present her two nieces'

---

* Our daily help at Weymouth Street.
† Parents of Henry Yorke, the novelist Henry Green.
‡ Henry and 'Dig' Yorke.

husbands, Lord O'Neill and Lord Long, and even Adrian was addressed as 'your Lordship' by the footman.

Here at Bradenham there is a bad drop in titles and also in the table fare. Boiled cod, quite tasteless, with a sauce like paste. The gossip is that Nigel Chapman and Hester are parted: and that she is coming to London, God help us all. He disappeared into space, and left a little debt of £2,000 behind him. I shall return to London on Saturday, but how am I ever going to see you at this rate?

(Julia's Diary)

April 21st, 1935. Easter at Biddesden. Randolph Churchill, Stanley Spencer, the Graham Bells* and the Julian Trevelyans are all staying here with Bryan Guinness. In the library after dinner Stanley perched himself on a high chair in the centre of the hearth and held the floor, talking all evening without stopping, while we all lolled round him on sofas and arm-chairs. He described his musician brother, said he was as obstinate as a mule and always refused to play the piano when family or visitors asked him.

" 'Music, what sort of music?' he'd say. 'Oh, I don't know,' someone would say, 'anything. I'm very fond of Mendelssohn.' So my brother sits down and plays all those terrible affairs—*Spring Song* and so on. And he plays these terrible pieces with this peculiar striking effect, y'know, like something moving about under a sheet of glass, y'know, something you can't get *down to* and yet you can feel it's *there*, y'know. *Amazing* really, come to think of it."

At Sunday lunch Stanley told us how his Academy picture of the crucifix and the weeping Magdalen came to be painted. He had heard or read a phrase, "women wept on the high roads and strong men broke down in the side streets", and it was this phrase which had inspired him. Afterwards he showed me photographs of his pictures; in one a dustman was being honoured "by a girl holding up a cabbage straight from the dustbin". He added that it had been painted with "an obscene urge. Some animal force which I never had in the old days is using me now. Of course anyone can see that. Just look at that old cabbage, for example; the stump is all cut away and there's a great tongue hanging out, isn't there? No *wonder* they consider me obscene at the Academy. Obscene is the very word, as a matter of fact."

* Painter of the Euston Road School, killed in the Second World War.

(Julia's Diary)

1935. In the Devas'* studio. A huge room, stylishly and solidly furnished, beautiful curtains; a feeling of space, leisure and freshness. A
fireplace like a huge megatherium. The two young people composed
and orderly—Nicolette voluptuous, steady and sturdy. Anthony's
ancient corduroy trowsers reveal an awkward boyish figure, his head
made too large by curly hair; bony wrists, large well-kept hands. He has
the raw, cold but sparkling and clearcut beauty of a hyacinth in a gale.
You feel the strong direction of a newly-sprung plant cutting its way up
through the hard earth.

(Julia to F.P.)

April 28th, 1935. It is really too hellish for words living day in and day out
with Marie. We don't get on together one bit. This morning another
row. We agreed to part—absolutely mutual, only of course she didn't
want to leave *you.* But if you'll leave it all to me I can get someone just as
good as Marie to work for us. I don't know *what* you'll say, and I am
fearfully sorry if you are upset and angry, but Frances, I think I am
going mad with Marie here. I cannot stand the woman. How are things
with you?

(Julia to F.P.)

May 10th, 1935. There is no reason why you should get the brunt of my
murderous feelings for Marie, dearest Frances! So she is staying on, as I
had no idea how awkward it was going to make matters for you in July.†
I will try and stay away in July, as it will make everything easier—a
week at Bradenham I hope, and a few days at Biddesden, also a night or
two at Lionel [Penrose's]. It is a very special occasion, and we must all
pull together, as described in the motto of our old school!‡ Roland
[Penrose] took me to see the Jubilee;§ we had seats in Piccadilly by
the Park railings—a superb view. The uniforms of the soldiers, and
their horses, were very marvellous. But *no music,* no bands. The King
and Queen were glorious, however: the Queen in huge white fluffy fur

---

* Anthony Devas, painter, and his wife.
† F.P.'s son Burgo was born on July 8th; Marie and the Partridge part of the house
were invaluable at this time.
‡ 'Work of each for weal of all'.
§ The Silver Jubilee of George V and Queen Mary.

and ablaze with diamonds in the bright sunlight, and a silver and opalescent toque: the King very sweet in a scarlet General's uniform. Bryan [Guinness] and I went roaring round London on top of a taxi at night, to see the decorations, floodlighting at St. Paul's, and so on. London looks like a provincial fair, that's all. Rather nice to see the place changed a bit, but the decorations are so hideous and so scrappy, messy and untidy. What other news? I have been getting into hot water all round for laying my hands on other women's men—it's too dreadful. All this hot weather, you know, is having a very demoralising effect on the citizens of London. G.B. is fairly dying of love for me, it appears. The telephone bell rings. "Are you alone?" "Yes." "Well, I must come round and make love to you." "That would hardly do. But would you care to come round and have a chat?" "No, I want sex, not conversation." And then P.'s young man appears every day with bunches of flowers *à l'Americaine*, and says—but no, I'm being vulgar. R. invites me to fly to Paris with him, and the only person I care to look at has gone to live in California! I ask you! Between all this spooning I have done quite an amount of writing. But there seems a good bit of gaiety up here, dinner parties, and driving to see Hampton Court floodlit afterwards and so on. I think you'd better both come up and join in with it.

(Julia's Diary)

August 15th, 1935. Odstock (staying with Hugo and Reine Pitman). A walk through Wardour Castle park. The impression of entering a new universe, a universe of trees, created by trees. The potent spell that the deserted woods exercised on me made me feel as if I was turning into a tree myself, and the pervasive smell of damp mosses and wet foliage penetrated my very soul. The sunlight, striking this way and that, helped construct a sort of architecture, with naves, arcades, pillars and galleries. The cooing of the turtle-doves echoed amongst the topmost branches of the trees, recalling with anguish the languor and thrill of high summer. I believe we are all aiming at emancipation from emotion. Not its annihilation but release from its thraldom. When sunk in a quagmire of feeling, no matter what that feeling is, one is a prisoner cut off from the rest of the world. Only through art can one experience feelings without being immersed and drowned in them. But oh horror and despair!—that nostalgia of summer recalled by the turtle-doves' cooing!

(Julia's Diary)

January 4th, 1936. Drunk at 8.30 p.m. after one of those lonely suppers at the Dutch Oven in Baker Street.

In the above-mentioned condition, it dawns on me that the secret of life is the Divine Afflatus—that is the pearl in the oyster, the gold in the slate rock; that is the value we are seeking. It swells the buds in Spring, the leaves in Summer, and fruit in Autumn.

Reflections about my boy friends: flirting around with all these young men, the games, the admiration, is all just a glittering drop-curtain, a design in the flat, mere symbols of the play itself and what is to be found in it. Or like a harlequinade as opposed to the pantomime proper. But in Graham [Bell] I feel something real—a human being in the raw. The divine afflatus blows through everyone—each person deals with this animating breeze differently. Heywood [Hill], for instance, is like a wonderful tent, firmly pegged to the ground; the divine afflatus bellies around and through him but he remains fixed. When people grow old the afflatus leaves them and they sag like the folds of a flag when the wind dies away.

Written when pretty drunk: Save us. Save us. Save us. We are all looking for something that will save us. We are drowning. What is there that will save us?

Why should love for others be better than love for self?

Answer (*later, when sober*): Because we are ourselves only part of the whole. We must love and cope with the *whole* or the machinery breaks down.

(Julia to F.P.)

April 1st, 1936. Thank you for a lovely visit, which I enjoyed enormously. I can't tell you what it was like returning to my new flat.* First the decorators had lost the keys; it was then discovered that they had forgotten to lay the carpets, so all furniture was dumped on bare boards. Then no geyser put in the bathroom, no electric light on either. Also a letter in the hall from my old charwoman saying she had scalded her leg (I don't think) and couldn't come for a long time. So here I am with no bath, no means of cooking, no help, no light, and I sleep under

---

* In Paddington Street, W.2.

all the dustbins and piles of kitchen utensils and can't put away *anything* while the gas men are tearing up the floor-boards like frenzied cats! I ask you. Also the paint is the wrong colour—utterly and hopelessly, and will have to be done again whilst I am sleeping there and everything. Which all shows what an owl I have been in hoping to rest quietly in the country, instead of keeping an eye on the workmen myself. *All* my news today is of gas inspectors and United Dairies, so I will lay off! Fondest love to both of you.

(Julia to F.P.)

May 6th, 1936. Ever since I wrote you last I have been living in a daze of horror. I really have been like a rabbit with a snake—mesmerised and unable to move hand or foot in a kind of stupor. The men simply *would* not come and put my room to rights, and other woes have come thick and fast, too. I am angling for two jobs—one at Robinson and Cleaver* if you please; nothing will come of either, I am sure. I am going on with my play (one of them) now, and go out to Regent's Park if the weather is fine, to write there.

(Julia to F.P.)

June, 1936. I enjoyed my Whitsun with Rachel and David [Cecil] very much indeed. They are both as angelically friendly and charming as ever. Anthony Asquith is a queer eaglet and one doesn't know how to react to him. He seemed very on the spot, understands all things and has a beautiful touch on the piano—played most meltingly. The only other excitement was when a contingent from the Wilton party descended on us—David Herbert in pansy raiment, two people in Tyrolean get-up and Lady Elizabeth Paget in horrible grey flannel trowsers. They were no sooner seated in the drawing-room than David Herbert in his most winning childlike manner demanded peppermint bullseyes. There were none, so we all had to troop off to the village to get some. ("Oh, *do* let's go and buy some. *What* fun! I'd *love* that! Would *you*, Lizzie? Oh *do* let's! *May* we? Hurrah!") Rachel, David and myself, pale, untidy and humdrum, struggled off amongst this flamboyant party of paroqueets in fancy costumes. Not a blade of grass, not a cottage, not a hen, not a villager escaped their piercing winsome comments: "*Oh*, how

---

* A large department store; she got this.

delicious! *Oh*, how I wish we had hens like that at Wilton! Lizzie, Lizzie, we must go *straight* home and buy hens like that for Wilton!" etcetera, etcetera.

(Julia to F.P.)

August, 1936. Thank you for one of the most enjoyable holidays I ever had. It was absolutely perfect from start to finish. I wanted to thank you both so very much also for being kind enough to ask down my young man*—very sweet of you indeed and much appreciated. My friend Heywood Hill has blossomed out into the most terrific and shee shee [sic] bookshop opposite the Curzon Cinema. Anne Gathorne-Hardy is working in it with him, and I am expecting to hear of their engagement any moment. My play progresses, but is not totally effected yet. Am quite halfway through the last scene, having written in an extra one into the bargain. Leonard refused it and evidently thought it most unfunny. He very nicely said by way of explanation that he and Virginia had a "blind spot about that particular genre of writing," and urged me to send it elsewhere.

(Julia to Bryan Guinness)

January 3rd, 1937. I had a very terrible Christmas, for on the Tuesday before, word came that Tommy had been rushed off in an ambulance to a hospital in Bournemouth, and was lying critically ill with blood-poisoning. His relatives were all wired for. My father and I went down there together, as it was considered possible that he might ask for me; and there we stayed all through Christmas week, visiting the hospital three times a day for news, and always learning that they expected him to die any moment. Oliver saw him often. He never asked for me, but I was glad to have gone. He is mending now, I believe, but slowly.

(Julia to F.P.)

January 7th, 1937. [Telegram] In case you had not heard Tommy died day before yesterday thought I would let you know love. Julia.

[Since his separation from Julia, Tommy had made little change in his way of life; mixing with most of his old friends, including Oliver, and

* Graham Bell.

going on with his psycho-analysis. The most important person in his life was probably a young man known as 'H'.

His major piece of sculpture was an over-life-size female figure cast in lead for Bryan Guinness's garden at Biddesden; he also worked at ceramics in the studio of Phyllis Keyes.

His death was quite unexpected. He had an aching tooth extracted under gas, and went home feeling none the worse, but a few days later became very ill with blood-poisoning and pneumonia, seemed to be recovering and suddenly got worse and died. One theory was that a piece of the decayed tooth had entered his lung. Another that his heavy drinking had weakened his resistance.]

(Julia to F.P.)

August 10th, 1937. Glengariff Castle, Co. Cork, Ireland.* My weekend at Oxford seemed to go off without any major mishaps—somehow the whole thing was a frantic steering of a P. and O. liner between rocks and coral reefs in a sea fog. What made the sea fog effect was that Solly [Zuckerman] is such an oriental, foreign to the *bone*, and looks it—a type I have never had anything to do with before. And suddenly to be clapped into a honeymoon weekend with him was unnerving. But when I explained that I belonged to a bourgeois tradition and that decorum was my middle name and moderation in all things was my motto, he was very nice, polight [sic] and gentlemanly about it. Although it took the entire three days to convince him I really meant it (perhaps because I failed to remain consistently bourgeois myself throughout), but I'll say no more for fear of the Irish Censor. Solly is tremendously alive in all ways, sensitive, kind-hearted and affectionate; he has great personality and temperament, and of course brains. We had a mad round of pleasure, music-halls every night, trips up the river, expeditions by car to picturesque inns where we drank cocktails among a mass of lobster-faced hikers. And in the background 50 monkeys, and as many guinea-pigs and rabbits, all having their ovaries grafted in behind their eyes and suchlike tricks played on them.

That's enough about Solly! Bantry Bay, and all round it, is very picturesque; dense tropical woods rise up the hillsides, in which bamboos, eucalyptus, wild fuchsias and monkey-puzzles all mingle.

* Julia was staying in a house taken by Heywood Hill and Anne Gathorne-Hardy.

The Castle is 17th century, with an Early Victorian wing in which we live. Stone-paved hall, many large deserted rooms papered in Victorian style, vases of long dried grasses. A doddering old butler served the dinner. All completely Irish and castle-like.

(Julia to Heywood Hill)

September 14th, 1937. Paddington Street. I meant to write ages ago and tell you how very much I had enjoyed the holiday at the Castle. I can't tell you how grateful I am for suggesting that I should come or how flattered I feel to have been one of the party. Everything in a letter sounds flat and meaningless, and so I'm afraid I shan't be able to convey to you what a pleasure it has been for me to get to know Sheila and John [Hill]*—and Anne. Anne I adored. She is truly one in a million —like finding gold at last after searching for years in the gravel of the Rand rivers. Now Heywood you're not to read that to Anne because it will simply sound stupid, it is for your eyes alone, and you will understand from it how I appreciated her quality. As for the romance of the castle itself—I am already writing about it, and so perhaps you will hear more of that later.

(Julia to F.P.)

November 14th, 1937. I wish you had been with me last night. Nicolette Devas and I first had basketfuls of oysters and champagne with old Hugo [Pitman] at the Café Royal, and then went on to a lecture on the Drama by Christopher Isherwood, and there we were with Day Lewis, Spender, Auden and all their admirers. He gave a stupid talk and said many tiresome things, but it was all quite a slice of life. Eddie Gathorne-Hardy has no doubt told you that Anne's engagement to Heywood Hill is now public. A delightful couple if ever there was one in my opinion.

(Julia to F.P.)

March 21st, 1938. Private and Confidential. I have decided to set off on my travels with Philip [Toynbee] on Thursday next, so that I don't think I shall be able to come to you Frances at the moment. I have planned to stay with him till 22nd April, but of course it may all break

---

* Heywood Hill's sister and her husband (interior decorator).

down. I dined with Raymond [Mortimer] and went to a play the other night. I enjoyed it very much, but I infuriated him by quoting Communist opinions culled from Philip, and he kept looking at me in horror and disgust over the creamy salmis and glowing purées on the marble dinner-table, saying, "Do pull yourself *together*, Julia! I thought you were quite a sensible woman!" Really I must make a resolution to keep my fingers out of politics. Raymond had just bought £10 worth of sardines and a bicycle to bicycle down the Great West Road on, in the event of war being declared, as he says all those with motor-cars will get stuck in a queue and never succeed in getting away.

(Julia to F.P.)

April 19th, 1938. Ebbesbourne, Wilts. I went to Weymouth with my young man, and then we came on here to Ebbesbourne Wake, where we discovered a sweet little cottage with sitting-room and bedroom and all meals for twenty-five shillings a week inclusive. Here we have been ever since, though Philip has gone back again now. It was very nice having him with me. I think I can't really tell you the whole saga of it now. So I will wait until we meet. Toynbee is a real duck, with a good dash of goose thrown in, for which I like him none the worse. He worked six hours a day as he wants to get a first it seems next term at Oxford. In the afternoons we went out, and after dinner we read aloud. At Weymouth we had a dear old lady with an ear-trumpet who couldn't hear a thing, which in certain cases is just as well. There we fed chiefly in the fried fish shop—a portion of fish and chips for fourpence, or else bought little pork pies and sausage rolls and ate them in a pub to the strains of 'Little Old Laydee' or 'Goodnight my Love'.

Esmond Romilly and Decca* came down (with the baby and all) and stayed one weekend. That was very strange. Somehow I really had forgotten the world at twenty years of age, and it was most curious being thrown into it again. The main horror of young people is that they can't foresee any of the snags that lie ahead, and go blundering along.

I had insisted on Philip being 'Stephen Tomlin', as I thought I might want to use this cottage later for my writing. Philip of course had made no arrangements, so letters, bills and parcels poured down in a steady stream for Philip Toynbee, and some even for Lord Tomlin, so

* Née Jessica Mitford.

altogether it was a fine mix-up I can tell you, trying to patch it up with the landlady, especially as Esmond Romilly would address him in front of her, "I say, Philip—or rather Stephen."

(Julia to F.P.)

June 7th, 1938. Paddington Street. I am now settled in to London life for good, and feeling there is firm ground under my feet on which to build. How sea-sick I felt all these last three months, not knowing from moment to moment what was happening to me upon my leaky raft of indigence. Somehow it has all taken years off my life in a curious way—I feel a completely different person: years older, middle-aged in fact in heart, and in *deed* also, with all that that state implies. I'm enjoying living quite alone and I really do some writing. I don't want to see anyone. Two cats have joined me here—one by day, one by night. The evening one comes on duty at about 8 o'clock, and when I walk into the kitchen I see a great *colossus*, as big as a *hotel*, and very very old, with one watering eye, sitting on top of my bath watching for mice. I never told you in my last letter how particularly I loved all the *weeding* at Ham Spray. It was perfect bliss.

July 11th, 1938. My young man has given me the chuck—Philip. We met again after three months' absence, as you know, and he came to dinner with me here. While he was drinking his glass of sherry he said he was engaged to be married. "O really," says I. "But I *do* congratulate you! How lovely!" and so on and so on. It all seemed to me a bit sudden at the time. Only a week or two before he had been writing to me in a state of despair because I hadn't written to him, and never a word in his letter of another love. Anyway the actual shock of trying to adapt myself so suddenly proved too much for me, and I found myself compelled after dinner to ask him to go away again. Of course I knew it would happen sooner or later, and yet when it happened I wasn't prepared. So that's that.

[The following is an account of the above episode, taken from Philip Toynbee's diary and printed thanks to the kindness of Mrs. Sally Toynbee. Philip was 21, Julia 36. The first scene took place in Julia's flat.]

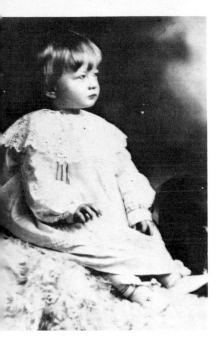

Above left: Julia aged one year

Above right: Julia in 1911 with friends at Miss Grüner's school

Right: Julia aged about 10 with Vincent Rendel

Mary Berenson, 'Aunt Mareeks',
in about 1890

Aunt Loo furthering 'The Cause'

Julia with Eddie Gathorne-Hardy at San Giminiano in 1922

Tommy, Julia and Carrington
in Ham Spray Garden

Julia and Tommy at the time
of their marriage

Breakfast at Swallowcliffe

Julia writing and (*below*) cogitating

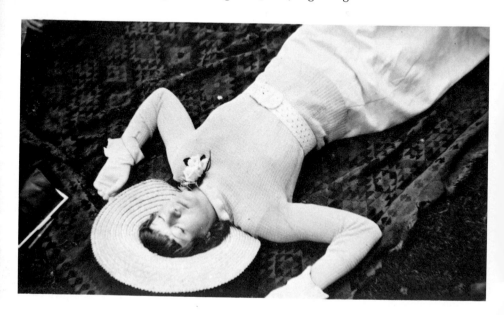

With Barbara Ker Seymer at her studio

Henry Lamb   Philip Toynbee

Pam Mitford   *Julia*   *M?s Cohen*   *F*   *Bryan*

(*Right to left*) Bryan Guinness, F.P., Mrs Cohen, Julia and
Pamela Mitford at Biddesden

Julia with Oliver Strachey
at Ham Spray

Julia at Barbara
Ker Seymer's studio

Julia with F.P. and Lawrence Gowing

Julia at Crescent Place, Newcastle. 'A stray passer-by stepping about through chaos, as if among the ruins of some big city. One sees strange glimpses of lives and cultures through the broken windows and carefully cultivated little spaces among the confusion.'

Julia with Lawrence at Lambourn

March 10th, 1938. How lovely Julia looked! She's not really beautiful but I love her face . . . I asked whether I might stay the night and Julia said she'd love me to. So I did. I shaved and lay down in her lovely big bed. Presently Julia came in dressed in a white dressing-gown with black embroidered edges. She turned out the light and took off her gown in the firelight. It was a wonderful night. Julia had such a lovely body and lovely scent. Not that we ever really made love properly.

[Julia wanted to take rooms in the country to write in for quite a time, and they planned to spend a month of it together.]

March 16th, 1938. It is rather terrifying to be alone for a month with someone one can't really pretend to know. We discussed intimacy and she said she didn't really feel intimate enough for 'making love', though she loved to be in bed with me. Then we talked about layers of the mind. Her lower layer was always melancholy, immutably melancholy, even when she was quite gay on the surface. She said, "I'd be bitterly disappointed if we didn't go together." And though I said it would be quite awful, I only meant I'd be disappointed too. What an odd sort of way to have a love affair—so cautious.

March 17th, 1938. Julia has written me a letter: "The important point is that we love to be together *now*; what happens the next moment is incalculable, one always knows that. So don't let's worry."

March 26th, 1938. Weymouth. A great deal of luggage, and I was very tired and frightened. We did at last find rooms, *chez* a dear deaf old lady. Once we were settled we lay exhausted on the bed, hugging and kissing. I was wildly attracted by Julia, far more passionate than she was.

Out for fish and chips. An empty pier. One of the steamers was called the *Empress of India*, and Julia said, "Does that go to India, I wonder?" I gasped. How *could* she think that a tiny steamer might go to India? Then she told me her husband had been furious with her once for not knowing what a nut and bolts were. She is an *extraordinary* woman. In her ignorance of the simplest everyday things she's quite unique.

Julia was lovely, lovelier in bed than anybody I've ever dreamed of. I made love to her in the morning. I *do* feel so fond of Julia, and so moved by her beauty. She's right that it's enough that we love to be together *now*. It's so easy to talk to her and yet so interesting and so amusing. It isn't *passionate* really on either side, but a very real and happy relationship.

March 27th, 1938. Sometimes Julia just looks lovable and dear, and at others *wonderfully* beautiful. It is still a joy to be here, in fact increasingly so. We are so gay—taking twopenny buses and then laughing at the awful suburban country.

March 28th. Last night we didn't even make love, but it didn't in the least matter. I love to be in bed with her and she I think with me. I love to walk and talk with her.

March 31st, 1938. We breakfast in our dressing-gowns, *very* comfortable. Julia, who always makes plans, has arranged to hire bicycles from a village three miles away. I mocked her all along the sunny road about her literary friends and suitors, her habit of writing down her plans in a note-book, her ignorance of—say—fish. The sun was hot on our necks, and everywhere the leaves were bursting out and there was hawthorn blossom in the hedges. Later we lay on a golden stack of straw with the sun on our faces. With her fringe blown back by the wind she looked quite different again, and very young and lovely.

We were very intimate last night, and in a way this is worrying. Some time this will end and I suppose every day makes it more painful to end.

April 1st. While washing Julia said, "The Daily Mirror Charm School says 'Never let him see you wash.'" This is the sort of delicious thing she's for ever saying. Today when I was nagging her to finish her play, she said, "It's just like poking a crocodile through the bars of its cage." Julia had a wonderful wash, every part of her, and came down to supper radiantly beautiful; we walked along to the pub with a torch through the pitch dark. I shone it on her face. Nice yokels, nice beer, nice darts. Back to lie dreamily on our bed in the fire and candlelight. She told me I have a mystic's face, and yet so sensual—like a Buddha! I reflected, as I often have, that I seldom feel cosmic and in touch with my creator, whereas she's as cosmic as can be.

April 2nd, 1938. "Weren't the birds *barking* this morning!" said Julia at breakfast. I wish I could remember all the things we say. We agree that we're very funny, and certainly we spend most of our time laughing. "I love to hear you playing away at the piano, like hundreds of mice." I read her *The Irish R.M.* by candle-light. She cuddled up against me. I'm happy as I write.

April 5th. Raining a little. Out though, and Julia trotted along the road in her speckled coat. Up onto a bleak hillside, and were quite insane —"A rolling dog gathers no moss," and "Every dog has a silver lining," screaming with laughter. Later Julia read some of my novel, and I took notes, getting on like a house on fire. Very drowsy on our bed after dinner. A cold and lovely moonlight night.

April 7th, 1938. I sing, 'I've got a new kind of love for you,' to Julia very sentimentally. She hates it. Last night I was suddenly afraid I'd been crude about something and not noticed things in myself which she disliked. But she assured me I was as sweet as could be, and (very relieved) I went to sleep.

April 8th, 1938. Sunny again and the gayest of a succession of gay days. The Cecils to lunch. They *were* nice. Somehow we were particularly affectionate that night.

April 14th, 1938. That night I felt restless and, I suppose, bored. But not when she began to tell me all about her artist friends when we were in bed. That was fascinating.

Next day we lay under a haystack in the sun. I felt vaguely unhappy that I didn't mind the thought of leaving much. Julia said we neither of us wanted a second-level affair, that was clear. What we didn't say was that a second-level affair would have been heart-breaking because of the fifteen years' difference. I suppose some mechanism in both of us has kept it affectionate and good-humoured because of that. In bed on that last night I said I really preferred the curtain not drawn (we'd had it drawn every night). She said, "Well, next time . ." very gaily, but it hurt me rather because I suspect we neither of us thought there'd be a next time.

April 16th, 1938. Julia came with me in the bus to Salisbury. There we walked in the sun and looked at fish in the clear little river. Pies in a pub, as at Weymouth, *three* weeks ago. We were our usual selves, bantering and gay. We kissed on the platform as off the train went.

I suppose I shall see this stay with Julia more clearly as time goes on. I know it's been a good thing, even if it ends now. In most ways she's the cleverest and most delightful woman I've ever known. I know that I shall always be devoted to her.

Chapter Thirteen

LAWRENCE

[In 1939 Julia was attending the St. Denis Drama School, with the admirable intention of learning as much as possible about all aspects of theatrical production before she got down to writing a play in earnest herself. This always remained one of her great ambitions, but the pages and pages of her archives devoted to ideas for dramatic writing, or their partial expression, are obviously impossible to include here. Michel St. Denis was one of Julia's heroes; she admired his theories, and I heard her defend them hotly against criticism on at least one occasion. His name and Tchekhov's were inclined to gravitate together in her remarks on the art of drama—the highest compliment of which she was capable. She even set up his photograph in her flat.

In her 'Coverless Diary for the Thirties' Julia noted: "I must have met Lawrence at Alison's flat in the very early Spring of 1939, when I was still in Paddington Street. During that Summer he and I moved in to 88 Charlotte Street—this was during my last term at the St. Denis Drama School, and we went to war that September."]

It took a long time to unpack my books from their packing-cases and arrange them in my shelves in my new flat. I vowed before starting the job that I would not linger and ruffle the pages, day-dreaming. But one old childhood possession, a volume of photographs of Pre-Raphaelite paintings, undermined my morale. It was the ambience of the pictures that drew me. The sorrow and rue of everyone, and the lush scenes in which all was set! And the youth and poetry of the characters, embowered in beautifully-curled, glossy, free-flowing hair—whether in marble halls or romantic green glades!

One evening a friend called round at my flat and took me along to a theatre, to see a revue whose producer was famous for her strong left-wing views. Every item had a political slant. One musical number, called 'Love on the Dole', was a lament of the times—the great slump of the thirties—and had a message as sorrowful as the times themselves. It was sung and danced by a pretty and suitably tearful-looking girl dressed in floating yellow gauzes, and her sweetheart. I don't know why but the pair reminded me of my Pre-Raphaelite book. The plaint of this number was cogent. It told how a man deprived of work and obliged to live on the dole cannot afford a room of his own, nor the luxury of privacy, and so cannot make love to his sweetheart, and certainly not make a home and raise a family: in short is debarred by society from taking part in the human condition.

The performers did their part well enough—sang and gestured adroitly, and wandered disconsolately hand in hand under the great trees. For behind the pair was an immense canvas drop-curtain stretching across the entire stage and painted to represent a city park on a summer's night.

I had not been sitting in my seat very long when I began to realise that it was in fact the painting of this night-time park, rather than the words, that expressed the poignancy of the lovers' predicament. It was not the usual stage-set for a song and dance act. The designer of tonight's set was evidently a fine and serious artist; he had engulfed us all—actors and audience alike—in a universe of dark peacock-blue-greenness. As in a dream one made out trees thronging—tall, aloof—giant presences existing in a chlorophyll universe of their own.

Never was a summer park painted in more *lonely* mood than this. But how had the painter achieved it? Between the leafy silhouetted branches yellow oblongs were visible, obviously representing the lighted windows of human dwellings. Within those lighted rooms the lovers knew that others, more fortunate than they, were even at this moment enjoying the normal human happiness and love from which they were exiled. The unknown artist had conjured up a rich, tragic metaphor of the sense of loss—had made me feel, as I sat there in the audience, as if someone long familiar, long intimate even, were talking with me from that wood.

In fact so great was the impression made on me by the painting that even before the house lights went on at the end of the number I raised my programme up close to my eyes, and peered at it sideways in the reflected glare of the footlights, endeavouring to decipher the name of the artist who had created this memorable picture: it was LAWRENCE GOWING.

The name was quite new to me. Opening up my handbag and taking out my diary I made a note of it there and then.

One evening a friend of mine, a painter called Alison Leplat,* asked me to dinner to meet an art student whose work interested her; he was called Lawrence Gowing.

Lawrence Gowing! At once I recognised the name I had memorised from my theatre programme—that of the artist who had painted the back-cloth of park trees at night which had affected me so much.

As my taxi approached Alison's house, I saw through its window a very tall, very thin greyhound of a young man, standing fidgetting upon the pavement, looking anxiously to right and left as if expecting someone. When I paid off my taxi he at once hurried up to me beaming, and asked if we could go up to Alison's flat together.

I remember very little about the evening that followed, except that at some point the painter told me that he had read my *Cheerful Weather for the Wedding* some years before and enjoyed it very much. I dare say I remember this because it turned out afterwards to be a whopping lie.

Lawrence walked me back to my flat in Paddington Street that night, and I invited him in for a drink. In order to amuse him, and also seeking to impress him with a certain light-hearted dandified quality I liked to think I possessed, I pulled out from my book-case a large and precious collection of old-fashioned and ridiculous picture postcards I had collected over the years. I watched my companion turning the pages languidly. I had noticed his love of paradox and absurdity, and waited expectantly for some admiring comment. Instead he shut up the album gently but firmly and placed it on the table beside him, saying coolly, "I'm afraid I prefer my sophisticated fun in rather smaller doses."

Good Lord! I thought. What a cheek! I was quite taken by surprise by this patronising speech.

A day or two passed. Then Lawrence invited me out to dinner at a Soho restaurant called Antoine's. He came to my flat to fetch me. As he entered the sitting-room I noticed two or three long stalks of oats sticking out from between the uppers and soles of his shoes, and trembling daintily at every stride.

* Née Debenham, sister of Audrey and Gilbert.

"Why, how did you come by those wonderful whiskery grasses in your shoes?" I asked. Lawrence looked down at his feet for a moment, then told me: "I must have picked them up walking across the waste ground round the derelict houses I sometimes visit, looking for subjects to paint, you know. Yes, it's true my shoes need mending." He bent down to pull the grasses out.

"Please don't remove them!" I cried. "They give you the appearance of some sort of rococo Edward Lear character—and could anything be more delightful than that?"

With his long, slender legs and arms, Lawrence reminded me of a daddy-long-legs. There was something very absent-minded about him, too, in spite of the fact that he kept on the move, both bodily and mentally, with unusual—almost explosive—celerity.

During the meal in the restaurant I held back from the more expensive dishes on the menu. (I knew that he was an impecunious art-student, and felt that we should not be dining out at such a restaurant at all.) But Lawrence soon spotted what I was up to, and insisted that I try some of the chocolate mousse.

"It's quite true I used not to have any money," he told me; "but now I have! Since my twenty-first birthday I'm not poor any longer! My grandmother gave me some money, and also my grandfather's overcoat, to go to his funeral in. (It was snowing at the time and I had none of my own.) I have it on tonight; I don't know if you've noticed it?" It was a Spring evening but with rather a chill wind, and I had indeed noticed and admired the big, inordinately fluffy blue overcoat he wore, with its many pleated pockets, buckled belt and leather buttons—the whole cut and style definitely not contemporary.

I couldn't resist getting Lawrence to tell me how much money his grandmother had given him. It was twenty-five pounds. Both pride and pleasure at her generous gift were clearly and warmly printed on his young and scholarly face.

The first time I visited Lawrence's studio I found him crouched on all fours on the handsome red plush carpet, another present from his grandmother. Beside him were paintbrushes of every size, palettes, cans of linseed oil and tubes of paint. A half-finished canvas was laid out on the floor in front of his knees. One could see he was short-sighted by the way he seemed to be putting the colours on the canvas with the end of his long finely-pointed nose, instead of with his brushes. I at once saw that his absorption in his work was *total*. He was lost to the world. It was a sight I was never to forget.

Beside him on the table stood a brightly-patterned cake-tin, containing a cake his mother had baked for him, so he told me, as he pressed a slice on me. It was a caraway-seed cake, his father's favourite kind. When Lawrence made tea I noticed that the teapot was covered in a close-fitting, circular, knitted cosy, and when I admired it he explained rather shyly that it was actually one of the many little caps his mother had knitted for him when he was a child, in which to go out in cold weather. "I'm apt to be forgetful when I'm working," he explained, "and I find it keeps the tea warm."

I was both flattered and delighted at being given all these items of domestic news from his family life, of which so many other signs were scattered about the room, lending it something of the look of an interior by Walter Sickert. And how I envied Lawrence for so evidently relishing the fond family feelings he had always experienced, in sharp contrast to my own bleak upbringing among cold-blooded, preoccupied intellectuals. I learned that the Gowing family had worked hard in their little shops in the suburbs where they lived. His grandfather was a pawnbroker, his father owned a small drapery; yet later on they were able to buy large roomy houses, all with gardens. How different from the London houses of my own relatives, in which the conversation never came round to subjects like the development of the raspberry crop that year! They had none. I remember I once asked my Aunt Philippa Strachey if she didn't feel how unnatural it was to be surrounded only by bricks and chimneys, with not an animal or vegetable in sight.

She stared, looked astounded, and replied, "No! Never!"

At this time Lawrence was living in a studio rented from a friend in a house only a few doors from my new flat.

Every morning he used to come round, mount the stone stairs to the second floor and chat with the decorators—two elderly men from an old-fashioned firm that had for many years been employed by the Strachey family. One of them, Sanders by name, was always dressed in a long white overall, with a fresh red rose in his buttonhole, picked from his garden at home. His co-decorator, an older man, short and stout and with grizzled hair, was Mr. Brownrigg. One could tell he was the boss partly by the black frockcoat and striped trousers he turned up in each day, and partly from the fact that he hardly touched a paint-brush himself but wandered about cogitating and giving orders.

The four of us—Lawrence and I, Sanders and Mr. Brownrigg, would talk together of many things.

"How did the bazaar in your home neighbourhood go off, Mr. Brownrigg?" I asked him.

"I won the lady's hat-trimming competition, Madam!"

We both congratulated him on this feat, while Sanders shook with laughter: "Ho! Ho! You're a great hand at women's competitions, aren't you, Bert?"

One morning a splendid pair of pilasters arrived, which I had bought for eight pounds at a junk shop. Everyone admired them. They ran from floor to ceiling, and were made of unpainted wood which had evidently attained its softly weathered silvery colour from having stood for many years out of doors—perhaps at the corner of a pub or cinema. I told the decorators I wanted them fixed to the sitting-room wall on either side of the fireplace. It was a large, airy room, built in fine eighteenth-century style, with panelled shutters, and the pilasters suited it well. Rumour had it that some of the houses in this street had been designed by the Adam brothers. Certainly the landlord was inordinately proud of the place. A cabinet-maker, evidently of the grandest sort, he repeated time and again that the Queen herself was one of his customers, and frequently came to see his carved cabinets and *éscritoires* in his ground floor front. He was obviously anxious to make it clear to his new tenants that he would stand for no running downstairs 'in unsuitable attire' (that's to say dressing-gowns) to look for letters in the morning, or any other nonsense, since one would always be liable to bump into Her Majesty as she entered his front door.

One day, when Sanders and Brownrigg had gone off for their mid-day meal, Lawrence was wandering round the flat inspecting it when he suddenly declared: "I *must* live here in this flat with you for at least one year!" His tone was urgent and very serious, and I was deeply flattered, though somewhat taken aback. Complimentary and heart-warming though this announcement was, it somehow amused me so much that I nearly burst out laughing: but then I looked at Lawrence's concerned and affectionate face, so innocent of all conventions, and at once agreed to the plan.

I had already arranged that the walls of my large bedroom should be painted sky blue—the deep blue of the rather louring sky that might hang over Venice in a stormy September.

"With all this blue you must have a moss green carpet stretching from wall to wall," Lawrence now pronounced.

"Oh no, never!" I cried. "I've always detested blue and green together!"

"Then you've made a great mistake," Lawrence explained. "These two colours are meant to go together. You've only got to go to the country to realise that."

"But this isn't the country! It's a bedroom in London!"

"*Never mind.* You go out and get a moss-green carpet and have it laid down here. It's RIGHT."

There was such conviction in his manner that I capitulated—partly persuaded and partly to please my new young friend. I duly went out and ordered the carpet.

When it had been laid on the bedroom floor—lo and behold! It looked most beautiful against the dull blue of the walls. The four-poster bed seemed to be standing in all its massive grandeur in the middle of what looked like a spacious field of moss. I was delighted—but it was not till some time later that I fully realised how important to Lawrence was this theme-song of the Blue and the Green.

[At the time they first met, Julia was thirty-eight and Lawrence an art student of twenty-one. This age difference did not remain noticeable for long, except perhaps in the emotional field. Lawrence's outstanding talent was soon spotted by the critics; intellectually he was very mature, and the two of them communicated on the same level and laughed at the same things. Much later, Julia added the following note to this account of meeting Lawrence: "I had already noticed the similarity in the way Lawrence and I reacted to the world around us; it was a prophetic sign that we would develop much—very much in common. But I did not then guess that we were to spend thirty years constantly in each other's company, and fifteen of those years actually married to each other; nor that, although there were to be unhappy as well as happy times thereafter, the similarity and community of our interests would outlast the break-up of our marriage, and Lawrence's foundation of a new family."]

Chapter Fourteen

WAR

Including Julia's *DISPLACED PERSONS*

[Lawrence's dream of spending a whole year with Julia in the blue and green flat in Charlotte Street was interrupted by the crash of public events in September 1939.

During the first few months of the war no-one knew what to expect or when, but it was generally believed that air-raids were likely, and many of those who were free to do so left London—particularly children and old people. Among the first to take refuge with Ralph and me at Ham Spray were Julia and my mother. Soon afterwards we were housing six small children and three nannies (including one of each of our own), as well as the parents who darted from London at week-ends like swallows to visit their fledglings. The nannies were far the most trouble; they carried on an internecine war among themselves. My mother was stoutly independent, and had always had a strong and humane interest in politics; she suffered a good deal, I fear, from the uncompromisingly pacifist views held by Ralph, Julia, myself and Phyllis Nichols* (mother of three of the children). It was a habit of the house to argue long and loud, and I remember her saying with some truth, "There's no-one so bellicose as a pacifist." In the general pandemonium Julia, as usual, provided solace and sometimes comic relief. Looking back, I feel sure that she must have exercised great control to adapt herself to this strange menagerie. She insisted that she must have a task allotted to her, and on Ralph's suggestion took over setting up the blackout each evening, quite an onerous task in a rambling house of many windows.

By January 1940, since no bombs had fallen, our refugees hankered for home, and left us; but in the following Spring the start of the

---

* Wife of Sir Philip Nichols, then at the Foreign Office.

blitzkrieg brought friends and some perfect strangers to our peaceful corner of Wiltshire once more—among them Julia.

From now on as well as extracts from Julia's letters, and diaries, I have introduced some from my own diary (begun during the war) whenever they seem to illuminate Julia's story.

The following chapter includes a sketch by Julia describing a scene on the lawn at Ham Spray, and her search for somewhere nearby, where she and Lawrence could live on their own. He had been staying partly in London and partly with his mother, and since he was in his early twenties, the question of whether he should register as a Conscientious Objector very soon arose. Julia's desire to preserve their names and separate identities without shocking their landladies' sense of decorum led to her describing the two of them as brother and widowed sister. But when she (but not Lawrence) was summoned to her father's possible deathbed, the web of deception grew tangled.]

DISPLACED PERSONS

They were all talking much too loudly, and at once.

"You mean to say you're prepared to sit back and watch the enemy flooding in and killing all your friends and relations, and do nothing —simply offer them cups of tea?"

"So you want us to rush abroad and murder everyone in sight in case they are planning to come across and have a go at us here?"

"How can you be so stupid? Everyone knows there's going to be an invasion!"

"*Everyone* knows nothing at all—never has done! History always takes an unexpected course . ."

"You'd talk in a different key if you had children of your own, my dear Julia." (A calm masculine voice.)

"Oh, thank you for the compliment of supposing I don't care a straw about what happens to other people's children. Charming! Charming!"

This was May, 1940, and Ham Spray House was filled to the brim with the London friends of its owners, Ralph and Frances Partridge. Out on the croquet lawn, sitting on a spread rug, with the evening sunlight glinting on half-empty cocktail glasses, sat the house-party (if you could call it that)—mostly mothers and grandmothers whose children were already tucked up in bed, while the fathers had been left behind in their London offices and weren't expected down till the weekend. Midweek or weekend, it was always the same—perpetual argumentation, raised voices, baleful prophecies and fierce controversy, all about the probable course of the war. Visiting neighbours also joined in; and the fact that there were a number of pacifists among them hardly helped to lower the temperature.

Lying prone on the brown plaid rug, a handsome young man explained: "Well, if you did have children you wouldn't be able to bear the thought of their growing up in a country of slaves, where everything we stand for had been destroyed."

" 'What we stand for', 'Country!' I just can't accept those packaged, factory-belt notions. The only country I stand for is the world; and the only fact I feel sure of is that every blow we deliver will lead to ten, twenty, a hundred in their turn."

"Julia, none of us *like* war," a middle-aged woman from the next village reminded me reproachfully.

"When people prophesied that another world war would end civilisation, I couldn't agree. Now I'm not so sure," said someone.

"Perhaps a *kind* of life will go on, hardly recognisable as such."

"Oh, good heavens, you mean we may all live in underground tunnels?"

"If not bodily then spiritually. Shall we escape our interior selves being blasted?"

"Well, good gracious, we've been through one world war all right."

"And you think we can repeat the process every twenty years?"

"Heaven defend us!"

"But Heaven does *not* defend us. How can there be a neat finish to global warfare? It will always leave wandering flames that sooner or later become a forest fire."

"If only we had had a larger standing army and more armaments!"

"Since when has piling up armaments led to peace?"

"But that's a horrible way to talk! You'd end as a pacifist like that. *Are* you a pacifist?"

"Yes, I am!"

Our host looked at his wrist-watch. "If we mean to see that film at the Regal we'd better move off now." He began hauling himself to his feet. The others drained their glasses, picked up their cigarettes and followed suit. Car doors banged. Wheels crunched on the gravel of the drive. They were on their way. All except me.

It was a grilling hot evening. Sunlight was still belting down on the wych-elms and sycamores; a flamboyant sea of rude vegetable health lay spread before me under the Italianate blue sky.

As I climbed the stairs to my shady bedroom at the back of the house I reflected that spontaneous happiness no longer seemed to me the natural response to the full richness of the summer scene, and this evening the passion of Nature all around me struck a great disharmony. I experienced the familiar sensation that I had fallen to the bottom of a well and the summer trees were stirring far overhead and out of reach. Did other people have this feeling? I didn't dare ask them, for fear of seeing on their faces that they thought I was emotionally ill. I could speak to my friend Frances, but she would reply that it was the normal result of two major catastrophes—a broken marriage and a world war. But as a matter of fact I could not remember a time, even as a small child, when I was not liable to such feelings—when I did not equate sorrow with the eloquence of Nature in a happy sunlit mood.

Next morning, while helping my old friend make up a bed with rugs in the nursery for yet another 'evacuee' from London, I told her I felt I had better go off and find country lodgings for myself and my friend Lawrence where we could work out a way of life for ourselves until the end of the war.

"But it would be nice to be not too far away from you," I said.

Leaving the bus-stop at Chilton, I crossed the bridge to the further bank where a printed notice nailed to a pole bore the word TEAROOMS. It stood beside the door of a long, squat brick armadillo of a building, having all its windows collected at one end—the river end—where its hexagonal head bulged all round with a number of embayed glass eyes and was finally tipped by a short conservatory snout. This snout rested on the green lawn of the river-bank, and seemed to be superintending some painted tin tables under striped umbrellas, which stood dotted over the grass, with country people sitting round them drinking tea. A further notice referred to pies and cakes which could be bought at the back, where meals were also provided for soldiers. From under the long brick body of the house water rushed out, gobbling and flinging itself under the roadway, and thence into the river itself. Of course! This building must long ago have been a mill! And indeed the gigantic mill wheel still stood in place, though motionless, while the swiftly-running water leaped and gurgled and splashed its way between the great spokes just as it always had, causing a tremendous uproar throughout the house and a perpetual trembling of its walls. I entered the front door.

A girl in a green turban was coming downstairs carrying what appeared to be a tray of family heirlooms. She sailed by with a welcoming word, pointing to her mother's drawing-room door. Mrs. Weight, the proprietor, was sitting in the bay window, looking out at the square where her elder daughter was unloading cakes from a bright orange van. In the drawing-room there were flowers everywhere, mostly sweet-peas—some in vases but even more pictured on the chintz of the armchairs and sofas, the pouf, the pleated silk screen in a corner. Orange marigolds were embroidered on the green velvet frill on the mantelpiece; pomegranates and pineapples on the curtains over the door. O yes, decidedly this place was designed for being buried alive in—a perfect mausoleum in which to remain respectably petrified, doggo, awaiting eternity. A place of shadow destined for shades.

I was tired by my journey over from Ham Spray. I would have a siesta. I went upstairs, lay on my bed, and was already dreaming when there came a sudden roar as if the house were being blown up by dynamite and collapsing in confusion. I leaped up and flew to the window. The Germans must have arrived at last! Armoured monsters, a hundred times too large to be tanks, were rounding the corner of the house heading for the bridge. Human heads in helmets were poking out of holes right at the top, and silhouetted against the sky. Guns were protruding everywhere. But only three of these fabulous vehicles went by, leaving behind a grinding, noxious din.

To the wars of Homo Sapiens, however, no other form of life pays any attention. As soon as the monster tanks had disappeared round the corner it was as if they had never been. There were the hedge sprays leaning out as before, listening peacefully to the shrill chirring of larks overhead in the blue air: the nettles and dandelions drowsed together among the grasses, together with the fidgetting stitchworts and clovers. The vegetable kingdom was relaxed in the warmth and damp, leaf at home with leaf. And of course it was the same with the animals, the insects, and the birds.

Just as well it was so, I reflected, for when two animals look at one another it won't be very long before it occurs to one of them to gobble the other up.

As I set off to the post office, a platoon of marching soldiers appeared from around the corner. Well, scarcely soldiers—they were more like children, their stunted bodies lost somewhere inside the dung-coloured weighty bagginess of their uniforms. An officer accompanied them. When they caught sight of me, wolf-whistling began automatically and some sort of sexy quipping, such as is expected of the soldiery: "Hey! Whoops! A skirt!" Each wanted to show off to his mates what a careless, easy, patronising way he had with females. It was just a daydream. None of them, had he been alone when he met me, would have ventured on such behaviour. I pretended not to notice them, but took stock of them surreptitiously all the same. Their plump faces were as healthy and innocent of human experience as the primroses in the woods. By joining the army these boys with almost grown-up bodies had been relieved of the harassment of their individual lives and responsibilities, found themselves tied up in a bundle like faggots of firewood, mercifully unable to move heart or head, told they were heroes. All this produced a look of good cheer on their faces, yet after being processed and prepared they would be packed into rolling-stock and despatched to the slaughter-place—soldier meat.

I felt deeply depressed; but, still wolf-whistling jauntily as in honour bound, the British primroses marched briskly by.

(Julia to Anne Hill)

August 31st, 1939. Ham Spray House. Ham Spray is taking in two families of children and all their nurses. Frances's old mother and myself are here already. Camp beds are being pulled out of cupboards, age-old window-blinds are hauled out of the store-room and laid out on the lawn, and being thoroughly sponged free of spiders' webs in preparation for darkening the windows. The telephone rings all day, scared friends from everywhere are scurrying all over the face of England, trying to find a port in the storm. We are all going into the mincing-machine. As what kind of sausages shall we emerge at the end of the war? With this rhetorical question it is fitting for me to close this letter, I fancy.

(Julia to Ralph and F.P.)

January 29th, 1940. 88 Charlotte Street. I have let a whole month go by before writing to tell you how awfully awfully grateful I am to you both for having taken me in as a refugee all those months. I don't know how to thank you. I was so happy there all those weeks (in so far as war will allow one to be). It was such a great thing to be living quite quietly with people who use their minds as you do; I have so long lived this very trying, scatty life in London of dinners 'out' with stray young men, interspersed with complete isolation, that your civilised home life was a really wonderful balm to the spirits I found. And I enjoyed it very deeply. Lawrence's tribunal is now fixed for next Wednesday. So that we may hear this week what his fate is to be. If he is banished to a farm somewhere I shall take exercise book and ink-bottle and string along also, hoping to find rooms in some cottage near. What a dance of dismal death it is to be sure! And with so very many thanks my dearest dears for all your friendliness and kindness which I am so much more melted and affected by than I can show.

(Julia to F.P.)

February 15th, 1940. Charlotte Street. Well, wasn't it a miracle about Lawrence's tribunal? When his turn came (last) they hardly asked him a thing; treated him with great respect, and very soon said, "Well, I think it is best that he should be allowed to return to that work which he is best fitted for." And gave him total exemption on condition that he continued painting! I have decided to stay on here for the present, for the simple reason that having spent all my money already, I now only have one pound a week cash to live on (for food, hair, fares and everything). So that I just have to stick here and cook and do housework all day, as I can't even afford a maid. It has been rather interesting working at the Unity Theatre (only working men, plumbers, electricians and so on, all giving their services free). I am helping Lawrence design the costumes for a new play by Sean O'Casey.

[When the blitzkrieg began in May, Julia returned to Ham Spray.]

(F.P.'s Diary)

May 22nd, 1940. Julia has been much disgruntled these few days, by war anxiety and other things.

"I don't know *what*'ll happen when the fatal moment comes," she said at breakfast. "You both have such totally different views on the subject. You'll never agree." (Julia doesn't like married couples to agree.) But when definitions had been made and the ground cleared, it was evident that we saw eye to eye on the subject after all.

Ralph: "Under the influence of fear one does one of two things. Either runs like a hare or squats like a hare." Julia: "Well, what lesson do we draw from the hare?" She said her plan was to make herself look very old and ugly so as not to be raped. Ralph laughed immoderately at this. From which it can be seen that it was a lively morning and not unfriendly.

Julia was in a state of shilly-shally all day about taking rooms for herself and Lawrence and where. Is it safe to live here, or there, or where? She asks over and over and *over* again the same questions: what are the chances of invasion, bombing, this or that contingency—as if such questions were as easily answered as: "What are the trains to London?"

Julia looked dumbly miserable after a letter from Lawrence. Afterwards she discussed her war problems with me. Lawrence writes in disgust at the idea of staying in the rooms she had taken for him. "Whoever heard of a painter living in Mill Tea Rooms?"

(F.P.'s Diary)

May 26th, 1940. Julia came down to breakfast with a remote unhappy look, and very inadvisedly began an argument on the fatal theme Town v. Country. The brightest country people do in fact gravitate to the towns, she said. Ralph broke into fierce partisanship of a country life; I tried in vain to set up a balance, but of course only received the blows of both. Oh, this teasing old Triangle!* "Why should I be put in a position to behave so badly?" said Ralph in the bathroom. After lunch another argument in which I became suddenly angry with Julia and she with me. I said I didn't agree that the sublimation of emotions provided the

---

* Fond as Julia and Ralph were of each other, I was sometimes the unwilling cause of jealousy between them.

only steam for scientific and intellectual activities. "Well, Freud thinks so," said Julia. I said I didn't agree with everything Freud says. Julia then took pains to show me she thought I had no right to criticise Freud's views as I couldn't possibly have his knowledge of human beings. Temper ran through us both like a fire catching heather. But it was an altogether quarrelsome day. We are all on edge.

"The situation is of increasing gravity from hour to hour," said the evening announcer. So it became one of those evenings when Ralph sighs, Julia and I yawn incessantly (a nervous symptom) and I end by falling asleep over my book.

(F.P.'s Diary)

June 1st, 1940. After tea Ralph drove Julia to the station. She goes back to London saying it is safer than Wiltshire, after seeing a lorry blazing through Hungerford yesterday, packed with uprooted signposts all pointing in different directions. We are told this is to confuse the invaders. Julia described it as "a blood-curdling sight".

(Julia to F.P.)

July 8th, 1940. Charlotte Street. I agree with what you say in this morning's letter, Frances, about the strange calm that has fallen—the calm before the storm, I suppose. I don't feel anxiety any more, personally—in any conscious form that is. I just feel that it is the end; a stiffening up of one's motor resistances to greet the hail of destruction ahead. Nonetheless there is a telltale nervous constriction all the while. Lawrence now wants to work in an ambulance, he says, and has gone off to find out what the chances are. So long as he stays in London, I shall stay and be with him. We are to go down to join the Anreps* in their coal-cellar below the pavement in the air-raids. Everyone here has bought themselves two-shilling boxes of ear-plugs, to prevent concussion, and we all have corks on strings to wear round our necks and put into our mouths to prevent damage to the ear-drums! What a go! Lawrence is going to buy an eight-and-sixpenny pickaxe and shovel.

I had a dinner-party here the other night to which came Helen Anrep, Dorelia John, Raymond [Mortimer] and John Hill, and it was great fun. But of course Raymond got up on his hind legs and bit the

---

* Helen and her daughter Anastasia.

left-wing John to bits and pieces. He also made a very fine speech about the beauty of airmen's courage, saying how strangely moving it was, how everybody must love an airman, and how he thought the whole feeling of rapture connected with airmen was an aesthetic enjoyment. Dorelia looked very nice indeed, and with her charming diffidence and natural manner showed up Helen rather, I thought. Like eating fresh salmon on the same plate as tinned. But I don't profess to know Helen intimately.

I shall be very sad not to be seeing you; and still, one really does not know from moment to moment what is going to happen next. I am waiting to hear exactly what Lawrence's position is before I definitely put off the Chilton Mill lady. First Aid classes go on apace. What a pity though that practice is so totally different to theory in this world.

[Shortly afterwards Julia and Lawrence did in fact leave London for the Mill House Tea Rooms at Chilton. This being only a dozen miles from Ham Spray, and within easy bicycling distance, letters ceased, but we met fairly often.]

(F.P.'s Diary)

July 14th, 1940. Julia and Lawrence arrived for lunch on bicycles. Helen Anrep was lying out on her boat-like bed on the verandah, and we all sat in two opposite rows talking to her as she lay like a queen with a Japanese sunshade and the blue flowers of the agapanthus making a bower behind her. I thought she must be enjoying this homage, but saw afterwards that she looked exhausted and fretful. Julia and I together walked to the foot of the downs while the others played bowls, and we looked back and saw their figures moving on the lawn, and sweet Ham Spray, pink among its greenery. In these dreary old days the stimulation of Julia's companionship is as reviving as an innoculation of strychnine. I asked how she and Lawrence were getting on. She told me she couldn't work and was oppressed by not being in her own house, and by the lorries full of soldiers hurtling along the road.

(F.P.'s Diary)

October 10th, 1940. Drove to Chilton, for we had seen that the lovely Queen Anne house opposite the Mill was for sale. Called at the Mill itself to see if Julia and Lawrence would like to come and look at it with us. We peered in at the window, and there in their sitting-room on a Victorian sofa drawn up before a roaring fire lay Julia with her face in a pillow fast asleep. She jumped up laughing and clawing with her hands: "Caught red-handed!" As we stood looking out of the window at the beautiful Bridge House opposite, it began to rain in slanting drops. "Do look at those gnats," said Julia. "They look just like rain!"

(F.P.'s Diary)

November 30th, 1940. Julia and I went for a walk in the afternoon, when she poured out her motherly worries about her big boy. He doesn't get enough to eat, he's terribly thin, he has so many colds, he won't take his cod-liver-oil, he will sit right in a draught and so on. Worst of all this awful car they've bought! He can't really drive it and he thinks he can. The other day when he had gone to the garage, Jimmy Bomford and Jonny Morris rushed into Julia's sitting-room at the Mill House saying, "Julia, you *must* keep Lawrence off the road. We saw him zig-zagging wildly along, and then I said, 'My God! It's Lawrence!' "

(F.P.'s Diary)

January 14th, 1941. Vicky*'s birthday. Burgo, wild with excitement, gave her a parcel containing two threepenny drawing-books. Julia and Lawrence were invited to come to the birthday tea in fancy dress. They stepped out of their little box of a car, unrolled various wrappings of old sacks and newspapers from their legs and waists (designed to keep out the draught) and appeared as Russians—Julia in full décolletage with jewels, Lawrence in a high fur cap. The first effect of this complex vision fading, the children looked dazed and expectant. Burgo started writing a story to be presented to Vicky, bound in gold paper and entitled 'Joan Spill, by Burgo Partridge'. It began: "Joan Spill was a young girl of 48".

---

* Strachey, aged about twelve, one of our child refugees, whom Burgo (five) adored, a cousin of Julia's.

(F.P.'s Diary)

April 21st, 1941. Heywood Hill came down for the night to see about being taken on at Tidcombe Manor as a market gardener, and I asked Julia over as well to cheer him up. The evening began rather formally, both Ralph and Heywood very silent. Then about eleven the conversation lit up. It was about *Madame Bovary* and disagreeable characters in literature. Julia has passed some invisible rubicon into middle age and become far more unconscious about her appearance. She looked very nice and very comic sitting on the sofa, with spectacles on nose and a hand running through and through her hair as she talked, producing complete chaos there. Her legs in thick stockings and eccentric boots completed the picture. She asked did we know anyone who would darn stockings? "*I'm* not going to do them, and as I can't find anyone else to, they just silt up in heaps in my drawer." It's characteristic that if a thing is disagreeable to her, she *cannot* make herself do it—and really doesn't attempt to. No, that's not entirely fair—it's mainly when the loss is hers that she can't summon energy. Her sense of duty to others often arouses her to phenomenal efforts.

Next day Ralph and Heywood went off to Tidcombe, and Julia and I started for a walk. We had hardly crossed the ha-ha when she began without preamble on the subject which had been filling her mind, and no wonder. Lawrence has for some weeks been turning over in his mind his position in relation to the war, and has now almost decided that he can no longer "stand outside", but wants "to share the common suffering"—in fact he wants to go and do warden's work in London. Also he says he can't paint any more and feels he needs the contact with other painters to stimulate him, rather than what he now has: Julia's middle-aged friends who take him as her adjunct, and the (to him) uninspiring fields and trees. Julia described all this with the most sympathetic understanding and modesty, painting I thought a far too humble picture of the life Lawrence has led with her, underestimating the great change she has wrought in him, his gained confidence and beaming look of well-being. The tragedy is that having at last found a relationship that suits and satisfies her, Julia seems likely to have it wrested away so soon. She said she wanted to find a female friend to share a house with her.

"I've not got husband or wife [sic] to build my life round, you see."

F: "No, but what about your writing?"

J: "Oh my hateful writing. I tell myself dozens of times a day that as a writer I could live for my work, but I can't. I've always looked upon my life as something separate, and more important than my writing . . ."

(F.P.'s Diary)

July 12th, 1941. The great heat-wave is breaking up at last, and seeing it go how bitterly one regrets it. Raymond [Mortimer], who is a sort of Witch-Doctor always bringing rain, arrived this afternoon, and with him the deluge. We went to the Mill House to tea with Julia and Lawrence, who had Aunty Loo with them. I had scarcely seen her since Julia and I were together at Ford Place, with Uncle Logan hovering inscrutably in the background. Aunty Loo had then seemed shockingly insensitive and relentless, though with a certain dry, eccentric charm, and I was surprised to see her today a handsome, distinguished figure with her grey hair and clothes. Recollections from the past drifted up. As we were leaving she drew me aside and said with tears in her eyes: "Don't you think Julia's happier than she's ever been? And I *adore* Lawrence."

(F.P.'s Diary)

July 17th, 1941. I was under the net this morning picking strawberries, when Julia arrived on her bicycle for the day, looking like a music-hall version of a French artist, in velveteen trowsers, with long hair on her shoulders and a large bow under her chin. She and I walked up the downs together. She said Aunty Loo had 'lost her head' utterly towards the end of her visit, and the greedy relentless egoist had come out. She had stripped their landlady's garden of flowers to take to London, without even asking, and when Julia protested said complacently, "I know it's awful of me but I'm like that."

(F.P.'s Diary)

September 28th, 1941. Julia and Lawrence to tea. Julia and I went for a walk while aeroplanes practised machine-gunnery overhead, and as we clambered through a gap in the hedge a shower of bullets, or bullet-cases, fell through the trees all round us, rattling against the branches. Julia looked up indignantly and shook her umbrella at them like an old lady in *Punch.*

(F.P.'s Diary)

November 9th, 1941. Bunny [Garnett] for the weekend. Julia and Lawrence to lunch. Bunny fixed on Julia the concentrated searchlight of his attention and admiration, and from the moment she came into the room had his head swivelled in her direction with a look of bursting delight on his face. When she had gone he seized a cushion and hugged it, saying, "Oh Julia, Julia, what a wonderful woman she is! I'd forgotten she existed!" Julia took his admiration very well, and so I must say did Lawrence.

(F.P.'s Diary)

November 13th, 1941. As Julia's old friend Hester Chapman has been staying here we asked her and Lawrence to tea. I can't help thinking they came as late as possible and left as early. As soon as they were gone Hester began saying how bitterly she felt Julia's departure from fashion, make-up and London. Ralph and I both said how much we preferred her present style, but Hester returned almost at once to the subject. She hates Julia's relationship with Lawrence, "although I'm very fond of him. He's a dear boy." One reason is that he's "common". I couldn't at first understand what she meant by this, she being the archetype of commonness herself—it turned out she referred to his plebeian origins, about which he makes no secret. All this is rationalisation, and I suppose she really feels, madly, that Lawrence has taken 'her' Julia away from her. It is difficult to realise that some people not only think but feel in clichés, and Hester rattles off in a casual way little gobbets like owl's pellets made of hair and bones, quickly plastered together and shoved out of the nest—such as "my kissing him means a lot to Lawrence," or "of course he doesn't really like very intelligent women like Rosamond and me."

(F.P.'s Diary)

November 28th, 1941. Our neighbour Dora Morris came to tea and told us how Julia gave her blood for transfusion, doing all she was told very carefully, resting and taking her recuperative pills. She thought it was to be used for civilian casualties, but after it had been taken the nurse said: "Well, you have the satisfaction of knowing it is going straight out

to Libya." Julia was horrified. "I had a good mind to ask for it back."
She always gets a bit confused about the implications of her pacifist
beliefs.

(F.P.'s Diary)

March 8th, 1942. Julia and Lawrence to lunch. Julia is laying her plans,
as she realises she will have to register this summer.

"I shall say," she said, with a preoccupied look like someone reciting
a part, "I'm not prepared to contribute to the war effort, but anything
else I will do."

A walk after lunch. Lawrence insists on Julia wearing her Wellingtons. "Julia *loves* her Wellingtons," he says beaming. Julia mutters:
"Lawrence *loves* to *think* I love my Wellingtons."

(F.P.'s Diary)

May 9th, 1942. Rang up Julia about something or other and she said in
an enigmatic tone: "We too have our problems." I asked what they
were. "Well, they aren't such as can be discussed on the telephone."
"Can't you give me a clue?" I said. Long pause. "I could not love thee
dear so much loved I not honour more." From this I deduce that
Lawrence has been called upon for war service.

We visited the Mill House and heard the details. It is rather a blow
than a problem; Lawrence has received notice that he will be called
upon to do full time Civil Defence work. Asked if he had any objection
he said he had none whatever, and was only waiting to be told what to
do. It is, I believe a sort of relief to him, for his conscience has long since
dictated to him that Civil Defence is not inconsistent with Conscientious Objection. Julia is much worried, but determined to follow him
wherever he may go. "I've got the feeling no-one else can look after him
properly—and he'll get ill, pneumonia or something."

(F.P.'s Diary)

June 26th, 1942. Julia and Lawrence to supper. Julia looked lovely and
blooming in a frock of pink linen, with a blowsy pink rose and silver
jewellery, and they both kept us amused and surprised by their
originality and outstanding intelligence. Julia made us laugh all the
evening with her scintillating stories about the sexual approaches of
American officers to the upper-class ladies of Chilton Foliat.

(F.P.'s Diary)

September 16th, 1942. Off in the car for a picnic with Julia and Lawrence. A conversation as we drove, about the Class War, etc. Getting away into a conversation is like scrambling on to the bare back of a horse and feeling its body start to move and rock beneath one as it carries one forward. We took our sandwiches up a hill and under a big tree looking out over Hungerford. Julia said, "How I dislike human beings. How hateful they are!"

(F.P.'s Diary)

October 16th, 1942. Julia and Lawrence's visit today was a tonic. We sat and talked by a log fire and then in the tepid sun of the verandah. Julia gave an amusing description of Aunty Loo and Logan Pearsall Smith each waiting for the other to die. They have lived together for at least thirty years but really dislike one another intensely, and hiss at each other like two cats who have decided for some reason to share the same kitchen.

(F.P.'s Diary)

October 28th, 1942. Julia and Lawrence have moved to new rooms in Shalbourne; we bicycled over and were offered a spread of ladylike cakes and buns. Later they came back with us and Julia and I went off and tried some violin and piano duets. She hadn't touched a piano for years and had forgotten her notes, but threw herself into it with gusto, calling out, "*One* and—two—*and*—three—*and*" throughout, as she peered at the music in a way reminiscent of her Aunt Marjorie Strachey.

I said to her how well and cheerful Lawrence looked, and that he must be enormously set up by the success of his show at the Leicester Galleries.

"Oh yes, he most certainly is. They called him 'the white hope of English painting'. I never knew I was going to be mixed up with a famous painter." We know from mutual friends that Lawrence complains of Julia refusing to marry him. Except for the fact that they have posed as brother and sister for so long down here I can easily envisage her agreeing. Ralph has the sense that there is 'something in the air' now when we see them. I couldn't detect anything, but was aware of a wave of affection for Lawrence as I looked at his scimitar-shaped profile against the dining-room window. He takes with great good humour the rough with the smooth from us and often gets the rough. However the signs of disturbance and unhappiness in Julia are all there. She has passed out of that contented pussy-cat concentration on the present which prevailed at Chilton, into a daydream unawareness of her surroundings. She lives in a state of phantasy, wherein talk of 'entertaining' has lately recurred, also certain clichés which one feels have been rolling round in her head, like "I like to get people to know each other," or, "I must before I die go to one of these South Sea Islands we hear about, in the Tahiti style". Another sign is a sharp crabbing note about others—for instance the new tenants of Ivy Cottage, because the poor girls had dressed up in her honour, one in black velvet, the other in "a kimono covered with Marshall and Snelgrove flowers", and so couldn't possibly say anything worth hearing.

(Julia to Anne Hill)

December 2nd, 1942. Have you seen anything of Hester since her bereavement, I wonder? She wrote me a series of amazing letters in the style of Queen Victoria, Queen Alexandra, Queen Mary, Ella Wheeler Wilcox and Patience Strong mixed—the letter beautiful as one might say. I was rather overpowered by the attitude of artless ancestor-worship therein displayed, and found myself in writing back impelled to answer in exactly the same style. This is at once a letter of congratulation and of great sympathy. The first on account of the most exciting news of the imminent arrival of a son or daughter. Tremendous congratulations upon this historic occasion. And the sympathy is of course on account of Heywood's having been taken.* Awful and abominable—I do hope he won't be too good at his work. The best thing is to have a nervous breakdown as soon as possible.

What news can I give you of Wiltshire? Frances and Ralph are only two miles away from our new house, a quarter of an hour by bicycle, which is much snugger, and we can walk over and see each other. I shall now tell you what was underneath both those scratchings out. In the first I wrote that Heywood didn't give the impression of a military type, and I thought therefore he had a better chance of some more intellec-

* For the Army.

tual job—then I wondered if you might be offended (and realised also
what a Napoleon Heywood in fact is) so I proceeded to write it all over
with the words, 'Peppery holly, peppery holly'! So now I have no secrets
from you.

(F.P.'s Diary)

February 4th, 1943. Julia to lunch after her crucial interview in Hungerford to register as a 'mobile woman' for National Service.

She arrived on her bicycle, preoccupied and tousled, her fringe awry
and a pensive look on her face, all vestiges of façade dropped. She had
lain awake all the night before, picturing herself in prison as a Conscientious Objector, which she might have spared herself had she mastered the fact that women of her age are not subject to actual conscrip-
tion. When she said she was writing a book the interviewer herself
suggested six months' postponement. "What sort of a book?" she asked.
"A novel," said Julia, "but not an *ordinary* novel—it's a novel with a
message." It isn't a novel at all, of course, but the same play she has
been writing for years.

She has worked out that her conscience forbids her taking any of the
jobs prescribed, except agriculture and civil defence. The interviewer
was quite agreeable, but the real trouble (according to Julia) is that
Lawrence has been thrown into a frenzy by this event, and says that he
couldn't bear it if she were to work on a farm. Julia also confided in us
that she was very doubtful if he could go on with their life here in any
case; he can't work at all, and she doesn't think he really likes it here,
but has accepted it for her sake.

(F.P.'s Diary)

February 9th, 1943. Sounds of a bicycle crunching on the gravel, and in
dashed Lawrence, sweat on his forehead and a look of frenzy. A new
calamity. Oliver [Strachey] has had a sudden violent heart attack, and
Julia was this morning summoned to his bedside at Woburn, where he
is working in the War Office Cipher Department, with indications that
the worst was to be expected. Poor Lawrence, quite at sea, said he felt
he must come to us for consolation, and there he sat—a lump of
misery—wondering what in the world to do without his 'Ju'. She had
gone off in such a hurry that she had no time to find out what her own
feelings were about this disaster, still less was it possible for Lawrence

to divine them. He didn't know what to be at, had a desire to munch but nothing to bite on. We feel responsible for him in Julia's absence. He presented a combination of loneliness and uncertainty, and could make no decisions, even about the wording of a telegram. His years with Julia, he said, had made him totally incapable of leading his own life without her constant support; it must indeed be a strange situation for him to live with someone so much older than himself, so pungently individual and (though so devoted to him) so egotistic. He presented us with a bleeding wound, and the only bandage I could find was an invitation to dinner tonight.

(Julia to F.P.)

February 11th, 1943. Woburn. I don't know whether Lawrence will have told you the sad catastrophe that overtook poor Oliver here on Tuesday night. Apparently he had a severe heart attack, and Barbara, Christopher and I all turned up as it was a highly dangerous position. I feel wretchedly sad at deserting Lawrence, and naturally he is my first loyalty, at the same time it *is* my old Dad that is causing the problem.

(Julia to Lawrence)

February 13th, 1943. Woburn. It was such a relief to see you again yesterday, and to hear that you had got good plans with which to tide over our terrible earthquake. I will write to you very very often—I will try for a line or two every day, like Henry Ponsonby to his wife from Balmoral! This doesn't mean that I expect you to answer every day of course—because to me scratching off a letter comes more easily than to you. I feel more deeply than I can say, darling, at your being left all by yourself like this so suddenly; and I too am horrified at the enforced parting. I do wonder if you will be able to stand being quite alone for six weeks you know—I doubt it. This morning Oliver was feeling so well and so 'himself' that he was able to indulge in an onslaught on pacifism and pacifists, pointing out what awful ogres we all were—he had me at his mercy because I am bound to humour him, so I had to swallow all the insults with a happy smile: "Bosh! Fiddle-de-dee! My child, *of course everything* you do is supporting the war effort—of course you can't pick and choose what you do conscientiously object to and what you don't. BALLS and Poppycock!!" But just let him wait till he is better again!

(Julia to Lawrence)

February 22nd, 1941. Woburn. Another lovely letter from you again this morning. I loved it—about the hedge clipping, the catmint and Mrs. Wheeler's* comments thereon, and finally about the pleasures of loneliness—that is a very nice idea indeed.

About your 'Porridge Oats'—I will not send it along until I get the word from you, as I am afraid you will think it just the kind of thing to infuriate Mrs. Wheeler. I have been picturing you in a panic at my tactlessness, and expecting a wire hourly from you: "At all costs hold back Porridge Oats."

(Julia to Lawrence)

February 24th, 1943. Woburn. Many thanks for your fine literary criticism, all of which I read with furrowed brow and deep cogitation. I think the acid test you set for books is very good indeed. Obsessional yes indeed. Your oatmeal will have arrived by now. I really tremble to think what a managing tactless woman I am becoming. I must *not* let myself be so high-handed. Hester wrote us a nice letter yesterday, and said she would send Oliver a game pie from Fortnum's, at which his eyes sparkled very brightly. She wants to come down here! We are caught like rats in a trap, and for that matter I think Oliver would enjoy her visit. She called him "my delicious old toad", which seemed to please him greatly.

(Julia to Lawrence)

February 26th, 1943. Woburn. Glad the oatmeal has arrived. Yesterday was rather an uncomfortable day, the psychological temperature being distinctly dry, hot and thundery. You must know that one of the things I suffered greatly with in my childhood was Oliver's forcibly feeding me with uplift and culture. Now of course his passion for 'educating' people against their wills is given full rein. Yesterday afternoon he rang his bell, and when I appeared before him looked at me with demoniac triumph in his face. At last he said: "NOW! Shall we try and give you a little education in decent music?" I gave a Chinese curtsey, or whatever they do in front of their ancestors, and nodded assent dumbly. Having ascertained that I loathed loud music he first insisted on a screeching

* The Shalbourne landlady.

trumpet affair. Then Beth* came into the room and he said to her slyly: "Shall we give Julia a shock? Shall we give her Delius' *Appalachia*?" and to me, "You certainly won't like it!"; roars of happy laughter, "You won't like it! You won't like it!" I said, "Now Oliver, you just tell us what you yourself would enjoy and we'll put it on for you. Let's leave education till another day. I'm not in the mood for it." He was foiled and looked bewildered, and cried loudly, "What? What? You *must* hear *Appalachia*. NONSENSE! Fiddle-de-dee! BOSH!" Wasn't it awful? Oliver was livid. He took up his detective story and turned us out of the room. Of course after a few minutes I felt desperately ashamed at having had my own selfish way as against the poor old invalid. At supper time I made a great apology to him, and vowed to myself I would be 'educated' up and down dale and teased and tortured without further protests for the duration of his illness. All the same it nearly kills me—at night I couldn't sleep properly; I get so wrought up with Oliver always!

(Julia to Lawrence)

February 28th, 1943. Woburn. Oliver is the most awful old thing, but yesterday my heart was warmed to him when he referred to something being "in the same pussygory" as something else.

My diatribes against my papa are meant for your eyes only, my dear—I let myself go to *you*; but I don't wish to send out the news publicly that I am so ill-natured about the poor old dear. Mind you I bear no *grudges*, only I just like to express myself roundly about all the silly nursing details. Yesterday I was again left alone in charge of the invalid. It was a *black* day, Oliver as testy as he has yet been.

(Julia to Lawrence)

March 4th, 1943. Woburn. Beth suggested that she and Nannie together do the nursing, and "would I like to go back home again? Why should I sacrifice my life any longer?" I was never in such an embarrassing position. Naturally my first loyalty is to you, and not to Beth—*but* my old dad has brought this burden on to her shoulders, and ought I to leave it absolutely to her like this? What do *you* feel? Would you like me

---

* The wife of a colleague, with whom Oliver was billeted.

to come home at once, or prefer to have the time to yourself to work in? I got *two* delightful letters from you today.

(Julia to Lawrence)

March 6th, 1943. Woburn. It's Hells Bells in the Sickroom today. And all my fault this time. I was told yesterday that the district nurse was coming early, but this morning the whole plan had left my head. Presently my nose began to bleed. That caused another little delay. However I jumped up later and took off my nightgown, at which moment Beth *flew* into the room, wild-eyed, dressed as if for a cocktail party, with bows in her hair, carrying a picnic basket choked with thermos flasks, and leading the puppy on a string. She thus confronted me—starkers and with my rats-tails of hair dripping over my shoulders.

"Twenty to NINE!" cries she. "And the district nurse arriving at NINE! And he hasn't been washed or had his breakfast! What *are* you thinking of?" A pretty kettle of fish, wasn't it? And Oliver, of course, not the man to show any mercy over a little accident of this sort. *Was* he mad? *Is* he mad still? And am *I* mad too? By the time Nurse came he had had his breakfast, but his hair was unbrushed and his teeth not done—but really, what *of* it? One would think he was a sort of Beau Brummell, shamed in front of the whole Court, by the way he went on about it all. Ah well. I was in the wrong, so best say no more about it.

(F.P.'s Diary)

March 10th, 1943. Lawrence had much to tell about Julia, who has been writing distracted letters saying how *frightful* it was looking after Oliver, she was worn to a frazzle by his relentless egotism and hostility. Letters and telegrams had been whizzing to and fro between Shalbourne and Woburn, and after many changes Julia announced her intention of returning tomorrow. Consternation on Mrs. Wheeler's part, for her two step-daughters had promised to come and occupy Julia's room. We told Lawrence she must come here. During lunch Mrs. Wheeler rang up in a hysterical voice announcing that two more telegrams had arrived from Julia, and she could make neither head nor tail of them. Others were dispatched by us to Julia, and long after Lawrence had left us the wires buzzed in expression of his anxiety. But from Woburn nothing but silence.

(F.P.'s Diary)

March 11th, 1943. We were expecting Julia at dinner time, but at about six o'clock Mrs. Wheeler rang up to say that she was not on the train. Shortly afterwards arrived Lawrence on his bicycle, almost in tears. "What *can* have happened to her?" Ralph, remaining calm throughout, had the brilliant idea of ringing up the Three Swans in Hungerford, and found she was expected there—having failed to receive a single one of our telephone messages and telegrams. Ralph drove in and fetched her, and she arrived dazed and bludgeoned by the hammering succession of events, yet holding tightly to her manners and remembering to ask us about ourselves—though all we wanted was to hear her own story.

It was pretty clear that irritation to frenzy-point had consumed both her and Oliver. Nor was she the only one to resent his need to have every tiny thing (a match struck or fishbones extracted) done in his own way. Both the cook and the District Nurse were heard exclaiming that they would rather die than work for him. Julia observed Oliver's egotism and desire to be constantly superior at every moment, with the needle-sharp acuteness got from so close a range.

(Julia to F.P.)

March 17th, 1943. Shalbourne. Once more, my dears, a hundred million thanks for having taken me in like that, a poor homeless waif.

I've been sitting all day amongst fifty brown quasi-chicken-henlets on the lawn in the sun, stupefied after my four weeks away from home. I don't know yet whether I'm on my head or my heels and can't concentrate on anything; and several times nearly rushed in like a mad thing and joined up with the hideous chick-henlets where I really belong now, so reduced have I become from the human level.

(Julia to F.P.)

April 10th, 1943. London. How delightful of you to send that delicious pot of cream from Cornwall. It was so much appreciated, it was simply heavenly. We gobbled it up with bread and butter and marmalade, with jam, with porridge, with everything. I hope you had a good time—I imagine you having great larks with your Indian friend* and

* Ronald Duncan, poet.

his lady. I 'went down' with German measles soon after I saw you, a
hellish disease. Poor Lawrence did his best, but doesn't know how to
cook at all, so I had to get up and do things myself. Well—all this seems
a bit over-shadowed now by the turn of European events. Life has been
very studious and quiet here. I have sent my story about a lady's maid
off to *Horizon*.* I am sending two other things in due course to John
Lehmann for *New Writing* and the 'Staggers' respectively. I have made
an Indian friend—met a *beautiful* Indian man at a sherry party; he is
such a disappointment though, in traditional Indian fashion.

(F.P.'s Diary)

April 21st, 1943. At last I received a summons to see Julia, who has been
quite ill with 'flu, pneumonia etc. for some weeks. Found her pale and
thin, wobbling about her little sitting-room. She told me Lawrence had
nursed her with wonderful devotion and patience and endless sympathy. As she began to get well a mood of despair settled on her, and she
burst into tears, declaring that their Shalbourne life was a prison and
she could endure it no longer. Lawrence consoled her, saying that they
must concentrate on literary and intellectual life.

(F.P.'s Diary)

May 11th, 1943. Rode off to see Julia. She had gone back to bed again
with a temperature, and was lying gazing around her with unsee-
ing eyes. She's very worried about herself, and also about Lawrence.
("No life for a young man.") Lawrence also expressed his worry to
Ralph downstairs. "I've painted nothing for weeks, and I shall be
ruined if I don't start again soon." Mrs. Wheeler made no attempt to
conceal the fact that she was furious with Julia for going back to bed
again.

"Really, Mr. Gowing, you shouldn't let her do it. She'll get soft."

Ralph and I have decided we must have her here for a bit and give
Lawrence a holiday.

[That summer Julia and Lawrence returned to London and took rooms
in Paulton Square.]

---

* Published in the *New Statesman* (or 'Staggers' as its contributors used to call it).

(Julia to F.P.)

August 2nd, 1943. Paulton Square. Greetings across the echoing spaces of chaos, across seas of packing-cases and above and through the rattle and roar of catastrophic events. It has all been like a drugged and feverish dream. The house stuffed full as a pincushion is of sawdust with *filthy* dirty rat-eaten objects—ten millions of them—and all piled up to the ceiling. The hot water heater has of course not put in an appearance, so no baths are possible. Then through it all the theme song of the Labour Exchange and my future in the War effort. The great thing to be avoided at all costs is to be sent away from London till the end of the war, so I have secured myself an offer of full-time work at St. Luke's Hospital (Civilian) in Chelsea and shall accept if the Labour Exchange give me their permission, but have begged for a few months to finish my play.

(Julia to F.P.)

October 22nd, 1943. Paulton Square. The air-raids are not bad at all really, they are so short, only last half an hour each night. It is somewhat like having a nightly purge—one is uncomfortable until one's had it (the raid I mean), one grits one's teeth and endeavours to bear up and numb oneself for the short period it is functioning, and then heaves a sigh of relief and happiness when the all clear goes. The noise is comparatively mild—nothing like a blitz, thank goodness. All the same! Germans circling overhead and trying to kill one are Germans overhead trying to kill one!

(Julia to F.P.)

December 2nd, 1943. Paulton Square. Anne and Heywood [Hill]'s baby has been christened. Never have duller-looking small moulting London sparrows been gathered together to celebrate. Osbert Sitwell was present in body but not in soul I thought. After having greeted one he said his piece, and then (as one was in the middle of replying) his eyes glazed over even more than before and he walked straight through me like a banshee, to talk to a young airman he saw standing behind. Miss Compton Burnett* looked handsome, not unlike Elinor Glyn. She

---

* The novelist.

stood, a solid blockbuster or blockhouse whichever way you look at it, in a navy Bradley's coat embroidered with winding strips of astrakhan like the carefully-designed paths in a municipal garden. Her portcullis, drawbridge and vizor were all down too. After an hour's hard work I elicited only two things from her that interested me, one that she never felt guilty about anything, and the other that she had no set working hours—"Oh no, nothing like *that*."

(Julia to F.P.)

[Early 1944.] We still have seen rather few people—and yet it seems one is perpetually preparing dinner-parties and recovering from the day before. Derek Hill* brought Molyneux, the dress designer, here to see Lawrence's pictures the other day. He bought two—"I'll have those please"—and whisked away. Lawrence and I are fire-watchers now. I have mastered the drill—stirrup pump, street parties, assembly points etc.—and know how to tie up your hands and drag you along on my stomach and on yours through a house filled with flames and smoke. And tomorrow I have to crawl through a tunnel of smoke and water, and play a hose as I go. Lawrence has to sleep in the basement of the public library on his nights. Là là! You should hear about the bombs we have to put out—one of them has 65 fire bombs in its belly; another is mortally dangerous for a radius of 300 yards, and so it goes on. Aren't you sorry for the residents of Chelsea who are supposed to be saved by me? I am.

(F.P.'s Diary)

February 28th, 1944. Julia and Lawrence's long-postponed visit came off at last. The fiendish cold unluckily continued and put Julia to a severe test. She wore her false leopard-skin and two pairs of woollen gloves even at meal times, and said that if Ham Spray was hers she would "have to sell it", which offended Ralph greatly. They were both heroic in the help they gave with bed-making and washing-up, and in Julia's case I know she hates it so much that it *does* amount to heroism. When I said I didn't want any help with the cooking, indeed would rather do it alone, she said, "Ah yes, I understand and respect that," in a voice of great relief. Yet there was on her part an undercurrent of criticism

---

* The painter.

which is hard for hosts to bear these days. This week of bad air-raids has been a horrible strain on Julia, and showed itself in ways that I now recognise: lack of interest in others (she asks one perfunctorily the same question over and over); a streak of waspishness in her criticism of mutual friends; a rather dazed glazed expression; letting her appearance become quite extraordinary (but having no notion of the fact). She has let her fringe grow so long that it falls into her eyes. In her old corduroy trowsers surmounted by an imitation fur coat, she looks like the sort of slum-woman who pushes her worldly goods in an old pram. I like this eccentricity and the unselfconsciousness that goes with it—it is in fact part of the side of Julia I am fondest of. But it is a bit odd to hear her at the same time criticise others for not taking enough trouble with their appearances, or speaking of how important 'elegance' is to her.

(Julia to F.P.)

March 5th, 1944. Paulton Square. So we are all still alive anyway. A whole week seems to have whizzed by since we parted, and the Blitz to have petered out. We have had only two alerts.

Bunny and Angelica [Garnett] dined with us, and helped us eat a haggis sent from Scotland one night last week. The haggis of course burst and went all to pieces, and the poor cook was in a terrible taking. Angelica looked like some romantic character out of opera or Persian charade, her yellow turban most skilfully arranged. Bunny was douce but beaming; and often in the long silences one looked and saw he was silently shaking all over like a jelly at his own thoughts.

We lunched with John Lehmann at his flat yesterday. He has been 'taken up' by the society hostesses and told us some quaint tales of their doings and sayings. He and Cyril Connolly were invited to dine with 'Emerald' (Lady Cunard) and go to *Uncle Vanya* afterwards. The Westminster Theatre was full of exhausted-looking old dowdys in dirty mackintoshes, and John also described Emerald's sables and flashing gems and thrice-lifted painted mask, and how—during the atmospheric pauses that are such a feature of Tchekhov's plays—she would invariably hiss out voluble remarks deafening everyone: "Have you ever *met* such people, Cyril? Really, they are *weird*! Are there really such Russians?", which is just what the Whiteley's shop girls used to ask each other, I remember. At the end, when Vanya weeps in the deserted lamplit room and says, "We must work—work—my dear, my darling ..." Emerald croaked out loudly: "What *is* this man's work as a matter of fact?" and Cyril barked out, "Estate" and the audience all started to laugh and the play was ruined!

(Julia to F.P.)

July 1st, 1944. Paulton Square. The famous secret weapon has begun. Last night these empty rocket-propelled airplanes had a good go from 11.45 till about 10 o'clock this morning—my fire-watching night too—and the endless sirens calling. I don't feel it's any good trying to escape, as goodness knows how long it will be kept up. So I just feel dismally philosophical. How lovely if you'd write a line and cheer us both up!

(F.P.'s Diary)

July 3rd, 1944. Soon after came Julia, our first Doodle-bug refugee. She was alone in London, as Lawrence's father had been suddenly killed by a lorry; she wrote sadly and we asked her down at once. Saxon [Sydney-Turner] arrived too, covered with dust from a Doodle-bug which had landed between Percy Street and Tottenham Court Road just as he was leaving for the station. On arrival Julia said, "I've not heard any good of them so far." So the refugee situation has returned again. Julia is here indefinitely, and obviously wants Lawrence to join the party.

(F.P.'s Diary)

September 9th, 1944. Julia at last got a letter from Lawrence, which threw her into a bit of a state, and caused her to ring up and arrange to go back to London. For it seems he had not left with his widowed mother at all. At one time this morning Ralph spoke of "end of war irritability". Julia said, "Yes, I know. Lawrence and I had some awful times in London." It is clear that things were not quite all right between them when Julia left. Some sort of slight tiff or difference. She may have been very *exigeante* about their coming move—Lawrence being expected to do all the hard work, carpentry and cooking every evening. How selfish is she, I wonder, towards him? She gives a lot of thought to his state of mind and other people's too, but I sometimes think her powers of penetration are not great.

(Julia to F.P.)

September 15th, 1944. 25 Wellington Square.* How long is it since we parted? Only a few days I believe, yet it already seems another life, I suppose because it *is* such a different life up here. Hungerford platform was packed like sardines; and when the London train came in, to our horror we saw people already jammed in the corridors. No seats. I had to stand all the way, stuffed in between a pram and a family of squalling children. *The Golden Bowl* read in such circumstances seems awfully eerie. At Paddington all platforms stacked with prams. So you see the refugees have all bolted back to London in spite of government warnings.

We are being shelled here, believe it or not, by *some* sort of V.2 rocket, evidently not buzz-bombs; but as we receive one shot every two days it hardly seems to count. We had a very loud one this morning. But they are not worth running away from *yet!* I'm writing this at Wellington Square, sitting facing a tin helmet reposing snugly in a chamber-pot, beside palettes, lampshades—but I propose to draw a veil.

(Julia to F.P.)

October 30th, 1944. Wellington Square. How overjoyed we were to get your letter! I was in despair at the lack of communication between us. As for us, we simply have not been human all this time. We are still furnishing automatons, it is really too degrading. We seem to have seen only the aged and failing folk whom we have henceforward got under our wings—i.e. Mrs. Gowing, Oliver and Aunty Loo. We talk of rheumatism with Aunty Loo, curtains and loose covers with Mrs. Gowing, and with Oliver it is like being with a humming-bird who darts from topic to topic. Oliver is settled in complete and majestic comfort in Gordon Square, in rooms as large as some sort of municipal buildings. In the centre of one or two chairs and sofas, interspersed with an Indian Victoria bronze toad or two (which used to contain Granny's† false teeth always soaking in Milton, I remember), and looking *tiny*, with a very cheerful red face and *snowy* white (Persil?) hair, sits Oliver like a twinkling Anglo-Indian God of some sort. He is utterly cheerful and well, and really does seem to have bobbed up on to the top of the wave

---

* Rented from the Desmond MacCarthys; later shared with Aunty Loo.
† Lady Strachey.

again; it is such a mercy. His talk is all about wanting to write a work on 'aesthetics' if you please! He who hasn't looked at anything but detective stories or 'Memoirs from the Highlands' for twenty years now! He is as naive as a Robin redbreast.

Rocket bombs seem to be getting a little more fast and furious here lately. We have an alert every night, usually for the old fly bombs, but they really don't bother one.

(Julia to F.P.)

January 15th, 1945. Desmond MacCarthy came to dinner with us yesterday, which was very enjoyable. Oh what an amazing small parakeet birdie he does look these days, his crest flying out behind him, red eyes—one bunged up tight shut, and the other peeping out at one slyly—and seeming to hop along and shift up and down his perch as he chatters. He was in very good spirits. Lawrence was much amused by him, as he'd never seen him in good form before; he particularly liked Desmond's way of getting to sleep at night (invented as a small boy) by repeating the phrase: "Fogger was puzzled where to go for his health," after which he starts to think of all the delightful places he knows of in fiction.

Yesterday morning Lawrence and I were snoozing in our respective bedrooms when suddenly an *almighty* earthquake and thunderclap of thunderclaps heaved at us out of nowhere, the sky blazed, the house was shaken like a medicine bottle and splintering glass from windows all round the square filled the air. When silence fell we lay and just waited for the walls to crumble and topple slowly on to us, but nothing happened. We shot downstairs—yes, it was a very near rocket shell, which fell on Chelsea Hospital. Immediately rang up Aunty Loo in St. Leonard's Terrace. She cried out, "Oh my dear, we've been blitzed *awfully* badly—the doors have all disappeared, but I'm going back to bed now to have my breakfast." Lawrence and I swallowed some food and ran round—to find St. Leonard's Terrace with every window and door blown away and all furniture overturned. In Aunty Loo's room glass everywhere and a two-pound pot of jam spread over the fallen books, you never saw anything so sickening. As a matter of fact the rockets seem to be coming thicker and faster now. I don't know why that should be. There has been another one ten minutes ago.

(F.P.'s Diary)

March 28th, 1945. Julia and Lawrence have been anxious to get out of London for a month or so, and wanted to find rooms near us, so I have been scouring round in the neighbourhood, and in spite of jeers from Ralph, who said it would all come to nothing, I took a lot of trouble, went to dozens of rooms, ordered coal and wood and rang Julia night after night to answer questions about the exact length of the arms of armchairs. We asked them down for the weekend to look at the best of them. Lawrence looked rather white and thin, and seemed keen on the rooms. "I'm sure the Swan will do, it'll be wonderful. We'll stay there two months." When they came back from their inspection there was frost in the air.

"Well?" I asked. "You'd better ask Ju," said Lawrence.

"Both absolutely *appalling*," she said shortly, and I thought pretty rudely. "One really can't be happy in what these cottage women think nice. And also the fact is I can't bear to be in any rooms that aren't *Georgian*." So she prefers to remain in London with the rockets, which naturally frighten her a great deal and quite prevent her sleeping at nights, to living in a non-Georgian room—heroic in her own peculiar way.

She told me privately that she was terribly worried about Lawrence's health. "Don't you think perhaps a stay in the country would have done him good?" I said with secret malice.

(Julia to F.P.)

May 25th, 1945. Wellington Square. V.E. Day, Lawrence and I decided to stay at home and read and forget about it; and all day things seemed utterly normal and dull. However when dusk fell, Major Barry at No. 27 began hauling out their wooden blackouts, old kitchen chairs and God knows what all, and piling them up in the centre of the square preparing for a great bonfire. Neighbours joined in and flags were hung out and about. After the news and the King we decided to step out and look at the decorations. So we walked to Buckingham Palace and found there a spectacular scene—all fountains, balustrades, not to mention trees and grass and everything, were crowded with these little pink penguins in their droves, all facing the Palace, which was brilliantly illuminated with beautiful golden light, and draped with red velvet over

the balcony. It was charmingly pretty. We walked on down the Mall
and through Admiralty Arch, threading a mazy course between shop
girls and their tiny, stunted shrimplike cavaliers, mostly in khaki; then
back to St. James's Park water, which looked very witchlike with
coloured lights hidden away in the bushes on all the islands. Home
again at one o'clock, finding that we had been on our feet about two and
a half hours. Everyone was fainting by the roadside, or rather sitting
down holding their stockinged feet in their hands and groaning. A few
faint upper-class cries of "Taxi!—Taxi!" came wailing through the air
from voices right down on the pavement, whilst cockney tones, slightly
more robust, could be heard: "I'm fucking well all-in now," also from
the pavement.

What a delight and somehow a relief to get your letter yesterday, as I
had the feeling that I was living inside a glass ball, and should never
again see or hear any of the old faces, voices, friends, or symptoms of a
former life. Why so? you will ask in surprise. I don't know, but it is
something to do with the fact that the war went on just *too* long—one
was at last crushed, and for me living in London fairly put the lid on it,
so that I feel no longer human any more. I mean the dynamic principle
has given way and one feels like a printed page, a sheet of newspaper or
a pressed dried grass.

[Two contrasting strains in Julia's character were courage and caution,
and I think the war years highlight the conflict between them. As a
child she was a bold—even reckless—climber of trees, and thought
nothing of looping the loop with a young friend in his small aeroplane.
Later on she developed a belief that one should not take unnecessary,
and above all irrational risks. This was a Strachey characteristic.
(Quite a few of them—including Lytton—never went in an aeroplane
in their lives.) But what *was* irrational? The extract from my diary dated
March 28th, 1945, gives an interesting example of how her cat sometimes jumped.]

Chapter Fifteen

OUTLOOK UNSETTLED

Including Julia's *COSMIC TOES*

[Julia and Lawrence had been living together for almost the entire duration of the war, moreover they had been living at very close quarters, first at the Mill House and then at Shalbourne, in ready-made boarding-house surroundings that allowed them none of those responsibilities for their joint life and for constructing their physical nest which bind people together, and with hardly any control over its aesthetic aspect. There had been short periods in London during the fear and strain of the Blitz, the Doodle-bugs and the rockets, and serious interruption of work for both of them—Lawrence lacking the stimulation got from other painters, and Julia (though she loved the country) not finding inspiration in it for her writing. Like some eighteenth-century botanical artist producing faithful reproductions of wild flowers, she sometimes lovingly described the doings of a cat or the sequence of plants along a hedge—*too* lovingly, *too* respectfully perhaps, without giving her observations the personal flavour got by subjecting them to her own critical cud-chewing.

The war itself was a theme too enormous and grim for her. She therefore turned her mind to a mammoth play which never seemed to end and was far removed from ghastly public events. When I asked for news of it her answers bewildered me: there were evidently a host of characters, a praying mantis among others, and in one scene an 'ice-mountain' slid on to the stage.

"Wouldn't that present difficulties for the producer?" I asked.

"Oh no. Stage-managers, electricians—they can deal with that sort of problem easily. Michel St. Denis would have made light of it."

Once the war was over, both Julia and Lawrence felt the need for more freedom. They had already rented the Desmond MacCarthys' house in Wellington Square, where there was plenty of room for expansion. Lawrence took over the top floor, leaving two others for Julia, even when (after the death of Uncle Logan in 1946) Aunt Loo appealed to Julia in her loneliness, and was allowed to occupy the ground floor and basement. Alys Russell was far from well, and led a sedentary life receiving devoted friends like Robert Gathorne-Hardy and playing innumerable games of patience.

"Do you often get it out?" I asked her once.

"Always. If it won't come out I cheat and *make* it." She looked at me out of her round blue eyes over red-threaded cheeks, with the expression of an innocent baby.

It is clear from Julia's letter to me of August, 1945, that in spite of all the happiness she had found in her relationship with Lawrence she did not despair of finding a mate of her own age. Why should she?

She was only forty-four, after all, and looked much younger. She was attracted by men; she attracted them, and enjoyed doing so. Meeting new people always meant a lot to her, and she had been short of social contacts during the war years, even though her country roots had developed and found rich sustenance. It was this half-unconscious search that was so disturbing. Soon after settling in Chelsea she was overcome by feelings of love largely based on phantasy. Ralph and I looked on with anxiety. We had watched the affection, the delight and amusement Lawrence and Julia got from each other's company, and listened to their lively conversational exchanges; it would be a tragedy if Julia threw away this real happiness for a chimera. For she was the most striking personification I ever came across of the truth that the far is more attractive than the near, but loses its charms as soon as attained.

Money was also a problem, but she miraculously avoided disaster by an eccentric form of 'budgetting' of her own invention: everything was treated separately—there was a budget for clothes, another for food, one for hairdressing, one for books and so on. Ralph, who enjoyed most aspects of finance, used to grow quite hysterical when he saw her painfully adding and re-adding long lines of figures, only to arrive at some conclusion such as that she could afford only half a pair of shoes in any one year. But it was not long before she was taken on to read novels for the publishers Secker and Warburg, one of whose partners, Roger Senhouse, was an old friend.

She used to sit in a small attic at the top of the building, reading manuscripts and writing reports on them. Another of the directors, David Farrer, became a great friend and spoke of Julia to me with warm affection and admiration. "Few small firms have been blessed with such a very remarkable reader as Julia," he said; it was partly owing to her recommendation that they published Angus Wilson.]

(Julia to F.P.)

[Spring, 1945.] Wellington Square. I visit Logan often nowadays since he has been ill. He is found in an armchair in his dressing-room wearing his flamboyant old check dressing-gown. Across the arms of his chair is a big board covered with piles of magazines and some of his own writings. The instant he sees me he starts off his long rigmarole on the subjects that obsess him at present.

"Well, you've heard all about our domestic troubles? I don't want to put our burdens on your shoulders, but I always say 'A woman in the drawing-room, Hell in the kitchen!' It seems that a woman finds it impossible to run a house without a lot of fuss and bother, tears, quarrels, the very devil to pay. Yet, as I was telling Ethel Sands this morning, with a man running things there's no sort of trouble at all. Aunty Loo spoils our Irish Mary, won't allow her to do any housework. When the door-bell goes, 'Oh, Mary musn't answer it, it's *far* too tiring!' She answers it herself, greets all my personal friends and pulls them into her sitting-room. They don't want to see her, they've come to see *me*. However, that's another story." Soon the subject changes to picture dealers and what sharks they are, and connoisseurs too. "Rattlesnakes! Take Kenneth Clark, now."

When I leave, his faithful attendant Hammond is waiting on the stairs to pour venom against Aunty Loo into my ears. She shows me a row of signatures in Logan's visitors' book. "All famous men! All enjoyed staying here and want to come back. Just look at all these distinguished writers—Edmund Blunden, Robert Bridges, Robert Gathorne-Hardy. And Mrs. Russell forbids them to come, because it's too much work for Irish Mary! But it's worth people's while being kind to Mr. Smith, you know—he can get any book published. Look at that last book of Mr. Osbert Sitwell's; Mr. Smith got it published in America." And so on.

(Julia to F.P.)

July 31st, 1945. Wellington Square. This house is now divided up for the new way of life. Lawrence's sitting-room on the top floor is very pretty, airy and charming, and he likes it very much. Unfortunately I feel no hope or enthusiasm for the future, but simply that I'm too old to catch the boat now. The events of the winter have taken it out of me and I feel crushed and ill. Age is coming over me in a rush. I look a thousand years old. My lifelong attempt to find a mate has failed once and for all, and all appetite for life is gone without that.

By the way I haven't yet told you about how I spent the Whitsun weekend with the Toynbees in their country cottage, and how one evening I told them of the new plans for independent living in Wellington Square. It seems that Philip and Ben [Nicolson] both took Lawrence and me for a married couple.

Tomorrow I start some sort of work at Secker and Warburg three days a week; but shifty old Roger Senhouse has glided silently away for his holiday, leaving his partner, Fred Warburg, to make all the 'arrangements'.

I always forget to tell you how dearly prized your glorious present to me is—the rainbow robe. I recline on the sofa in it every evening, and it is so light and fleecy and warm. With fondest love and to Ralph too, Juliaroo.

(Julia to F.P.)

August 10th, 1945. I wanted to thank you for your most sympathetic and delightful last letter to me. I feel you must be rather flabbergasted at the coolness with which I talk of Lawrence and myself parting company; I think the question—of parting—might not arise if there were indeed any chance of an independent existence here. The only way for me to make a new sex relationship would be to be living on my own hook, so that people could ask me to dine and spend the evening alone. But I don't care for sex devoid of sentimental emotion in any case—I'm far too shy.

So the alternatives are as follows:

i. To stay with Lawrence à la Siamese Twin in spinsterhood, and probably find him breaking free in a few years anyhow, as I gather the psycho-analysis has begun to make him flutter his wings already.

ii. Part from him as soon as he can find a studio to live in, and very likely be lonely from that moment onwards until I die.

iii. To do one or other of these and *try* to forget myself in my writing.

The whole prospect is bleak and doesn't bear embarrassing one's friends with. Drink and money would help one to forget the horror, but where to get them? How I envy rich people, who are able to distract themselves with house parties and theatres ad infinitum. So fuck the whole bleeding set-up and let's *try* and forget it! Please forgive this horrid letter, my dear. About having been happy with Lawrence in the past, as you point out all my friends noticed: yes, but the past is past.

(F.P.'s Diary)

September 1st, 1945. The day was mouvementé; as soon as lunch was swallowed I drove in to fetch Julia and Lawrence, and no sooner had they arrived than Alix [Strachey] and Julia were plunged in their classic argument: Elegance and Individualism versus Utility and Tins. Lawrence, wearing a new pair of very massive horn-rimmed spectacles seemed in some subtle way changed.

After tea Julia and I walked very briskly to Shalbourne and back, under a grey sky which dotted us with warm raindrops, and I asked her about the effect of psycho-analysis on Lawrence. She spoke sadly, saying she lay awake often at night staring into a future which she felt was all too likely to be a lonely one, with her happy relation with him gone. For if the psycho-analysis were successful he would probably fall in love, and it would be the end for her. She hates London and can't write there, and feels cynically that she is only living there for the sake of Lawrence's analysis, which will probably sign her own death warrant. Of course a good deal of this is just externalising her own difficulties as a writer. If she is in rooms she could only write in her own carefully planned surroundings; if in a house it is quite impossible to work with the housekeeping to attend to. If in the country she needs the stimulus of the town; if in a town she misses the peace of the country, and its animal and vegetable life. She gave a comic description of Lawrence trying to get out of his daily task, which is to cook supper. He has passed the enthusiastic cookery-book stage and now simply *loathes* it. He puts off, and feebly suggests 'going out' every evening, but is relentlessly driven by Julia to lope off into the kitchen; however, some evenings it is more than he can bear and he comes out again saying in tones not to be denied: "Julia, put on your hat and coat; we are going to supper at the Queens!"

It's delightful having Julia here, and we pass quiet homely evenings —paper games with Burgo, and then reading.

(F.P.'s Diary)

January 22nd, 1946. When I saw Julia in London she confided in me a strange and pitiful fact. She has fallen in love again, and in that romantic, unreal way that all Stracheys incline to. As she is constitutionally incapable of being attracted to any but a young man, her passions grow more unsuitable as she grows older. This time their object is a friend of Lawrence's and a homosexual, whom she has only seen once since Christmas, and that for two minutes accidentally in a restaurant. One would think that on such meagre fare her love must expire. And she feels it ought to. "Oh no, it won't do," she says. "So there's nothing for it but to try with might and main to strangle and stifle my emotional nature, become a corpse, and step backwards into my coffin, putting the heavy lid down and lying alone in the darkness." It is too tragic. Then comes the inevitable Charley's Aunt touch. Could I, she asks, when writing about the subject, send my letter to Poste Restante, Sloane Square. Then I could send the code word 'turnip' on a postcard to Wellington Square, and she would go off and get it. "Anyway if I hear of your maid cooking turnips badly I shall hie me away to the Sloane Square post office." The pathos and absurdity of it, and now of course my pen is paralysed. *Turnip!*

(Julia to F.P.)

January 31st, 1946. Wellington Square. It was very nice to be able to get my last long wail off my chest to you, and I'm only sorry for you receiving it. Anyway the picture has changed, and I thought I'd send you a scratch to let you know that I have clambered out of my coffin after all, as on second thoughts it dawned on me that acts of renunciation aren't really part of the main stream of my way of life. As for my remarks about my writing—it is true that when I'm upset I feel like that, but when I get back on to my old level I enjoy writing, as perhaps you've realised. The fact is that when one is in my state of mind it is very hard to understand *objectively* what is happening at all. Don't you agree? I feel like a submarine that has submerged in some tropical ocean and is obliged to put up a periscope to take my bearings. These I painstaking-ly record by the swinging ship's lantern, in my log book—but then the periscope sees such peculiar things: stares into the rainbow face of a flying fish for instance. Well, I invited my young man to lunch and to go to a picture exhibition with me, and instead of a God of peerless beauty and mystery turning up, he appeared in the guise of a simple-hearted teddy-bear, with dirty nails, unshaved, and hair cut much too short. He came and sat beside me, and at once I received the most unmistakeably warm, trusting friendly smiles. So that was a relief. At the picture exhibition he waxed mysterious in the extreme—the more we looked the more sphinx-like did he become. At the same time he kept calling my attention to this and the other one with a magician's wave of the hand. I've tried to give you my impression of the afternoon. Do write and tell me what you felt on reading it. Don't say words of cheer, I beg you. I ask for the sake of our mutual interest in the spectacle of life to tell me what your thoughts genuinely are. I do hope your maid is doing all right, my dear. And how does she cook TURNIPS, pray?

(Julia to F.P.)

February 4th, 1946. Thank you tremendously for your lovely long, full-bodied letter, in which you threw yourself into the subject in hand in the most moving way, believe me. No point but had been fully taken most practically and wisely imagined and worked out by you. Of course just what I had been craving for. I'm sorry about the password I chose. Your card was indeed ingenious, but took me so by surprise that I dissolved into giggles upon reading it, much to Lawrence's amazement. I want to tell you that it seems to me that I have just received my *congé* from the young man, and I wonder so much what you would say. I realise that from this very second onwards, for good, I must do what I can to obliterate the whole ghastly construction that has grown up inside me during these last ten months. Well I'll say no more—the rest is silence for me I suppose now. Please do forgive this awful scratch; you can imagine I'm at my wits' end to know how I'm going to arrange myself emotionally from now on. Do write soon. You're such a great comfort to me.

P.S. Whatever do you think, Uncle Logan summoned me round the other morning and informed me that he has just left me £500 in his Will, isn't it lovely? He has done it, as he confessed to me with glee, "to annoy the rest of them. I don't like Christopher, and I don't like Barbara, and I don't like Karin and I never liked Ray, but I *do* like you," says he, and adds, "Aunty Loo will be FURIOUS!" However perhaps his doctor will up and say that he was of unsound mind when the Will was drawn up (and certainly no voice will be raised to deny it). Anyway, the arrangement is that Logan is turning Loo *out of the house* on May 1st, as he can't stick her any longer. She has begged me with tears in her eyes to have her as tenant downstairs—I had to agree. So she comes on May 1st. Logan has gone mad in all literalness; it is very trying for us all.

(Julia to F.P.)

February 23rd, 1946. Wellington Square. I'm afraid I must again, Frances, take up the tale of my personal difficulties—if you *will* be so kind and patient in letting me pour out, well, out it pours. On the Friday that my young man had said he *might* ring me up, but didn't, I wept in the afternoon, and then at night rushed rather abruptly up to bed with a sleeping draught, with the result that when I *did* wake up the whole thing broke over me again and I wept all through breakfast. In the end I told Lawrence the whole truth, and that the celibate life I had led for the last six years was really unnatural for me. I assured him it made no difference to my feelings for him. He was extraordinarily kind and friendly, but the point is I begin to wonder if I really can face settling down into my old age in this sort of celibate life with him—he so much younger and all. It makes me unhappy to be in *a false position*, I am not a happily paired-off female, but just as emotionally unsatisfied as if I was living with a girl friend. I should, as you know, feel awfully sad at leaving Lawrence and should miss him. Can I ask you to write me yet another line to the poste restante and tell me your thoughts on reading this letter? You may ask how much my young man is responsible for my desire to part from Lawrence. The answer is that if it hadn't been him it would have been another, for I'm no nun by nature.

(Julia to F.P.)

March 11th, 1946. Wellington Square. Logan's death you saw. So Ralph was very shrewd!* There has been a certain tohu-bohu and brouhaha over the Will question.

* He had guessed it was imminent from Julia's letter of February 4th.

I have talked over our future life with Lawrence—nothing conclusive (as you were afraid) but we have both agreed that a certain independence from each other is desirable. Different roofs over our heads. I have given up all idea of planning for another mate or husband, but I want to mix with my own generation and lose myself in some kind of work. Thank God there have been no tears and sorrows or rupture in our close friendship. Lawrence is sad, but still his mood is *not* cast down, and I feel really horrified and numbed, but I want it all the same.

(Julia to F.P.)

April 21st, 1946. What news here? We all missed you at Eddie [Gathorne-Hardy]'s cocktail party, very much. There was Eddie, embedded somewhere inside a mound of close-textured pink fat. I found it very sad to see him lost away in there. It was rather amazing meeting one's past again. I dreaded it, because I have changed so much—the old rebel days of shouting dirty songs in night-clubs seem so off the point now. He was decorous and quiet and wonderfully sensible and dry as of old. Awfully nice.

Our own news: Well, Frances, we have decided to live under different roofs, that Lawrence shall go and live in a studio as soon as he can find one, but make no other sort of break in our relationship, and we hope to see a very great deal of each other indeed, nursing each other when we are ill and as affectionate as ever. This has not been decided upon, as you can imagine, without great sadness on either side, yet it *has* been decided. I feel extraordinary. Quite uprooted and lost; it is terrifying and *triste*, and calls for a lot of philosophy and summing-up of 'principles'. But I want it all the same.

(Julia to F.P.)

June 2nd, 1946. I haven't seen Eddie again. I do feel such a great gap has yawned between us, and though I admire his mind as much as ever, the utter cold haddock fishyness in his eye puts me off. Lawrence and I have finally decided against a formal separation, instead he is to have a 'flat' at the top of this house, and also of course keep his studio. I really don't want to go into it all again. I feel a leaden depression not to say despair. I am still in love with my young man, and still weeping bitter tears daily over the whole affair. Enough. I must go down to lunch with Aunty Loo now. Pray God she allows me pudding; as it is Sunday perhaps she will.

(Julia to F.P.)

October 15th, 1946. Yet once again you have thrown yourself into my problem in magnificent style, 'sparing neither pains nor cost', and the result most classical and limpid. I'm really in the position of someone attempting to co-habit (forgive the frankness) with a stone wall—or a Morison shelter, shall we say. Shall I throw up the sponge, as it is clearly hopeless? I don't know. I do so hate to feel I've wasted so much time and emotion on him with so little result. Pride or something, or rather vanity perhaps.

We have had tea-parties and dinner-parties with a number of friends —two nights ago a very worldly outing in white tie and tails given by Roger Senhouse at the Ritz. There were present Peter de Polnay and his Holloway-style wife, who was truly gorgeous; rising nakedly out of a smoked-salmon evening gown, her coils of lustrous blue-black hair polished with Cherry Blossom boot-polish and crowned with a huge emerald-green palm tree. Nothing but gibberish transpired from this little set-up, and I've seldom heard such rapid vapidity of a baroque theatrical kind before. John Hayward* lives around the corner (with T. S. Eliot) and I've seen him three times lately. Tom Eliot goes off to Mass every morning at 6.30 and kneels on the cold stone floor, winter and summer, he says; but is secretly jealous of other converts like Graham Greene and poetess Kathleen Raine, who he feels haven't done the thing in style like him. Catty this; but John is nothing if not *that.*

(Julia to F.P.)

July 18th, 1947. Wellington Square. *How* I enjoyed my weekend. Somehow you treat one like a Queen—better, some Oriental Begum or Llamaette—*every* consideration, and I assure you it is not lost on me and I am deeply touched. You both looked very well, and I was pleased to find Burgo growing into such a sturdy plant, with his husky gallant habit.

Well, I went to the great Ivor Novello feast. I got quite hysterical as the time approached, for I realised I had simply nothing to say to him and no meeting ground. However, when the time came, he and his boy friend entertained us in fine style; having removed their greasepaint and appearing, thank the Lord, as perfectly ordinary, good-hearted old

* Writer and bibliographer.

folk, with a lot of theatrical tales it's true, but interesting and amusing. I liked them both very much. Rosamond was *éblouissante* in a dazzling tea-gown of silk, striped broadly in sulphur yellow, pale green and shocking pink, and Ivor was all over her, raving about her beauty. I felt I'd dropped behind badly, decked up for the occasion in Aunty Loo's jumbles (bits of old Berénson lace pinned on to an old pink jumper, and a black skirt from a bazaar) and unable to mimic any celebrities. When I'd left, so Hester told me later, "Who *was* she?" they enquired. Fortunately she thought of saying, "A niece of Lytton Strachey's". "*Ah!*"

(Julia to F.P.)

February 23rd, 1948. Wellington Square. The bright spot in my own personal life is really Carlyle Mansions, where dwell John Hayward and T. S. Eliot, and they really are congenial souls, and seeing them *does* cheer one up. Yes, the dinner I gave with Tom Eliot was delightful; Bunny and Rosamond came. Everybody was very amusing. Eliot and Bunny reminisced about past times they'd had with a comic character, one Lady Rothermere; and Eliot told us about his American friend who wrote the books of the words for a lot of the Marx brothers' films, and all was great fun. The food was mercifully fairly successful and drinks abounded. Bunny was in his quiet, charming, slyly humorous vein; Rosamond glowed like a gorgeous peach with hoarfrost on its head. I get on with John Hayward like a house on fire. When I was visiting him one night at Carlyle Mansions Eliot came in to see me. He was in his dressing-gown, having just had a bath, and seemed utterly distracted and Strindbergian, with his at-all-times remarkable manner accentuated into something quite ghostly and weird. I wondered for a moment if he was dead drunk; but I fancy not.

[Early in 1948 Lawrence was appointed Professor of Fine Arts at Newcastle, a post which he took up in the Spring Term. He also had a very successful exhibition at the Leicester Galleries. Meanwhile Julia began working a full week at Secker and Warburg, as fiction reader. Things seemed to be looking up, in so far as work was concerned at least. The new regime also automatically solved the problem of 'separate roofs'.]

(F.P.'s Diary)

March 25th, 1948. First day of the holidays. Fetched Burgo from school, and Julia and Lawrence have come for a week. They are here explicitly as 'inmates' and can be absorbed into the house far less exhaustingly than when an effort has to be made to entertain them. But they are neither of them people with whom one can relax, and I feel myself tingling with the effort of supporting life for them.

Divinely hot, fine, crystal clear. Julia took her work on to the verandah, and lifting her face to heaven snoozed off with a rapt, blissful expression on her face. Lawrence shambles off to paint—a morning picture in the fields, an afternoon picture on the downs.

Ralph, Burgo, Julia and I set out after lunch in the direction of Sadler's Farm, but as we climbed the first sloping field Julia exclaimed that she was weak and exhausted and could hardly go any further.

"I wonder why rich people never spend their money on really useful things," she said, "such as an invalid chair to carry them over ploughed fields." Reaching the top, new energy seized her, and she led us on for miles.

This evening: "Marshall plan? Which Marshall plan is that?" she wanted to know. It is little short of genius to have avoided hearing about the damn thing.

(Julia to F.P.)

April 17th, 1948. Secker and Warburg. Lawrence's exhibition was as successful as it could well be. Oliver Brown was heard telling the *Evening Standard* representative that its success was well-nigh unique in the annals of the Gallery. So there now. Only very few pictures were left unbought when it officially opened, and those few went that day. I gave him a celebration lunch during the proceedings, and we had a celebration dinner with Bill Coldstream.* Lawrence has been beaming for three weeks without stopping. Now he has left for Newcastle. I am much pleased with my new regime of office every day of the week; the feeling that work stops at 6 and is over and done with is a marvellous sensation.

---

* Painter, later Sir William and head of the Slade.

(Julia to F.P.)

September 13th, 1948. Fiesole. Lawrence and I are exactly halfway through our holiday, and it has been a welcome experience returning to the sunlight and heat. Lawrence has insisted on breakfast at 8.15 daily; and immediately the last mouthful is swallowed he leaps from the table and is off like greased lightning round the churches and galleries, never drawing breath till dinner-time at night. I don't attempt to follow in his aesthetic footsteps, but potter vaguely around and try to sit in the sun. All the same I have enjoyed some things very much—notably the Sansovino and Palladian churches. I prefer the architecture and sculpture to the pictures you know.

We are just back from motoring up to Vallombrosa to lunch with Berenson. He was truly fascinating. A seductive, dreamy, far-away gaze, and a slow natural manner, accompanied certainly by a veritable cannonade of philosophical witticisms and epigrams, more than one of which must have been tried out before: "I have been reading the most up-to-date and fashionable periodical in the world this morning. Now, can you tell me what that is?"

"Tell us. We don't know."

"Thucydides. I read him daily for thirty minutes; that is all I can stand. And I have to nerve myself beforehand as if getting into a cold bath—he describes so exactly the horrors of the present day."

Of what it feels like to be old, B.B. said: "One loses the sense of space, time and distance. Yes, the great spaces are gone—and with them all nostalgia, all romance. Time whirrs by, and life seems to be only a rapid buttoning, unbuttoning and buttoning-up again. It hardly seems worth while." Now we have been invited to stay on our next visit, so perhaps I have retrieved my old reputation of the *bête noir* of *I Tatti*.

[During the winter term Lawrence told Julia that he had fallen in love with one of his Newcastle students and wanted to marry her. A month or so later he became ill, TB was diagnosed, and he was sent to a sanatorium where he remained for about nine months. There are surprisingly few references to this whole episode in Julia's letters.]

(Julia to F.P.)

January 3rd, 1949. Wellington Square. Lawrence came down to London on Thursday, and brought his girl* to tea with me on the Saturday. Let me say at once that I judge her to be loving and kind-hearted, with something of the brightness of a hospital-nurse, handsome though thin—half hospital-nurse and half a very young witch on a broomstick —a witch in the moonlight, only twenty-one years old. It's his choice and there you are. I am so fearfully glad that he has found a mate that gratifies him in fundamental ways, at last.

These last weeks have been the first time I've actually emotionally faced the end of our relationship. When he left me to return for the last fortnight of the Newcastle term it had been with earnest proposals of marriage to *me*, and protestations of eternal love, saying that sex didn't matter, he and I were a case apart, etc. So that, after fourteen days, to be faced with his engagement and made to realise that I was only to have his company for ten more days—*ever*! was a great emotional shock. By May his flat will be empty and hollowly echoing. You can imagine I have been in a daze of sorrow, with tears frequently flowing. À propos, I realise it wasn't a volte face on Lawrence's part at all, for I had categorically refused in all firmness to marry him. But he is, as I've often said I expect, the only person I've ever lived with who was really fond of me, since I left my mother in India; and you can imagine what I feel at going back to the old solitary state.

(F.P.'s Diary)

January 15th, 1949. Quentin [Bell] and Julia for the weekend. The weather is mild and unseasonable—probably as warm as a normal May; the sweetness of spring is in the wind. Julia doesn't of course notice this, and goes on as if it were fabulously cold, wearing a coat in the house, two eiderdowns and a quilted dressing-gown all night. This morning she and I went for a walk and she began at once to unpack her heart. She spoke with deep emotion and a trembling voice, and I glimpsed that Lawrence's visit to London must have been miserable for them both. He even said that he couldn't bear to see her again at present. Presumably he feels agonies of guilt, and perhaps regret towards her, though there is no grounds for the first at least. And she is

---

* The Newcastle student with whom he had fallen in love.

bitterly sad at losing him, for she doesn't believe it will be possible to continue friends. I feel her tragedy deeply.

Julia showed me a temperature chart which she has been keeping for the guidance of her new doctor. Impossible to guess that such an abstract thing could bear such marks of character. It was studded with little comments: "Attack of flue here, or feverish cold," and (when the line went dead straight for a span): "Bought new thermometer here and couldn't shake it down below this point."

Unhappiness makes her egotistical, and (interested and sympathetic though I feel) I have been aware of the exhaustion of being all the weekend like a hospital nurse watching the patient and ready with hot bottle and ice-pack.

(F.P.'s Diary)

March 18th, 1949. Julia arrived this morning. After tea Ralph, she and I drove to Euphemia [Lamb]'s,* and stood for half an hour in her pale blue kitchen, which is entirely surrounded by baskets full of smelly dogs, mostly Pekinese, to which Euphemia throws an occasional bone or remark. Julia was fascinated by the extraordinary atmosphere, and I could see a short story curdling behind her inscrutable expression. She couldn't bring herself to shout at Euphemia—who is distinctly deaf —and was paralysed to the verge of nausea by the stench emanating from the dogs; so she stood silent and bolt upright, clutching her fur coat round her.

She lay in bed all morning and was still there just before lunch, with her eiderdown drawn up to her nose and her eyes staring owlishly over the top—not reading. She has been very much herself on this visit and given Ralph and me great pleasure thereby.

(F.P.'s Diary)

November 12th, 1949. Julia has now moved from Wellington Square into a flat above the George Kennedys in Oakley Street. David Wolfers occupies a large bed sitting-room underneath her, shares some of her meals and provides some sort of substitute for Lawrence. He is young, good-looking, and seems fond of her. How odd that she always chooses a young man half her age for her companion! She has taken on his

* First wife of Henry Lamb.

shopping and even promises to cook for his evenings with others. He on his side provides affection and appreciation, the pleasure of his good looks and undoubted, if rather dreamy charm. He appears to be a character without a sting, a sweet slightly sleepy pear. But Julia is not happy—when has she ever been? Perhaps less so than usual. She feels ill and works harder than she ever has in her life; she complains of having no thoughts too, though her company and conversation is as amusing as usual.

She asked if she might bring David this weekend; they have been the minimum of trouble. The height of Julia's desire has been to have breakfast in bed and lie dreaming there most of the morning.

In the evening a conversation, on ground often covered before, as to whether being rich (or 'wealthy' as Julia calls it) would provide what she describes as "wider vistas", and the ability to get to know people of real importance, who wield power. Such as whom? we asked. Kenneth Clark and Mr. Neroò (Nehru), Lord Beaverbrook, and—surprisingly—the bee-man from Ham village!

On Monday we all caught the early train to London. Ralph teased Julia a little about 'wealthy' people with 'costly' possessions, but I don't think she disliked it.

Back in the evening, convalescent from London, Ralph and I talked about Julia. We decided between us to send her a largish sum of money, and wondered if it would do her any good.

(Julia to F.P. and R.P.)

December 1st, 1949. The Office. Oh my dears, my dears, my *dears*!!!!!!! Was there *ever* such a handsome present! You could have knocked me down with a feather when I opened your casual little note. It comes at a most opportune moment I must say. Somehow one takes and takes and takes from you both—spiritual support, physical support, financial support, every kind of up-bolstering, my dears, comes from Ham Spray in a *steady* stream down the long years (I nearly wrote 'ears'). And what does one give in return? However, if (now) you should ever find your beloved Paddington Hotel full up, you must know that there will always be a spare bedroom with canopied double bed (breakfast in bed served daily) and a warm and cosy sitting-room below waiting with open paws and doors, eagerly to receive the King and Queen of Birds. Ten billion thanks from your ever faithful and loving Juliaroo.

(F.P.'s Diary)

February 8th, 1950. Our weekend visitors were Julia, Vicky [Strachey] and Richard Garnett*—the last asked by inspiration of Ralph's to provide youthful male company for Vicky. I think everyone enjoyed it. Julia greatly appreciated the younger ones. I took her breakfast in bed each morning, and found her some time later lying with her nose over the sheet "thinking about Richard and Vicky", and with such intensity as to be lost and absorbed.

(Julia to F.P.)

April 29th, 1950. I wrote you a long letter a fortnight ago—I have suppressed it. The truth is I was going through a final psychological crisis comparable to that in the old-fashioned type of pneumonia, and I wrote the letter at its very head—blank despair, an 'unctuous cater-wauling', to borrow an excellent phrase from Pritchett in this week's *Statesman.* Now I am so glad I didn't send it, because all's over and I have come out the other side. I decided that it was really quite impossible to live out the last twenty-odd years of one's life in such a gloomy state as I have been doing the last year or so. It had got to stop. So I hit on the conclusion that I would never think of my misfortunes again. If I catch myself beginning to brood I switch off like lightning and rush away to do something practical. If one really *is* a chicken with its head cut off, well, so be it. One *is* a headless chicken and catastrophe has come, but the last few hours can either be funereal and solemn *or* uncaring and sprightly. I have plumped for the latter.

Last week I went down to John Lehmann's new cottage; he is very pleased with it, dear fellow. I have managed to get an advance out of him to pay my Universal Aunts to take down my ill-fated story to my dictation. All still goes pretty well and I think it will be done this summer. But do you know I just can't write a line with my own hand or even on a typewriter, but have to have a human being there like a wardress, to stand over me and flog me on.

(F.P.'s Diary)

June 7th, 1950. It is a long time since I saw two such successful, well-adjusted, *victorious* people as those we met at dinner with Julia last

---

* Son of David Garnett, and my nephew.

night—Veronica Wedgwood and Freddie Ayer. They make some of our friends seem dim and uncertain. No "sort of's" and appealing "d'you know?'s" but an even flow of words fluently expressing their eager and complicated thoughts. Each has the confidence which is solidly based on knowing they are extremely clever. Both are frankly delighted to talk about themselves and their work; but whereas *she* emitted a great breath of candour, an air of putting her cards on the table, and when talking of Love at once took a back seat and volunteered that she had endured fifteen years of unrequited love, and "been quite unable to charm the undergraduates," Freddie declared that the greatest misery was to be loved by someone you couldn't love. It might be said he flattered us by not talking down to us—or on the other hand that he took delight in using his superior knowledge to take every remark in a philosophical sense if possible, turn it and twist it, rapidly producing (as a Variety artist produces Napoleon's hat out of a poke-bonnet) a neat, paradoxical conclusion. These two at once took the limelight they deserved, and I think Ralph and I both enjoyed turning it on them, at the same time we managed to keep afloat in the conversation, which was of a kind we like. But Julia, who was anyhow worn out by preparing and serving our meal, was a bit out of the talk, which was anyhow not her sort. And looking at these two confident, successful people and then at the infinite sadness and world-shattering despair in her face I felt enormously touched. She seemed like a battered moth that had beaten itself for hours against a lamp-shade, beside two glossy winged beetles. I felt she must long for us to go, yet didn't want her to think the evening wasn't a success. It was.

(F.P.'s Diary)

November 20th, 1950. Julia for the weekend. Though her *brain* is not of a masculine or logical sort, she has a tremendously individual, original and active *intelligence.* She kept us all stimulated, and general topics were always springing up at her touch ... She brought her all-but finished story, and I read it and made my criticisms and comments. It excited me greatly—oh, how I hope it is a success.* Even though her effects are sometimes incompletely carried through, her writing seems to me to be aiming a long way above the normal level of fiction, and

* A first draft of *The Man on the Pier.*

there is hardly a paragraph that has not gone through some process of soaking in a marinade composed of imagination, poetry and general reflections. Not to mention the humour of it all.

Julia told a story about a meeting between Rose Macaulay and Ivor Novello at Hester's, when the conversation turned somehow or other on things written on walls. Rose Macaulay said: "Then there's another *very* good word one sometimes sees—Fug. It seems an excellent word. I wonder what it can possibly mean."

[I have mentioned Julia's favourite conditions for 'thinking' or 'cogitating' as she liked to call it—lying flat on her back in bed with her nose over the sheet. She would remain thus for hours; I have never met anyone else who had this habit. I suppose I was particularly aware of this penchant of hers because I myself have always found it more conducive to thought to have a pen in my hand, or be stimulated by conversation.

Lawrence left his sanatorium completely cured, but all was over between him and 'the young witch on a broomstick' when he returned to work at Newcastle, visiting Wellington Square in the vacation. Aunt Loo died in 1950, and her death was one theme of the sketch that follows: *Cosmic Toes.*]

COSMIC TOES

I arrived at the picture gallery in Chelsea, opened the door and walked in. It was a private view; the room was already crowded. A man in a white linen waiter's jacket came up to me holding a tray of glasses containing some sort of golden-brown liquid.

"Sherry, madam?"

"Thank you very much." I reached out my gloved hand, took a glass and began to sip.

A brash glare, deflected from the sunlit, wind-jigging treetops of Carlyle Square immediately opposite, clattered and bucketted round the pictures on the walls. I looked about among the crowd and spotted only one or two acquaintances. One way and another the atmosphere didn't seem very congenial. I felt low. But a few glasses of sherry later,

an elderly man was brought up to me and introduced by a lady in a
flowered frock, who murmured in my ear that he and I had mutual and
cultured friends near Hungerford. She then disappeared in the crowd.

My new companion had a long, pale, distinguished face. We looked
at each other for a moment or two, during which I received the
impression that though he wore a most amiable expression he had no
intention of starting up a topic of conversation; then I found myself
launching into a long, boring anecdote about one of our mutual friends,
who was very absent-minded. During my narration the face of the
gentleman opposite remained immobile, his eyes fixed on mine with
always the same affable, expectant look. I began to be slightly anxious
at the fact that he didn't seem to be registering the humour of my tale,
while out of the corner of my eye I saw my black-begloved hand moving
about unexpectedly high in the air, still holding a half-filled sherry
glass, and endeavouring to mime—striving to communicate by hook
or crook with my companion, who had not as yet responded in any
way.

"And do *you* like London?" my new friend suddenly interrupted, still
smiling with obvious bonhomie.

"Do *I* like London?" I repeated blankly. The question had taken me
by surprise. What could I answer? I had lived in London on and off for
most of my life. London formed a part of my mind.

I shot a glance down at my feet. Then at last I answered: "If you
should ask me, 'Do I like living with my *toes?*' I should have to tell you
that in the past I have sometimes been horrified by my toes. But at other
times taken a certain delight in them; and then at other periods I have
forgotten their very existence! (Or imagined I had done so, though I
should have been brought to my senses fast enough if they had suddenly
been chopped off by a passing lorry, and I had to face my whole future
without them!) Well—it is really the same with my feelings about
London."

Silence greeted this statement; yet my companion still went on
looking at me in the friendliest fashion and smiling expectantly. I
plugged on: "At times I have been terrified, simply appalled, at being
so very closely pegged on to all ten of them—my toes, I mean. Pegged
on to them without even a by-your-leave, as the saying goes. Nobody
has ever asked me if I wanted to be attached to all these toes, and there
is something oppressively ineluctable—don't you think?—about this

whole position." I waited for his answer. None came. I went on: "But my toes after all only belong to a temporary order, and at such time as they vanish, are finally done for—why, the whole Cosmos will in fact have been permanently affected! Bound to be! I mean everything that happens alters everything else in the world, once and for all. Something to do with the Second Law of Thermodynamics I believe—don't ask me to explain the matter just at the moment."

I should say that I have been apt, for some years now, to cut back to the Cosmos whenever possible, in order to orientate even the tiniest details of my life. Yes, I feel unsafe, feel I should be proceeding on an artificial basis and likely to fall through some hidden trap-door, unless I keep my tabs on the Cosmos, you know, every step of the way . . .

I confess that during this long rigmarole about my toes I had hoped to spark off a reaction of some sort or other at last from this so-uncommunicative gentleman. But he was still facing me in serene silence, and still wearing the same expression of mild expectancy.

Who was he? I felt stumped. At this point I noticed that from his ear there dangled a pink cord. He was wearing a deaf-aid! Ah well, that explained a lot. He had not caught a word of all the nonsense I had been talking! Just as well. Meanwhile of course, he was still waiting amiably for the answer to the first question he had asked me. What had it been, though? Suddenly I remembered. I bent down and shouted at the top of my voice: "*You asked me do I like London?*"

At once he smiled assent. Good! I had found the key.

"I first came to live in London you see," I bawled, "when I was six years old."

"Ah yes, yes, yes, of course! I understand. I too! I lived here all my youth."

It was a lady who had spoken these last words, having come up from behind and decided to join in. "My wife," said my companion. "I think you've met each other." I turned and recognised a figure from the past—Lucila Japp, the beautiful Spanish woman who had once endeavoured to teach my Uncle Lytton the tango.

It had been many years ago, on just such a summer evening as this, in my uncle's country house, Ham Spray: the rest of us had been profiting from this Spanish dancer's exquisite style and learning some new steps, when on an impulse we all surrounded my uncle, who was watching the dancing with a guarded expression, and tried to induce him to join in.

But he simply threw up his long thin ribbon-like arms with the gesture of a drowning man and quickly bowed himself from the room. Now here at this picture gallery this same Spanish lady was informing me that it was her husband, Darsie Japp, the man to whom I had been holding forth at such length about my toes, who had painted all the pictures on exhibition around us!

A little later I was rattling down the King's Road to Wellington Square in a number 19 bus. I had rented a house in this square from Desmond MacCarthy's wife Molly in 1944, with my Aunty Loo as occupant of the ground floor. But this handsome old lady—my tenant—was now lying on a table in her bedroom, having been laid out by the nurse in her winding-sheet, cerements, or whatever is the modern name for the clothes in which people are buried.

I met the nurse outside the bedroom, and was told that all was ready for me now within. I could go in and pay my last respects to my Aunty Loo. As is I suppose understandable, I was half afraid to enter for my last of all interviews with her. Not that it was the first time I had looked upon someone I had known long and well, after their death. Not so very long ago I had been taken to see the body of Loo's brother, Logan Pearsall Smith, where it was laid out in the little study where he used to write his books. Anyway, standing outside my adopted aunt's bedroom door, I was fearful of just what aspect of our new relationship was about to strike me. The last time I had visited her in this room she had been alive. Now she would be different.

I am at present only concerned with the difference between a particular aunt alive, and that very same aunt dead.

Aunty Loo had subscribed to no religion. Neither did I. An agnostic's conscience commands him at such times as these to be on guard against any sinful wishful-thinking—any intimations of personal immortality, and this line of thought leaves the unbeliever a prey to a certain degree of floating despondency—to put it in a general way. I opened the bedroom door. Went in. Saw the long, narrow coffin in the centre of her bedroom, placed upon an unexpectedly high table—a piece of furniture that I did not recognise, probably provided by the undertaker. I walked round to the further side, and stood looking down at the startlingly white waxen substance, so splendidly moulded and bodied forth. The Pearsall Smiths had been a very handsome family indeed

—their fleshly architecture, with its terraced plateaux, escarpments, convexes and concaves, all of the finest.

However, I could tell after my very first glance that my Aunty Loo *herself* was simply not present in this room. Strange! To look at the hands and the mouth, the legs and the feet that this lady had once used: strange to see them parted from her personality so completely for the first time, and yet not to feel any melancholy at that fact. But as she was not present herself—having abdicated—it was not so bad to be left alone with this marvellously created form, of which she had for so long made good use.

Aunt Loo's doctor had told me that I must give notice of her death at the local Registrar's, and bring back the death certificate. I therefore left the house and headed off towards the office of the Registrar of Deaths at Chelsea Town Hall.

I entered the main door of the big building hesitantly, not knowing which way to turn when I got inside. There seemed to be many mile-long, door-studded corridors leading off in different directions. I threaded my way among a number of notices embellished with hands pointing to such remarks as: "Taxes", "Pensions", "Registration of Marriages", and a host of others. Ah! At last here we were: "Registration of Deaths". I found my way into a narrow waiting-room with wooden benches round the walls. This was *my* room. On the benches five or six people were sitting waiting. As I entered, another person who by his assured and commanding air was plainly a Town Hall official was bustling out on his way somewhere else. His face was flushed a beetroot red; he seemed to be fleeing from a hornets' nest. He passed rapidly through a glass-topped door at the far end of the room, and then after a moment shot back again, this time plainly making for a second door at the side of the room. But before he was able to reach it, a tiny old fellow, a member of what used to be called 'the working classes', attired in a suit of clothes belonging to a much bigger person, and with a huge cloth cap slipping down over his eyebrows, sprang up from one of the wooden benches, and throwing himself in front of the desperate-looking official (who was now trying to escape from the hornets' nest through this second door) succeeded in cutting off his retreat, at the same time bending back his neck as far as he was able so as to stare into this face so far above his own, and crying out, "Would you like to see my toes *right away*?"

It was an offer from a very shy man who meant only to be helpful, as one glance at his pale old face revealed.

A pause ensued, while we all awaited the outcome of this suggestion. When it came it was a violent explosion, carrying a ring of unmistakable sincerity:

"I don't care if I never see your toes as long as I live!"

I think we were all somewhat dazed by this answer. The tiny man himself seemed completely stunned, and stood there turned to stone. Meanwhile the furious-faced official disappeared through the door.

"The Pedicure Clinic is down the passage and turn left. You're in the wrong room!" shouted one of the people waiting on the benches—the first to pull himself together.

At this the small man's pale visage cleared somewhat. He shuffled hastily out of the room. Silence fell.

When my turn came I was determined not to put a foot wrong. I found the official with the scarlet face glaring across his desk, strung up taut as a fiddle-string, quivering all over, and his hands shaking with hostility and aggression. I told him politely that my Aunt's doctor had told me to announce her death. He reacted as if I had thrown a bucketful of slops over him. "What the devil do you mean by that?" was roughly his come-back to every statement I made; no remark of mine passed without a jeer. He refused to allow me to register Aunty Loo's death, and finally shooed me out of the room without a word of explanation or advice.

On my return home I rang up the Chelsea County Council, and told them that I considered the Registrar of Deaths in the Town Hall was on the edge of a nervous breakdown, and required a long holiday as soon as possible.

Next morning there was a ring at our doorbell in Wellington Square. I opened the door. There, clutching a sheaf of forms, was my Registrar. Bowing low, he apologised for yesterday's behaviour, and begged me to permit him the honour of helping me register my Aunt's death forthwith.

(F.P.'s Diary)

December 27th, 1950. At the last moment we invited Julia and Lawrence for Christmas, and they seemed pleased to come. Lawrence appeared to be in very good, not to say boyish spirits and entered into everything

—jigsaw puzzles, poetry game, etc. Both of them slept a good deal and Julia was obsessed by fear of cold. We did what we could, two fires each in sitting-room and dining-room, but all was fruitless. She sat in an armchair drawn close to the fire, in fur coat, my woollen stockings, and a rug pulled round her knees, casting something of a blight by her unhappiness, which I instinctively knew was laid at our door. I took her several walks at her request—out into the steely colourless air of the avenue and along the lane. Once, when a sudden flurry of snow struck us, she exclaimed: "Oh, this is *too* awful! I can't help feeling it's *your* fault, Frances." Really she was very nice most of the time, but feeling cornered by the cold brought out her most critical mood, and she often sat with narrowed eyes gazing bleakly and disapprovingly at the outside world. On Christmas Day we went to tea with the Brenans,* who had forgotten they had asked us. This Julia would not forgive—the iced cakes should be *there* although she never eats them; nor did their warm welcome and the snugness of their little room, charmingly decorated with a few sprigs of holly and some silver balls, and the great cat before the fire like a picture in a child's reader, succeed in thawing her. None of this went unnoticed by Lawrence, and when next day he cancelled his invitation to Julia to spend the first week of the New Year in his house at Newcastle, on the grounds that she would be too cold and he would hate to see her look unhappy, I suspected cause and effect.

* Gerald and Gamel.

Chapter Sixteen

SECOND MARRIAGE

Including Julia's *BREAKFAST IN PERCY STREET*

[1951 was not a happy year for Julia. Lawrence was now absorbed in virtually creating the Art School in far-away Newcastle; and though of course they corresponded, he visited her in London and took her once to Paris, the link between them seemed to be growing more tenuous. Julia's company was always sought-after; she was never short of friends—but of love, possibly yes. Nor did her present relation with Lawrence, or anyone else, represent the 'family life' she so constantly longed for. She was in fact haunted by the spectre of loneliness. Meanwhile the little flat at the top of many stairs in Oakley Street was very constricted: David Wolfers, living on the floor below, was always a kind and sympathetic friend, but had ceased to be anything more through no fault of his own. He it was who advised Julia to see a consultant psychologist, and this lady gave her some support. Among other advice, she explained to Julia why she so often dreamed of small furry animals, clamouring for affection and caresses: "You see, they are all projections of yourself," she said. "It is you who longs for these things." This interpretation entirely convinced Julia, and for a while any autobiographical writing about her adult life was transferred to the third person and attributed to someone called "Racoon". (She afterwards altered this.) It is tempting to think that her intense, almost obsessive passion for cats and other creatures, and interest in everything they did, came from the same source.

She still had her reader's job at Secker and Warburg; moreover she must also have been working at her second novel, for it was published in 1952 by John Lehmann, as *The Man on the Pier*. Twice as long as *Cheerful Weather for the Wedding*, and rather more ambitious, it is—as Philip Toynbee brilliantly expressed it*—"a book about passion and it is

---

* In a review of her work for the *Observer* in April, 1978, when Penguin Books brought out a paperback edition of both her novels.

passionately told, a modern fable in which Priapus plays the part of Nemesis." In the course of what might be called 'working walks' when Julia visited us in the country, she admitted (as was obvious to me) that the décor of the new novel was inspired by Ham Spray, its surrounding fields of cows, its daily input of book catalogues and flies, the thatched cottages of Ham and even the contents of the village shop. But she stoutly denied that Ralph and I were the models for two of the chief characters, although their son Coco was very clearly a portrait of Burgo.

On Julia's visits to Newcastle she began taking a deep and detailed interest in the administrative side of the art world. Her five years with Lawrence had developed her taste for studying pictures, and thinking about aesthetics. She had, as well, a never-failing respect for all sorts of intellectual techniques—moving on from that of literature to a more amateurish exploration of science, for instance.

Three years of living on her own came to a climax of loneliness and misery. A passage in *The Man on the Pier* sounds the note of silent appeal which was only dissipated by her marriage to Lawrence in March 1952:

He had expected reproach, indignation, frank outrage, perhaps a sense of loss. But there was nothing so passive in Marina's eyes as a mere awareness or any such acceptance of her situation. They were simply alight with uncontainable pain. She seemed to be shrieking to be released. He was looking at an animal in a trap, crying out to be saved.]

(Julia to F.P.)

February 16th, 1951. Wellington Square. I haven't seen Lawrence again; he keeps putting off his visit to London. But he declares he *is* coming later.

I've made two nice new friends since I saw you last. One is David Gascoyne, the poet, who lives round the corner; the other, Terry Kilmartin, works on the *Observer*, a charming Irish young man. They are diametrical opposites—which is refreshing. David Gascoyne romantic, tall, haggard (very), beautiful (very), and mad (very). He is an Alice-in-Wonderland animal rather than a man, but does the thing in slap-up style. I suspect him of being a genius. Terry is nothing if not sound in wind and limb, but really delightful company. Both are about thirty. I still don't seem able to find any friends of my own age for some reason, except the charming Edith Finch, Bertie Russell's American girl friend.

[In the winter of 1951–2 Julia visited Lawrence in Newcastle, and discussed with him the possibility of a joint ménage.]

(Julia to F.P.)

December 4th, 1951. Wellington Square. I decided to ask Lawrence if he would care to make his headquarters with me—i.e. rent a room under the same roof as me, and he said he certainly wanted to do that very thing. At the same time he has decided to leave Newcastle at the end of the Summer term. He plans we shall have a flat together in some shape or form. But I do feel that he's not in the mood to cross the Rubicon and throw in his lot with me quite *definitely*. Newcastle seemed much more enjoyable this time. Really this little group of his friends who run the Art School is utterly delightful, and you wouldn't believe the fun it all is. They were hanging up a marvellous show of Poussins in the gallery there.

(F.P.'s Diary)

New Year, 1952. Our visitors, Lawrence and Julia, look like joining forces again, though Julia, perhaps because her security is returning, at once lets a scintilla of doubt creep into everything. One feels a trace of irritation at her Nannyesque (though perfectly unconscious) movements to signify she is cold—rubbing her hands or shaking her shoulders; or the way she counts the blankets on her bed under one's very eyes or says, "Do you happen to know, Frances, where that book on such-and-such is?" I *know* she hopes I'll leap up and get it for her. So I can't resist saying: "Yes, I know exactly where it is. On the table just inside the front sitting-room." Of course she had not the energy to get it herself, and it remains where it is. All this constitutes the pea under the mattress, an essential part of Julia, but when I say it doesn't make the slightest difference to my affection for her, nor to her company being the best in the world, I mean it.

(F.P.'s Diary)

January 18, 1952. Lunched with Julia at Favas. She was very sad and low. Tears crept into her eyes when she told me that Lawrence, having had a fine social time with her in London, had written to say that he thought he would rather she didn't visit him in Newcastle, as he was "not sure he liked having the different elements of his private life heaped on the floor in hopeless confusion". She had been looking forward to going up and of course this was all horribly snubbing. She now thinks the project of life together in London will melt away indefinitely, and all her lost and lonely feelings come crowding back. She had been living closeted in her room in the Lord knows what state of dismal reflection, poor creature.

(F.P.'s Diary)

February 17th, 1952. Yesterday evening Julia came for a week's visit, and at lunch today she said, "Well, I want you to be the first to hear the news that Lawrence and I are getting married next holidays." (We had all dined together, plus Bunny and Angelica [Garnett], after the wedding party for Quentin and Olivier [Bell] last week, and Lawrence had made us roar with laughter over a dream about playing the piano in a quartet at the Wigmore Hall.)

I heard the full story on a walk in the afternoon. After my lunch with her at Favas she fell into unutterable gloom and terrible fits of crying. She wrote to Lawrence telling him how unhappy she had been; and affectionate, consoling, regretful letters came back, saying he was coming to London and they would talk over their future together. He did, and the night after Quentin's wedding party he asked her to marry him. She seems immensely relieved and able to look into the future with interest; planning has taken the place of the hollow echoing tin of loneliness she stared into before.

(F.P.'s Diary)

February 21st, 1952. Julia got a most encouraging letter from Lawrence, full of affection, saying that he had been unable to avoid telling all his Newcastle friends the news, and how pleased they are and want to make '*delightful fusses*'.

(F.P.'s Diary)

March 28th, 1952. A piercing cold morning with a freezing wind, as Ralph and I took the 9.36 to London for Julia and Lawrence's wedding. Arrived, we went straight to Oakley Street. No reply to our repeated rings. "Julia's bungled it again," said Ralph. "Oh dear, oh dear; what shall we do *now?*" We were about to set off for the Registry Office in the teeth of the cold wind, when we caught sight of Lawrence stooping his way along, talking to a very nice young woman called Catherine Sinclair. Julia was upstairs all right, and we all went into her tiny room, now altered by the presence of a second bed. Julia on her wedding day, how touching she was! The years had rolled away from her and she appeared Lawrence's coeval; no-one could have carried off the age discrepancy better, and she and Lawrence were both in an agreeable fluster.

"Ju! Good gracious! Where is it? I knew I'd lose it. I *have*. The ring! I left it on the table here, I'm positive. In a screw of paper." "Oh, was that it?" asked Julia serenely—"Why, I threw it away, of course. Just a dirty old screw of paper, I thought." It came to light in the waste-paper basket. Julia was wearing a ring of diamonds and pink stones, a buttonhole of a pink rose and stephanotis, while white carnations were provided for male lapels. George Kennedy* arrived from below like some odd sort of diver, with a bottle of champagne. David Wolfers, with a sweet and benign expression, completed the party that went to the Registry Office. The registrar evidently took an artist's pride in his trade, and recited the words in a deathly slow, mystical sing-song, with his eyes fixed aloft. It was a near thing to a *fou-rire* with several of us, and didn't make things easier for Lawrence, who however got it all out in the end—even "impediment" which stumped him for a while. Kisses all round, and off to Prunier's for lunch, joined there by Bill Coldstream. The wedded pair are to come to Ham Spray for the weekend, in their car.

(F.P.'s Diary)

March 31st. Lawrence has given Julia a fur coat for a wedding-present. How she basks in it! The weekend only confirmed our view that this is the best thing that has happened to either of them for years. "All my

---

* Architect, owner of the Oakley Street house.

worries and glooms have rolled away," said Julia to me on a walk. "These last few years I've enjoyed *nothing*. Now I haven't a care in the world."

(Julia to F.P.)

May 19th, 1952. Newcastle. I just couldn't write before—you may, in fact of course you will disbelieve me, but the fact is I haven't had one second's spare time since I got here *in which I was not so dog-tired* that I just sat with my feet up and turned the pages of the *Listener*. This was because my life here is so new to me that it has taken me all this time to learn a possible routine. But I have achieved my main object—to preserve Lawrence's health, and he tells me that never before this term has he felt so absolutely well and not at all tired. He is in roaringly good form and spirits, bursting with dynamic energy. With a great effort I have railed off three hours every morning in which to do my own writing—but this means I must shop, arrange, cook and cope in the last half of the day until I'm too tired to do anything else.

Lawrence has been perfect to me. We are both very happy. I am *thankful* to have escaped that ghastly hell of a life in London, which I look back on with a shudder, as into some infernal sulphurous pit. Here I have someone to live for, affection, and a very interesting life indeed. I just don't care a hoot for anyone except three or four people—you and Ralph and Lawrence about finish it—oh, and Philip [Toynbee] and Robert [Kee] come in as well, and Adrian Beckett and Olivier [Bell]. Everyone else can disappear with a melodious twang as far as I'm concerned.

(Julia to F.P.)

May 26th, 1952. Newcastle. Quentin [Bell] has been a great success with all. He is to teach teachers to teach art to children, as I think you know. He is an angel in the house of course, has such a sweet nature. He helps me all he can; and encourages Lawrence much by his gales of giggling at every word L. says. His *appearance* is much admired by all the painters up here, who sit around gazing moonstruck at his honey and auburn tone-values and his seal-like contours. But *my*! what an eater! He is busy trying to find a nice flat or house for himself and Olivier. But you know Newcastle is an awful spot whatever they tell you, and I just can't imagine Olivier not being depressed when she first settles in here.

There is this frightfully busy, very dirty, sooty town. And immediately you leave the main streets, which admittedly are of fine architecture, you are at once into drab, hateful suburbs. Our own house, between you and me, is quite a depressing, prim little villa of a low type. But outside it and all round grow trees, and there is very fresh, pure sweet air outside the town which I enjoy, like Scottish air.

We are both unsociable; all the same we had an enjoyable evening with a couple of philosophers called Midgely, only about twenty-eight, but brilliant both. They are the Lionel Penrose,* Christopher Strachey† type of intellectual, a perfectly shattering, bleak house and bad food, yet delightfully warm, ingenious and brainy. Hoping to get a return from *you*, dear, about the world outside.

[Disillusion with Newcastle was not slow to appear.]

(Julia to F.P.)

November 19th, 1952. Newcastle. I have just taken your blue letter out of my bag where it has rested since it first gladdened our eyes almost a month ago. However I feel it befits Arctic travellers to issue their bulletins at long intervals only. So now I have re-perused your first page; and find a most glamorous description of your shining soggy avenue entwined with ivy leaves—and a request to know what Newcastle looks like in the Autumn.

You are right to ask, *pardi* or *parbleu*, as it is so entirely foreign and different from the South. When we drove up here at the beginning of term we were both appalled at the hideous change in things as we approached the town. The air loses all body, all rich juices, all mellow overtones; mature undertones and human know-how are withdrawn from everything. Newcastle itself is a world of footballers, industrialists and slums; the air is filled with a network of tram overhead wires; the ground is flat and consists of hundreds of football fields with their withered grasses wilted by the rough sea-winds. In between these things are soot-stained factories, breweries and filthy *sheds* above

* Geneticist, married to Julia's schoolfriend Margaret.
† Julia's half-brother.

all—all sizes and shapes they come, these millions of dirty, industrial sheds.

Our own little villa has a brewery slap up against the back, and waste land opens out from our bathroom windows on one side, in the puddles of which the mud flings back the icy light from the ravaged sky, whilst old planks and piles of bricks glitter wet and soggy as your avenue trees—but no ivy wreathed around them, alas. If I want to take a little 'constitutional' there is just one round one can make (barring the blasted town moor, with its industrial golfers and cosh-boys kicking footballs) and that consists of about six football fields diversified by glum allotments, with warehouses and factories and football stadiums, tramlines and winding about between them! I don't really complain of the gale force of the north wind, a thing I've always detested, because it keeps the clouds chasing away, and every two or three days there is one of brilliant, clear sunlight.

You will want to hear about Olivier and Quentin. Well, up came Olivier, only three weeks after the actual birth; what with the all-night train journey and new baby and everything, she was exhausted and looked pitiful, white and trembling, and promptly went down with 'flu. We did all we could of course, but it wasn't much. But Olivier was MAGNIFICENT. She wouldn't go to bed, she had too much to do. Now she is well and very chic and radiant in a cherry candy-striped apron, with a baby on one arm and a carpentry saw on the other. In between feeding the baby she has made marvellous carpentry miracles.

Is there a chance that you and Ralph could bear to come and stay? We have been longing to ask you. Do, do come.

P.S. It strikes me that I have said nothing at all about what goes on inside my head up here, which is what really counts—all the football fields and tram wires are superficial, comparatively.

Lawrence and I are getting on together marvellously well, and not a day passes but I thank my stars that I had the luck to get married to him in the end. My life is now a human being's life and not a suicidal spooky drudge's. I am still feeling the effects of shock of having lived through three of the most tortured years I can well imagine.

I'm still afraid the dream will break and let me fall through into that other sort of reality, in which as a matter of fact most of my life has been spent. This cosiness is so foreign to me. I have lived on the outside rim or crust of life for so long that I have acquired the habit of being an outsider, and viewing the world from a thousand miles away.*

(F.P.'s Diary)

December 30th, 1952. December has been unusually full of social occasions, and ended with a five days Christmas visit from the Gowings. This left us exhausted and—asking each other why?—we decided it was because when Julia goes visiting she takes with her not only her criticism—but her pessimism: she expects things not to measure up to her standard, so of course it is a wonder if they do.

On Boxing Day, perhaps as a result of this unobtrusively-imposed but distinctly-felt strain, Ralph awoke in something of a rage, whose purpose and direction he himself hardly felt aware of. Having suggested a walk to Julia in vain, I walked off into the muddy fields alone, and discovered that it was a day of rare and peculiar sweetness. The intense silence of a National Holiday hung over everything, leaving the cheep of birds, the crow of cocks to be heard. A mild and tender light came blooming through the clouds, and laid a beam of great softness and delicacy along the line of the downs for a moment. I was *mad* about the day, and after lunch went out again, somehow communicating my insanity to Julia, who came too. A discussion about people's philosophies of life: and whether optimists lack some finer awareness of life's value. Julia said they do, and described what they miss as "the epic nature of life's tragedy, of which is it a privilege to be allowed to partake"!

(Julia's 'Newcastle Diary')

January 19th, 1953. I mean to incorporate myself much more fully in Lawrence's academic life at the College. I must avoid being the housewife full of shopping and food problems, to whom he returns every evening. As at present, I shall spend the whole morning in the College library. Walking down in the frost and slight mist, I congratulated myself on living in a town where one can hear seagulls crying all the time. They were swooping over the field beside the medical school. It is pleasant picking one's way through crowds of little student nurses on this path, with their floating capes and fluttering white caps, and always running and laughing hysterically.

* This splendid letter ran to ten pages in all

(Julia's Diary)

January 21st, 1953. Before continuing I really must make a note of the great Hamster revelation which I received whilst walking round Harrods' Zoo at Christmas. Seeing the little Hamster, all but human with his plain business man's face and his long elegant useful human hands and feet, and bursting busy enthusiasm and vitality, I went on into the snack bar for coffee. Sitting there, suddenly my eyes were opened. Looking around the tables of middle-aged shoppers, a sight that usually weighs me down and deflates me, I saw them all, lo and behold—as Hamsters! They were actually big but I saw them as small—and miraculously they became neatly made, comically marvellous little machines and puppets for me. The Hamster in Human Beings and the Human Being in Hamsters suddenly magnetised each other in my mind, like two drops of water coming together, and this fascinating life-enhancing Hamster principle has quite changed the face of industrial civilisation to my eyes. I see Hamsters everywhere now—walking down the streets, sitting in tea-shops, in the buses— where before I saw only huge, unhealthy, heavy, coarse ogres walking about. A red letter day when I saw that Hamster in the Zoo.

(Julia's Diary)

January 24th, 1953. Casson* lecture yesterday. Lawrence dined with him and came back quite unimpressed. I had been completely swept away by his oratory, serenity and humour. I must take a lesson from Casson's exemplary attitude. I seem to be so vinegary by nature. What can I do about it? (This is the sixth day in succession that I have felt sick and dizzy all day long.)

(Julia's Diary)

January 27th, 1953. In a low and depressed mood. Complete lack of enthusiasm for the world—the newspapers deluging one every morning with stories of savagery and stupidity and starvation. I felt so sorry that I really made Lawrence weep with depression when I expressed my point of view to him. I hoped he'd put the other, cheerful side. But then the alternative to frankness—putting up an artificial face of cheerfulness—surely that leads to great emptiness and boredom?

* Sir Hugh.

[Julia's diaries frequently refer to feeling ill, low, sick and so on, during the early Newcastle years. This was to have extremely unfortunate consequences: her doctor prescribed amphetemines ('purple hearts'), which she found so raised her spirits that she increased the dose, and gradually became 'hooked' on them. Indeed she constantly recommended them to her friends as a cure for all ills. Later on, when she had serious cause for depression they were to be a disastrous factor in the decline in her health.]

(Julia's Diary)

February 3rd, 1953. After a terrible Sunday, trying to make the new pressure cooker work and failing dismally, now on Monday I am still too tired to think.

I stayed supine, resting all afternoon, quilt over knees by the fire, watching the daylight fade and the lamps come on outside and shine on the sitting-room wall. Such a melancholy lost mood. I allowed my thoughts free to ramble round—my main feeling being that I had taken such a long journey through the world, starting in India and on and on and on from pillar to post, I felt I had come too far from my original 'centre', and it was time for the journey to finish. A traveller too exhausted is no good for anything. Then Lawrence returned, so full of enthusiasm and happiness after a magnificently successful day's painting; and that, together with the good tea, and his being so loving, and making the toast with me, revived me. I felt that through staying quietly thinking by myself I had retrieved my disintegrated spirit. My new book, *Man's Place in the Universe*, set my thoughts in motion again. Some beautiful lyrical passages all through it. All the same I can't think he is right to prefer Beauty to Truth. I still prefer Truth, however ugly—only one needs such bravery to stand it without withering up in terror and being blasted by its thunderbolts.

(Julia's Diary)

February 8th, 1953. This morning Lawrence and I woke up to a snow-powdered landscape. Walking down Framlington Terrace was delicious—the trees, ground, the railings of the little gardens and the house-tops as if sifted with white icing sugar, the sky across the field diamond-like, a refreshing morning sweetness of air. Big birds were hopping as tame and as large as domestic cats, on the railings and everywhere, asking for crumbs.

(Julia's Diary)

February 18th, 1953. Having been feeling ill for months and under sleeping-drugs all the time, I am today really well, or anyway convalescing, and feel the urge to write again. One gains experience and new vision from *everything* that happens—illnesses and troubles included. From this seemingly inert period I have got a glimpse of what it is not to be emotional about everything. I was told to keep calm and cool, and drugged to that end.

My philosophy of what life is for: living creatures seem to be in the process of dragging their inner dreams into reality and making them substantial, just as a mother giving physical birth to a baby tugs it gradually and painfully out into the world. I must not waste emotion in *hating* this Northern atmosphere as I do; I must ignore it and carry on with my private birth, establish my dreams for all the world to see.

[This year the Gowings took a small flat in Percy Street, W.1., to stay in when they came to London, and Lawrence encouraged Julia to decorate it just as she liked best. It is the scene of *Breakfast in Percy Street*.]

(F.P.'s Diary)

September 15th, 1953. The Gowings, whom we lunched with in their new Percy Street flat, were the only cheerful people we saw, but the décor—so much talked about, and with such eager planning by Julia, is a great disappointment. She has tried to be modern, and so failed to express her own taste at all. The bedroom has a wallpaper of small bright checks. "The trouble is one can't *look* at it, it's so dazzling to the eyes. So we don't any more." The sitting-room walls are each painted a different colour; it has furniture from Heal's and a characterless wall-mirror with no frame. The little dining-room is nursing-home green. Lawrence (who had said that Julia "was the best interior decorator in England, and I feel she ought to have free play") seems quite disappointed in the most good-humoured way, and says he is tired of the dining-room already. "I'm going to paper it with *Financial Timeses.*"

(Julia's Diary)

*November 27th, 1953.*A short London visit. Bill Coldstream came back with Lawrence after the Tate Gallery meeting. Bill was very interesting about Picasso. "He is a jazz band player," he kept saying, "by which I mean that he spends his time playing obbligatos on a given theme—it all wells up from the bowels as he goes along. He may take someone else's theme and play a jazz melody on it." He reached this conclusion after having met Picasso in the flesh, when sent to bring him back from the station in a taxi to the Peace Conference. "He has the gaiety and the spontaneity of a small bird," said Bill.

(Julia to F.P.)

December 15th, 1953. Newcastle. We had a hectic day or two in London; of course one meets everyone in the world strolling down Percy Street. We went to a cocktail party in Bill Coldstream's rooms at the Slade, afterwards dined at Antoine's and on to dance at the Gargoyle (which has become quite gay and luxurious, with scarlet wall-sofas and a very good, danceable little band). Strange figures were there, behaving strangely. Very strangely. All the sexy beauties nowadays are juvenile delinquents, so it was explained to us; and certainly I've never seen anything so wild, so bedraggled, so fey, so dirty, so slummy. I hopped around the room with Bill most of'the time—he dances like some puppet nigger-minstrel, with agile, chattering feet, most lively. But staying up to the small hours quite killed us and we've sworn never to go to the Gargoyle again.

I see that at such close quarters with old friends as the Memoir Club* a special technique of polite writing will have to be evolved. I shall not be able to say all the *terrible* things I would have said in a book. How unlike my attitude to my childhood is to yours. Yours was so friendly and warm and nice, whereas I felt myself surrounded by ugly birds of prey all the while. I can't say *that*, however, at the Memoir Club, especially with Oliver there.

I must try and summarise the life here in the briefest way. In this tiny

* Julia had just been elected to this Bloomsbury club, and attended her first meeting, at which I had read a paper.

villa in an awfully ugly street lined with what appear to be miners' houses, with the aid of a rough slum 'daily', and with abominable Newcastle victuals—the ubiquitous frozen meat, huge old cabbages and codfish in the shops—with these straws one works like a black every minute to try and establish (you know the game) food worth eating, and general comfort and glow. I sit in the sitting-room always with a quilt round my knees and often in my duffle-coat and mufflers to counteract the North Sea draughts which lance one from twenty directions at once through cracks in doors and windows. I do want you to realise what it is all like.

Today I am in bed because the week was so hectic. Victor Pasmore, who is coming up here as Painting Master, and his wife Wendy, had to come up to be given the O.K. by the University Appointments Board. It was refreshing to see such a regulation artistic couple—bohemians of the Sickert sort. Wendy with her yellow hair streaming down over her face, like a Yorkshire terrier or a Yak, right down to her waist. Hard on their heels came Dawick Haig,* who is utterly inarticulate, but makes up for it by being ideally handsome, and also very snug, kindly and comical, like a mad Earl in a play.

Now Lawrence has come back from work and is staggering round the room, cursing and wrapping up Christmas presents for the five secretaries in hollyed paper; when I tell him he has put the wrong thing on the accompanying note he curses louder than ever, and begins to wail.

(Julia's Diary)

January 18th, 1954. I returned to consciousness this morning in bed with a familiar sense of guilt and corruption. I feel outside the world, clawing for a foothold—yet not perhaps clutching hard *enough*. What kind of life do I imagine I should find wholly to my taste? Answer: One in a beautiful house and garden, in beautiful country and climate, all distracting and exhausting household things quite removed, and to be occupied in something really thrilling (playwriting, say), surrounded by really interesting people.

Lawrence's memorable phrase: "I don't want to have people about me who are engaged in a honeymoon with failure; I want people who court success." Thinking of Aunty Loo in this connection; she kept a

* Second Earl Haig, painter.

balance between both. Split souls, like her and Tommy, have a kind of double vision—each eye perceives only what it wants to.

(Julia's Diary)

January 23rd, 1954. Early morning thoughts: An artist's vocation is surely to hand on, in or by his work, the impressions he gets of life. Such impressions are dim and full of mystery, received in glimpses, sunlit sequins of meaning, peppered through huge dim shadowy foliage belonging to heaven knows what gigantic trees in antediluvian forests, hidden by mists and cavernous shadows and shot through with calls and cries of unknown animals. Living, the process, feels like fumbling one's way along an Ariadne thread of significance.

(Julia to F.P.)

January 24th, 1954. Newcastle. I am really turning into a Moon Cow, you know. You spotted it yourself when you exclaimed indignantly on the 'phone, "Well, you're turning into Absolute Northerners!" What an accusation! No, never, never! I loathe the North, as such, as much as I always have; all the same I do feel that I have, in a sense, turned into a foreigner towards my old life; looking back to only two years ago I feel I'm looking back at a different animal—and I *am* looking back at a different animal. It is the difference between being a performer on the stage when the play is in full spate, and being old, in darkness in the wings. So, feeling that I have 'closed up the shutters', to use one of Desmond MacCarthy's phrases, my only thought now is to try and make sense of my life *in retrospect*, by writing about it, and to perform this task I have to keep away from the stage itself—the lights, the noise, the actors.

But why all this? Sending you my 'elephant egotism' in a great parcel suddenly?? Well, simply because you asked me to tell you what kind of things were interesting me.

(F.P.'s Diary)

February 8th, 1954. To lunch with Julia and Lawrence in Percy Street. The crisis at the Tate Gallery fills their thoughts, Lawrence being a trustee. Julia, cooking away in the background, explained that her watch was an hour slow—and lunch indeed appeared about two. Very delicious it was, but we saw little of Julia. Meanwhile Lawrence flapped out of his bedroom wearing a jacket and pyjama legs. He is put to bed by Julia at every moment when the Tate Trustees are not meeting, fed with glasses of milk and most carefully ministered-to.

(Julia's Diary)

March 2nd, 1954. Some artists are living martyrs to their ideals; such a one is Henry Lamb. He is too full of hate for his own comfort, is shocked by his real feelings. Art can grow equally out of hate, which is merely the reverse side of the coin of love. Henry is too 'good' to allow himself his evil demon, but it is there. Such people make stimulating companions—one senses in all they say and do, in their expressions and gestures, the wealth of creative passion that lies within them. I believe it was the same with Carrington—undoubtedly there was much hate in her, but rigorously kept under. People thought her an angel, and there was something of that too, but it was the devil in her that made her exceptional.

Dinner party last night: Eric Dobsons to meet Ceri Richards. What is the secret of Dobson's being such good company? He's not a talker; no panache; yet his 'bouquet' is very fine, and rare and delicate to the palate.

[The Gowings spent several of their vacations at Stokke Manor, Wiltshire, staying with Robin and Mary Campbell—two fairly new and extremely sympathetic friends. Robin shared Lawrence's dedication to Art (he later became Director of Art for the Arts Council), while Mary farmed their land, and entertained numerous friends and children with delicious meals at her long kitchen table. Julia seemed to breathe more freely at Stokke than anywhere else.]

(Julia's Diary)

April 2nd, 1954. Visiting Mary and Robin Campbell at Stokke in the vacation. First morning: This place is bliss, really perfect. It is the same Russian country house system as Ham Spray, but the house itself is really more interesting. Large rooms at the end of long winding corridors, centres of civilisation to sleep or sit in among wildernesses of peeling walls, where nature at times takes over and paints her own colours and moulds her infinite variety everywhere, giving the house the relaxed and easy quality of woodland glades and rides, and feeding the imagination far better than the flat monotonies of the 'well kept-up house'.

Even in the sitting-room there are two universes—the main large part for formal occasions, and (round the corner) a Russian stove surrounded by windows looking over the woods, and filled with comfortable old chairs and sofas where the family and friends usually sit. In the middle is Mary's desk, chock-a-block with letters, bills and leaflets connected with farm business. Conversation in this corner is interestingly interrupted by her telephone chats with figures from the farm world, from whom she orders hay and cattle food.

At breakfast there is a feeling of a whole world starting up. At the end of the long kitchen table sit all the children (by Robin and Mary's first marriages) who chatter all at once, none of them silent for a moment yet managing to hear the others through their own burble; the girls' voices sound like the creaking of ropes and timbers on a ship, or the dry squeak of saddles and harness.

Robin and Lawrence, side by side, go through Sotheby's catalogue item by item, apparently discussing values and prices, but really excitedly building castles in the air. Mary joins in mainly with the children, and the whole thing is a lively babel. After breakfast everyone goes off to Marlborough by car, leaving me alone in the garden. A cold wind roughly buffeting, but brilliant summer sunlight; the chestnut buds looking at one ostentatiously. Six or seven rowdy little heifers keep racing up and down the field beyond, flapping their tails and cantering like stiff rocking-horses.

Later in the morning, while Mary stitched at her black and white tablecloth, or darned—entirely with scarlet wool—she told me the story of how she lost her Catholic faith.

(F.P.'s Diary)

April 8th, 1954. Julia and Lawrence are now at Stokke, but Julia is so deeply plunged in what I can only call her maternal feelings that there's barely room for her friends. Dorothy* described how when she pressed three of her paperback books on Lawrence as light reading,

* Wife of V.S., now Sir Victor, Pritchett.

Julia snatched them away, saying, "Lawrence, you know you're not allowed to carry heavy weights."

(F.P.'s Diary)

April 16th, 1954. Delightful evening here with the Campbells and Gowings to dinner. That experimental ménage is evidently a great success. I had forgotten how brilliantly amusing Lawrence could be and what a good mimic. Julia has suddenly got the idea that they must have a third establishment—a country cottage which is fast turning into a house, in Wiltshire. She is possessed by this dream. Lawrence's face is inscrutable. "Julia's got straws in her beak," is his comment, and I guess by his expression that he is confident of circumventing her desires by painless diplomacy.

(Julia's Diary)

May 18th, 1954. Newcastle. It is great fun having Victor and Wendy Pasmore staying here. At first Victor's complete oral stultification was somehow oppressive, but by the second evening his wonderful vivacity and great liquid black eyes had begun to fascinate me. He *does* communicate—but hardly at all by words; it just shows how conventional one is not to be on the lookout for different modes and manners of expression. Victor uses a whole language of gesture and mime, such as foreigners deploy, mainly with arms, hands and fingers. In repose his dark head (in which his golden face seems to glow and smoulder) and the velvety fur of his beard, give out a warmth and melancholy such as one gets from peat bogs. Wendy's looks have the freshness of a dew-drenched wild rose growing in a rural hedge in the sunshine. Her sweet smile comes and goes, revealing her even white teeth.

Lawrence has two great talents—one for optimism and one for grieving. Out of his optimism comes his gift for administration; out of his grief comes his best painting, in which there seems to me a tender feeling not far from sorrow—something poignant and veiled.

Sometimes he goes out of the room in the middle of a conversation and disappears for a long time; if I go out to find him, lo and behold he is washing and ironing some ties all by himself in the kitchen. Or he runs round to the Bells in the morning, and is found after his return putting new castors on the dining-room table or taking the bathroom taps to pieces. All these projects are carried out in brackets, as it were—in the middle of something else and with never a word to me.

(F.P.'s Diary)

July 8th, 1954. There have been tough moments in these last weeks, and I feel as if I had been juggling with different heavy objects including my own angst, though at the moment I seem to have poked my head through it (the angst) as a clown does through a paper disc. Meanwhile crash! bang! boom! the telephone has never stopped ringing. In token of the scatty state of things, I found on a piece of paper by the telephone the absurd words, "Trot out to pub" scribbled in my own writing! Then I remembered a call from Julia. Could we investigate a possible nursing-home for Oliver near East Ilsley? Yes, certainly, but what were the special needs to consider? I asked. "Well, he must be able to trot out to the pub."

(F.P.'s Diary)

July 18th, 1954. It is one thing after another, and I trot along as best I can, but not "out to pub". The Gowings came to stay yesterday but are in moderate disgrace. Expected to arrive for lunch—at 12.30 Julia rang up from London and said dreamily that they hadn't yet started, and supposed they wouldn't "make it". No apology or word of sorrow for the succulent leg of lamb cooking, nor the tender broad beans I had struggled out in the rain to pick. They arrived after tea, and today Julia went straight to her room and lay down all the morning, while Lawrence did the same all the afternoon. No way to treat one's friends—the truth is we are offended.

(F.P.'s Diary)

July 19th, 1954. Gowings much more human this morning—perhaps they were really dead beat and are just reviving. Amusing accounts of taking Oliver from nursing-home to nursing-home in the car.

O: Where *is* this place we're going through?

J: (peering) I see Norwood Police Station written up there, so I suppose it must be Norwood.

O: *Nonsense*, nothing of the kind!

J: (peering again) Well, this seems to be Norwood Post Office we're just passing.

O: (fiercely) I tell you we're *nowhere near* Norwood.

J: Well, you know best, I'm sure—all the same this does say Norwood Fire Station.

Julia told Oliver they were spending seven weeks with the Campbells at Great Bedwyn this vacation, "and it'll be nice as it's quite near Ham Spray, and we hope to see a lot of the Partridges."

O: Julia's *always* thinking everywhere's near Ham Spray. Great Bedwyn's *nowhere* near Ham Spray.* It's the other end of England.

When they arrived at a Convalescent Home in London they found some very old ladies sitting about. Oliver put on his 'hatchet face' and said, "They're all crocodiles. Waiting to *gobble* me *up!*"

J: Well, you know what Freud would say to that.

O: What would he say?

J: That if you see crocodiles everywhere it's because you're a crocodile yourself!

"Luckily," Julia said, "Oliver saw the funny side and burst into loud guffaws." She went on, "I think we'd better insert an advertisement as you do to get rid of your kittens—'Retired civil servant with cultivated tastes, very distinguished and rather crotchetty, wants good home.'"

"No," said Lawrence, "very crotchetty and rather distinguished."

(Julia's Diary)

July 29th, 1954. Stokke again. Such joy and pleasure to be here, pacing around this delicious house and gazing out at the countryside, that it's awfully hard to settle to work. I revel in the peace, the furniture, books and cooking arrangements. I'm gluttonising in fact; I have been so long starved of my rightful nourishment. It alarms me to realise how little use I can make of contemporary life in Newcastle and London. How I hate it all!

(Julia's Diary)

August 8th, 1954. Conversation with Wynne Godley and Robin over mid-morning tea, about choosing a profession (example the girl visitor). Should she think of the community's welfare or what brings her in more money, holidays and general happiness? Is one *ipso facto* better than the other? Wynne says no.

---

* It was six miles away.

Mary's two girls are interesting to compare. Both Serena and Nell* let all their feelings show on their faces. Nell's outstanding, angelic goodness is a dynamic thing, and her whole face obeys its force, as an electric light bulb when the switch is turned on. Serena touches one deeply because she often looks personally hurt, but remains vital and sparkling, though with a faculty of dropping a safety curtain between herself and sad facts. Mary's personality, seen from inside as it were, gives me the same euphoria as my blue pills—excitement, gaiety and joy, but she can't stick to the same subject for more than a second. This euphoria stops me writing and anyway my nature is not euphoric, though there is a layer of excitement just below the surface, which I've always felt it imperative to keep in its proper place.

(F.P.'s Diary)

September 2nd, 1954. An afternoon spent with Julia. In contrast to the glowing day through which we walked for nearly two hours, how grey and drab seemed her inner landscape as she unfolded it. She feels, and admits herself to be, full of bitterness; resents the man-made world, the 'selfishness of men', feels stupefied and dazed by the drugs her doctor makes her take, cannot write to her own satisfaction and feels she no longer wants to, yet still talks as if writing were the centre of her life. What is it she is *really* bitter about, I ask myself? Her mother's desertion when she was four; or the fact that she has never "got the man she loved," nor had a child? I found that she thinks me much more fortunate, because I had done both (and so I suppose I am). She still feels aggrieved because some time each day has to be spent on household things; "and then I can't help worrying, if Lawrence was run over by a bus tomorrow what *would* I do? I couldn't go back to that awful bed-sitter life. I should just have to jump off Westminster Cathedral." Poor Lawrence was to blame for getting her up too early, failing to teach her to drive a car, and keeping his painting hours sacrosanct—how very dismal all this is!

(Julia's Diary)

September 13th, 1954. It was like breakfast on any other day to the yellow basenji bitch. I found her alone in the kitchen when I went in to cook

* Nell Dunn, now well-known as novelist and dramatist.

and eat my breakfast, as is the custom for visitors in this house. As I
returned carrying my egg and coffee, she sprang on the chair beside the
window, and there remained with arched neck and long stiff paws
looking out upon the farm's *va-et-vient*, which consisted at this hour of a
lot of reproachful ducks and hopeful kittens going the rounds of the
empty pig-buckets. One had to admit she was a very stupid dog. It was
her blank and bemused countenance rather than her so notorious moral
delinquency which had at first put me against her. All the same, later on
I came to notice her unwavering civility to everyone and the cordial
bonhomie which she preserved throughout all, and somehow I was
melted. She had the bloom of a truly hopeless innocence. After breakfast out at the back door we went, she and I, to sniff the summer day.
Marigold in the sunlight, she stepped out high on stilt legs. At the end of
the greenhouse I spied Archie, the little boy of five of one of the farm
hands, kneeling on the path and bent over a toy cart into which he had
piled stones and gravel, from which he seemed to be doing some kind of
sorting.

Robin emerged from the trees in his faded Italian workman's
shirt and trousers, carrying a hose. He passed the little boy and
halted.

"What are you doing?" he asked Archie curiously.

"Mincing."

"*What?*"

"Mincing."

"I see," said Robin without seeing, and passed on in the direction of
the house. But the boy stood up and bawled after him: "We got ter do as
our Lord done!"

Robin turned, startled. "Er . . . Ye-es," he said doubtfully. Now here
came the basenji hurtling from the croquet lawn. She fairly flung herself
on her master, to whom she was devoted. He and Mary were going
away that afternoon, and Lawrence and I were to drive her to the
kennels where she was to be boarded until they came home. She was
shut up in the back sitting-room so as not to see them drive away; and it
was not until she had raced round the passage and kitchen and finally
the empty bedrooms that her intimations of disaster began to mount—
the wild fear of Calamity and Desertion. I felt like a combination of
Dalilah and Judas Iscariot. She had been deserted by the ones she
loved.

As for me, as I lay in bed that night I felt as if a meat axe had been thrown into my soul and was sticking there undislodgeable.*

(Julia to F.P.)

September 21st, 1954. I am still half in Paris, and wish I was wholly so. You may have noticed that before going I was quite tepid about the idea; indeed I was in rather low spirits (and I'm afraid you bore the brunt on our walk, which was a great shame for you). Then I suddenly realised that Paris had so much more in common with Rome (still my peerless ideal) than it had to London, and Hey Presto! all clouds lifted and I was in my glory and enjoying every moment. The fresh morning air (so balmy compared to England) wafting over the wide wide streets, the emptiness, the forests of trees everywhere, all this made me feel human again. The Cézanne exhibition was extremely fascinating, and Lawrence and I had many interesting discussions about him—interesting to me, that's to say, though he probably found them very small beer. I wouldn't have missed Rameau's *Indes Galantes* at the Opéra for anything, the designs and costumes were *whizzing*. We had got fifty pounds to spend, so by going only to inexpensive restaurants, we managed to buy two Picasso plates, six second-Empire plates, and a beautiful necklace for me.

(Julia to F.P.)

December 24, 1954. La Souco, Roquebrune. We got here safely, and a very pleasant journey. The magic of the place is as strong as ever it was for me, although I haven't been here since the early thirties. Looking at the villas around here is my chief delight. Yesterday I went off by bus to Monte Carlo, whose villas are delightfully accurate translations of the big-bosomed, big-bottomed, stiffly corsetted royalties and Edwardian aristocrats and gamblers for whom the place was originally built. There is a hauntingly rigid and frigid splendiferousness about them; they are all painted a cold shining white, and stand there snobbishly isolated from one another by their thickly palm-treed and cactusified gardens.

Janie and little bowed old marmoset Dorothy [Bussy] ding-dong along here together in a rather scarifying manner. Dorothy is now so weak she can hardly totter across the room without an arm to support

* This entry was the basis for *Can't You Get Me Out Of Here?* (*New Yorker*).

her, and if you don't watch out to see where each foot is landing (as with a child of eighteen months) she is swinging sideways and falling into an armchair or something. Conversation with her, too, is quite an ordeal, as she hears nothing lower than megaphone pitch, but expects to join in everything. Janie, who is at her wits' end, and patience quite exhausted, never fails to come back with crushing contradictions of everything her mother says, as you know.

Burgo's brilliant Christmas card has just arrived—it is *too* dazzling and glorious. What a talented boy he is! Do write to me.

(Julia to F.P.)

February 22nd, 1955. Newcastle. I wonder if Vanessa [Bell] will stand by for Saxon's flat in Percy Street. One doesn't know quite how it would pan out from our point of view to have that dignified great cathedral, Vanessa, settled in Percy Street, although I should welcome the twittering Duncan [Grant]. It will of course hardly affect us, as we are always up in Newcastle. I dream of Roquebrune every night—and long to be there. It seems so sordid and unnatural to be boxed-up in a stuffy house month after month, with no air or exercise, and no beauty—as here. Awfully like a concentration camp.

(Julia's Diary)

July 30th, 1955. Stokke. Nell and Serena have two friends staying—Jane Willoughby and Jonny Gathorne-Hardy. Nell sits still and quiet, a baby's pink-and-white complexion, and on her face a singlehearted goodness and kindness, sober attention to everybody's words and needs—a little angel in fact. Serena whirls around the room, switching on the wireless, dancing, or down on all fours like a plump bear or bush baby; volatile, defiant, full of warmth and simplicity; leaving the room suddenly with tears in her eyes when annoyed ("I must ask you to take that back").

Conversation on Sunday evening about what art was about and artists up to:

Jonny Gathorne-Hardy: "Beauty."

Lawrence: "It's by no means certain that all artists are engaged in the same activity, and I'm bored stiff with this art talk, anyhow."

Mary: "But you must box on, Lawrence, because hearing people like you talk is the only way the young people pick up or learn anything."

Meanwhile Nell, Jane, Robin and I are discussing women's position in the home.

Nell: "I can't think *why* women give themselves up to servitude. I shall never turn to and spend all my time washing and cooking."

(Julia's Diary)

August 22nd, 1955. How to describe these wonderful summer mornings? The heat wave has hit us again, and before the day has got under way one is aware of a steady brilliance, of the comfortable *safety and reliability* of the fine weather. Golden warmth, no wind, silence. Flickering white butterflies. From the far side of the hedge the low 'Quoi, quoi, quoi' of ducks.

(Julia's Diary)

September 3rd, 1955. Newcastle. I have been thinking about rather an interesting subject—that is: what connection there is between a person's mood and its context. The basic moods of characters in literature—their temperaments, whether sanguine, jittery, lethargic or buoyant—how far are they explainable by circumstances?

Looking back on my own life, it seems to me that I have always had the most enormous struggle to stabilise my emotional states of mind. In my childhood and adolescence particularly, I was so frequently borne along on a tide of melancholy, which it was my occupation to delve into and grapple with. As a child, before I grappled, I merely passively allowed floods of tears to sweep over me—what else could I do? To wit, the day I had to leave Aunty Loo's lunch table, sick and weary from her rebuffs, which caught me in a weak and vulnerable moment. Her friend Gertrude Heaton-Ellis was there, and she smiled one of her charming affectionate smiles. I was quite unmanned and taken by surprise by this message from someone 'alive', imaginative and affectionate—as opposed to Loo's terrifying, mad, stony and unnatural presence.

(Julia to F.P.)

November 11th, 1955. I have completely and utterly disgraced myself, I realise, in having shelved my correspondence for so long. What was so undeserved was that your letters to me were so glorious, and stuffed full of goodness as an egg is full of meat, as old Scotch Nan used to say. Now this is why: for *ages* now I have been in a perfect fever and frenzy of *frustrated* attempts to be allowed to do my own writing. What could stop my writing, indeed, you ask yourself? Well, Frances, if you saw what the end of the summer term here was like, with the entertaining of outside examiners and others, and in between whiles Lawrence taking to his bed with exhaustion, and having to be waited on hand and foot in the bedroom with his trays. Very well! Our maid Peggy suddenly got the high strikes, and told me off about having too much work to do, and "why did I not do a hand's turn in the house to help her?" A new lady, Mrs. Ferguson, is coming tomorrow instead of Peggy. Of course I shall have to spend the first week running up and down and in and out showing her how we like everything done; well then the second week Mrs. Ferguson's twins will have fallen ill and she will have to stay at home to nurse them; the third week Mrs. Ferguson herself will fall ill; during the fourth week I shall be ill; during the fifth Lawrence will be ill, and so on and so forth.

Our new plan for living: we are staying up here, *in situ*, trying to get some work done. But we greatly hope that that will not deter you from inviting us to Ham Spray, any time you might happen to feel in the mood. So *do* ask us in the Xmas Vac!

(F.P.'s Diary)

April 4th, 1956. Looking back over the last few months we seem to have taken a hand almost incessantly in the affairs of others. Now it has been the Gowings and Campbells. Not long ago Julia suddenly got into action and rang up Mary to ask if they could go there as P.G.'s for the Easter vacation. Hearing this was no go until after Easter she rang me up and invited herself somewhat dictatorially here. The sad thing was that neither Ham Spray nor Stokke was dying to receive them. Mary and Robin have had almost no time alone, and the last visit of the Gowings, six weeks long, had taxed them severely. "Julia began coming into my kitchen, and I can't bear that." But out of the goodness of her heart, Mary said Yes. Then Julia made her fatal mistake and wrote Mary a letter which made us all roar with laughter, but also hurt Mary deeply, saying how Lawrence needed "heaped plates, schoolboy style, plenty of green vegetables, mounds of cabbage, quantity more important than quality" and ending (as Ralph thought most tactlessly of all) "silence means consent". Mary began to dread the visit, and get crosser and crosser about the letter. Meanwhile, during their visit to Ham

Spray, Julia came into *my* kitchen and was all remorse and contrition, indeed in such distress that I confined myself to saying I thought they should either accept the Stokke way of life or not go there. In most ways, she loves it better than anywhere else. Well, poor Julia paid for her thoughtlessness by a very bad night, and in the morning wrote an excellent letter of apology, which Lawrence took over to Stokke in person.

Julia's mental processes are an unfailing source of interest and surprise. After four years of marriage, Lawrence gives her a good testimonial. He is a dear, good fellow, and delights one by his joyful, boyish laugh at Julia's characteristic sallies—as when she described Quentin as "a golden-hearted copy-cat".

(Julia to F.P.)

November 8th, 1956. Newcastle. It was nice, and comforting, to see your 'blue paw' stretched out on the doormat in all this clatter of 'dementia and doom',* to quote you all the way. Well, my dear, I was just going to stretch out *my* paw for the very same reason. We are like you deeply depressed. I don't think there is real justification for all those ghastly feelings of hate and bitterness that well up in one (in me, anyway) when one contemplates all the villains of the piece, and I'm sure it will do no-one any good to let them out. But of course the great thing that has shaken and moved us in your letter is your news about Ralph's health.† Dearest Frances, it has been absolutely desolating and crushing for you; I go through the whole thing in imagination. Now I shall shut up all my prissy pep-talk and give you some news:

Bells. Olivier has no nursemaid of any sort, and her two children (brought up in the modern way whereby they are never never corrected or told to pipe down) are *always* sprawling all over her lap and bawling at the tops of their voices whenever I go to see her. Not one word of sense can be said, because it literally can't be *heard!*

Another excitement in this house has been reading Joe Ackerley's little book *My Dog Tulip*, which though entirely about dogs and bitches is a veritable little marvel of brilliance and shockingness. I don't know when I read anything so indecent, disgusting, touching, beautiful and stylish; I do fervently recommend it. Now I am telling all the tweedy,

---

* The Suez Crisis.
† He had had his first of several heart-attacks.

philistine old crabs up here to read this sweet book about a man and his loyal doggy, and revelling in the idea of their scarification as they proceed. Will you give Ralph a great many messages from me? Please convey to him the utmost desolation we felt at hearing about his ill-health.

(F.P.'s Diary)

December 31st, 1956. The first day for some time that Ralph and I have been ALONE together, and the fact is we absolutely *love* it.

Julia, Lawrence and Burgo came for Christmas and stayed until the 27th. It was a muffled affair, kept at a slow, safe pace, and as such it chugged along pretty well, though much too cold for Julia, who sat in two jerseys, tweed jacket and fur coat in our hot music-room. In other ways, too, she made us well aware of her criticisms and displeasures, but we were forewarned and had our mental macintoshes on. True, she got under my skin one day by lecturing me about not understanding my own oven; however the vast turkey turned out very succulent and was washed down by champagne. Also I had two confidential and very friendly walks with her. She is unhappy, suspects herself of being 'melancholic', has no energy, and wakes up in deep gloom each morning. When Lawrence goes to America for two months in the Spring she feels she can't stay in Newcastle. "I would almost die of depression and never get up in the mornings." In fact she really hates Newcastle, can't bear to go out, or even look out of the window; can't write at all and hates the household commitments. I advised her to go and see another doctor and discover if it's really a good thing for her to take luminol every night, and 'purple hearts' for her depression. I feel very sorry for her indeed—a woman with nothing tangible to complain of, yet so desperately unhappy.

(Julia to F.P.)

March 29th, 1957. A splendid letter from Lawrence* awaited me at the flat. Enthusiastic about New York, and meeting all the nobs; and he says it is so comforting and glorious to be in a place which is a going concern. Undoubtedly, should he be offered a job at one of the Art schools or universities, he would jump at it. So I now realise, *finally*, that

---

* Lawrence spent two months in America, during which Julia paid a long and very successful visit to Ham Spray.

I shall never be able to lead the quiet country life in a nice home of my own with a studious painter working in the next room, which is the only way I can do any work myself. Lawrence is a nomad, a sort of Julius Caesar, and it's eternally up stakes and at 'em, so to speak. I feel very dismal, as vacation begins at the end of June, and then it'll be up stakes again and back to London, of all impossible places, and spend July there. He's off painting landscapes at present. How I regret our lovely quiet days at Shalbourne.

(F.P.'s Diary)

July 21st, 1957. Heywood Hills and Gowings for the weekend. Julia complained of last week's Memoir Club, particularly of Bunny [Garnett]'s deadly slowness and complete absorption in his own preoccupations, 'as in a glass bell'. All of which is true, but I love him and enjoy his company in spite of it. Julia said he filled her with horror, but then she is probably the most censorious woman alive. I think her dissatisfaction with her life, which doesn't falter or slacken for a moment, is beginning to get Lawrence down. He has done everything he can to give her security and happiness and time to write in—yet *nothing* fully pleases her. The truth is that the dissatisfaction is meant for herself, but has to be externalised on to the outside world. For nearly thirty years she has been telling herself that she can't write because she has too much cooking to do, never sees the sun or goes to bed early enough. It's farcical in a way, but cannot be to anyone who suffers her endless complaints. I took her for a walk on Saturday morning with the object of letting her vent some of them, and out they all came. After some time she said: "I know one can't have everything in this life and I've chosen Lawrence." I asked what her idea of a perfect life would be. "Great wealth" was the first necessity; perhaps "a house in the country, but Lawrence is set on a teeny thatched cottage, and that I couldn't abide." He felt that Stokke was his spiritual home, and Julia thinks (rightly I believe) that he blames its being impossible now on to Julia's tactless behaviour over the green vegetables. But both Ralph and I thought she returned from our walk in a sunnier and less acidulated frame of mind.

(Julia to Robert Kee)

August 15th, 1957. All right, Robert—I'll have a shot at the Beckett.* I shouldn't think there's a more difficult fellow to assess though anywhere on the globe. I suppose that's what makes it attractive. As a matter of fact, why do you not do it yourself? I'd much rather see your piece on him than do one myself. Go on—Do.

We've just had the Partridges staying here. At last—after six years—they decided to come up and have a look. They were the perfect visitors, seeming enthralled in every least detail of everything—every old Northern dog and cat in the streets was marked and inwardly digested. How I wish we could hold high carnival here with open house to all friends. Because we'd greatly like to welcome *you* here. But of course it's simply a grim workshop where we have high tea at 6 o'clock and drop into bed, done for, at ten each night—and also no-one can afford the fare, which is all of four pounds.

(Julia to F.P.)

November 6th, 1957. Newcastle. I was most grateful to get a line from you. As you know, Lawrence and I are dog-kennelled and space-suited in our teeny sputnik here, so feel out of things as a result. I think one must face up to the fact that one is living in a different country; hence I am staying firm up here until the Christmas holidays, so shall miss you both, which I do very greatly regret.

We have been very social up here, in that we seem to have had a steady stream of lecturers, for whom we gave numerous dinner-parties. The last two were K. Clark and Stephen Spender. K.'s visit was a trial. He is so glassy (*and glossy*), and 'U', and brilliantly urbane on his own ground, without taking the faintest interest in the lives or words of anyone around him. Thus—as symptoms only of this non-humanity that emanates ice-berg-wise out of his every pore—he not only did not once ask after Lawrence's painting but did not once refer to anything to do with our lives here. It was the same with Olivier and Quentin. In his bread-and-butter letter he said that the visit had been too short, and was like a "transatlantic telephone call", which was a capital description of how it had seemed, and I picture that he must go all through life

* Robert Kee was literary editor of *The Spectator* and had asked Julia to write a piece on Samuel Beckett, which she did.

aware of this unsatisfactory long-distance remote-control element, but never tumbles to the fact that it is all his doing. Nevertheless—Clark remains one of my favourite writers. I adore his ideas, which I suppose are essentially literary and philosophical, and not visual ones.

Stephen Spender was the same adorable good doggy that he always is—a sheepdog of the old-fashioned breed, a sofa-sized 'Nana' as in *Peter Pan*. And the joy of him is that underneath his tangled cerebrations and his golden heart is an extremely sharp and perceptive and laconic slapstick artist; one half of him is struggling to rid himself of a heavy burden of social and political guilt, while the other is an imaginative and entertaining debunker. What a Punch and Judy show we do all of us make, to be sure!

(Julia to F.P.)

January 26th, 1958. I had promised myself to write you a full and colourful description of our Xmas holiday, when I received this fearful *coup de téléphone* telling me that Oliver was dangerously ill with pernicious anaemia, and the whole Strachey tribe had gone down like ninepins with flu; I hadn't the face, or heart really, to allow that to go on, so I turned right round and went down south again for a fortnight. Oliver is now considered to have 'turned the corner', and the Stracheys are beginning to stumble to their feet again. It reminds me of a French poem Aunt Dorothy used to make me recite as a child, in the manner of the Comédie Française:

"Hjalmar se soulève entre les morts sanglants . ." (which I always tended to continue with "tenant en son bec un fromage"*).

And now, about Oliver, I dread going into all the pathos and horror, but will just say that I was reminded of the Rake's Progress. Those four bottles of neat whiskey a week, which he has accustomed himself to consuming, had resulted in his system being unable to manufacture Vitamin B12—in other words developing pernicious anaemia. This has been cured by injections. But Marjorie and Pippa, when they hear the word "Vitamin" think it refers to some modern quack religion like Mrs. Besant or Nudism, so they wouldn't believe me when I told them what the disease really was. I do think I have got a most *inhuman* family! Does everyone?

* La Fontaine.

(Julia to F.P.)

April 20th, 1958. Newcastle. After we left Ham Spray we had a quiet and pleasant week in London. Duncan rang up from across the road, and came over for a drink, as (deceptively) and engagingly soft and sweet as ever. We saw that furrowed autumnal leaf of the rustling silken voice, Adrian Stokes;* he seems a figure out of some other age and time—an ancient Druid perhaps, and I really can't picture living in a domestic way with him for six long weeks, as we have planned to do. I had rather an interesting visit to Pippa [Strachey], who has just been honoured in the House of Commons, and publicly presented with Henry Lamb's portrait of her, together with a large fish-footman's envelope containing a hundred and fifty pounds in notes. And why? Because, it appears, the men of England are undyingly grateful to her for having achieved equal pay for the sexes. Then I went to see Oliver of course. This was one of the most ruinous interviews I have as yet had with him. He greeted me with a face scarlet with Anglo-Indian rage, and behaved throughout as Victorian sugar-planters did to their blackamoors. He is, alas, fearfully confused in his head, to put it no higher than that, and at one point informed me that "his daughter Julia, who used to support him, never came to see him any more". However, "let us pass away from that" (as Oliver kept saying to me whenever I started a new topic). He said this so often that he soon shortened it to "Pass away!", "Pass on!" or just "Pass!" Well, I must go down and deal with Sunday lunch now, so "Pass!"

(Julia to F.P.)

July 7th, 1958. Newcastle. This is only a note to let you know that my letter will be coming from *Italy* whither we go the day after tomorrow. I had no visit to London in the end, as Lawrence really needed me up at Newcastle at his long end-of-term functions. His friend the economist Lionel Robbins, also Fuchs (if you'll forgive the name) of Arctic Geophysical fame, were both given doctorates, and Lawrence had to be present with bell, book and candle, and long Great Agrippa robes. Then there were hundreds of student parties and so on. Yes, Mary did indeed find us the house, which belongs to Kitty Godley's aunt, Signora Scafalti, and we're sharing with Adrian Stokes as I think I told you. It

* Painter and writer.

sounds too perfect. But I dare say the whole thing is just a hoax, and we shall find ourselves on a great autobahn in a rabbit hutch, and simply hating it.

FOR YOUR EAR ALONE—things to come may be shaping themselves very differently indeed next Spring—we shall know either way in September, when Lawrence is being interviewed by the London County Council about taking up the principalship of Chelsea Art School next year. Fearfully exciting if he does get the job, and we come south. I should then look for a country rectory in all seriousness, where Lawrence would join me at weekends. I shall write you a proper letter from Torridi-Benaco, Verona, where we shall be from 14th July onwards.

[The horrors awaiting poor Julia in the Italian house exceeded even her expectations. I had two letters from her—the first consisting of *fourteen* pages of closely packed, detailed despair; it is only possible to give an idea of it by a few disjointed extracts:

"It has really been rather rough going. Lawrence set off from England at the last gasp of exhaustion . . . Driving the car on the Continent appears to be most exacerbating for the nerves, and Adrian Stokes too is a whirling inferno of persistent anxiety . . . There were words and strained tempers . . . Our house was a ghastly English Wordsworth cottage with heavy black beams, chocolate woodwork and all light kept out by a thick Virginia creeper . . . filled with surly workmen, plaster and buckets of paint in every room . . . nothing to cook with, no electric light, no note or message from the Signora . . . A shattering heat wave . . . mosquitoes and flies . . . Then Adrian, who behaved like a perfect fool, of *course* got ill, with a high temperature . . . I kept Lawrence away, so I was the only person to catch it . . . Finally I saw the doctor who gave me antibiotics and kept me incarcerated like a sick dog in a kennel. Italy is awful in August."]

BREAKFAST IN PERCY STREET

I had been aware of Lawrence leaving the bedroom some time before I was properly awake. When I finally came to, the flat was silent. I got out of bed and went to draw the curtains. The daylight fell on the dressing-table, on powder boxes and glass bottles, and lingered on an enormous bunch of keys surrounded by a lake of silver and copper coins, a pipe, matchboxes, and a tube of throat lozenges.

I went into the sitting-room, where the cloth was already laid for breakfast on the folding table. Early May, but cold. The peace of our attic sitting-room was partly due to its thick carpet and the society of potted plants, partly to the pictures of hills and woods surrounding the walls.

Stretched out along the carpet under the electric fire lay something that looked like an empty hot-water-bottle cover, made of black plush. "So Fishman is here already," I murmured, shifting back the chair the better to see her. The white tip of a tail and four white paws were curling and uncurling rhythmically, in the manner of white water-lily buds fluctuating on some deep swinging tide. Fishman was the cat from next door; she belonged to the family of a waiter who worked in the restaurant opposite, and visited our flat daily, treading her way along the broad stone parapet that ran outside the top floor windows down the full length of Percy Street. I watched our black visitor for a few minutes in silence.

A blast of wildly gay, thunderous dance-music suddenly hit the flat through the open sitting-room door. It was half past nine, and the mops and buckets of the cleaners of the cinema below us were already under way. Every morning somebody, the head cleaner perhaps, switched on the same records—designed for Titan robots to dance to by the sound of it. Through habit or association of ideas, I bethought myself of my overall and blue rubber gloves, and automatically rose and went into the kitchenette, accompanied by the cat.

If an action is abominable enough and yet inevitable, if one is cast for the role of both victim and agent—as for instance, let us say, in the case of a Japanese soldier about to commit hara-kiri, or a thinking and fastidious person on the point of washing up, there comes a moment when all normal apprehensions and impressions have to be switched off like a light, so that the victim, already as good as dead, can fling himself mindlessly upon his agonising task. And so it was with me at nine-thirty on Thursday morning when faced with Wednesday night's washing-up in the kitchen sink.

I worked away.

"Art is NOT an enlargement but a concentration! Degas said so."

These words, spoken loudly and with a certain triumph, as of someone scoring a winning point in a rather tricky argument, came from the small doorway connecting the kitchenette with the bathroom. I looked up from the sink in surprise. There stood Lawrence in his pyjamas, a mask of shaving-soap surrounding his eyes and rendering them unintelligible. He had evidently been capping some discussion taking place inside his head.

A few minutes later the door to the tiny kitchen was blocked by the figure of Lawrence himself. He waved a piece of toast back and forth in the air to fan the steam out of it as was his custom, while with his free hand he made pencil notes on the pages of an open journal propped up on the plate-rack over the sink.

"I've done all the toast now," he told me.

"Oh, you should have let me do it." I knew he had to attend a board meeting of the directors of his art school.

"I didn't want to wake you," Lawrence said, "but I've left the eggs for you to do while I go and dress . . ."

First thing in the morning, before donning his public face, and with his long black hair flying from around his head, like snakes trying to escape, and his large loose mouth fantasticating songs or gibberish, Lawrence presented a bacchic effect. He might have been a member of a pagan rout streaming through the woods of some Italian painting.

"Where is Fishman?" I asked, as I laid the plates and knives on the table.

"I don't know. I haven't seen her."

It was my belief that Lawrence had never positively succeeded in seeing Fishman in his life, but knew of her existence only from hearsay, although she spent her days wandering around the flat, nibbling the potted plants or sniffing the bottles of varnish and linseed oil in his studio, and snoozing for long hours in the armchairs. More than once I had seen him absently sit heavily down upon Fishman when she had been in one of those chairs, and even after all the ensuing disharmony, squirming and squawks as she extracted herself with a mighty effort from under him, I judged that Lawrence was unaware of what had happened.

"You sat on the cat, Lawrence!!"

"What?"

"That was the *cat*—the CAT! Why did you?"

"I didn't see it."

I knew this was true. Ever on the lookout for signals of a totally different order from those for which most people keep watch—his mind absorbed with 'tone-values', 'multi-focal linear perspective' or 'black-upon-black'—Lawrence decoded the messages received by his senses in a way unlike that of other folk. I had come to the conclusion that the ordinary concept 'cat' was missing from his spiritual vocabulary. The same, at times, applied to such things as suitcases, film-stars etcetera, depending on the circumstances or rather upon the fall of the light.

As for me, I was constantly watching the cat. Not that that was an easy thing to do. For a feline on the prowl observes an obscure Stygian silhouette as much as possible. Usually the first sign of her arrival in the morning was a black, lacquered glitter, eeling in and out between the legs of chairs and tables, keeping mostly in shadow. Then, from underneath a chair perhaps, there would poke out a black face with frantic dazzling yellow eyes, and a blunt nose embowered in a white jet-spray of sickle-shaped whiskers, and withdraw again immediately.

I laid out the breakfast plates and the cutlery. Now I put down the marmalade and the apricot jam on the table. The telephone rang and I sped away.

Lawrence was shaking something out of his shoe when I returned. I asked him how he would like his egg cooked.

"I'll have a figurative egg."

"What d'you mean—scrambled?"

"NO! Not a *tachiste* egg—streaking all over the toast and everywhere!"

"Well, what's a figurative egg?"

"Why, poached, of course!"

I went out to the kitchen, pondering this, but at the door turned back to say: "A real figurative egg is a boiled egg, surely?"

"Never!"

"What, then?"

"I'd like one with a static inside shapeliness undisturbed by elaborate gesture."

"You mean a kind of neo-classical egg?"

"Could be . . ."

Breakfast ready, I smiled at Lawrence's transformation as he made his entrance. He was now fully attired in his disguise as civil servant, all set up for the Committee Meeting—hair plastered flat beyond imagining (at least for those familar with the original material). A pair of executive spectacles on his nose, black leather brief-case under his arm, and a rolled umbrella in his hand.

Aware of my eyes fixed on him trance-like, he smiled at me as he took his seat at the breakfast table:

"I expect you're admiring my fine line of quivering Establishment fruit!" he remarked cheerfully, helping himself to toast and butter. Where had the bacchic roisterer of a few moments before gone now?

Fishman was no longer asleep. Aware of my presence now she rolled over on to her back, then opened her neat triangular mouth in a yawn, and gave me a gooseberry yellow upside down stare.

"Hallo, Fish!"

Long centuries since, Fishman's ancestors had bequeathed her a legacy—a life spent hunting mice, and there was no opting out of it. Unfortunately there *were* no mice in our top floor flat. All the Percy Street mice had congregated on the ground floors and basements, where numerous little delicatessen shops and restaurants kept them busy and happy. Furthermore I had been told by old Mrs. Jopson, the solicitor's wife in the flat below ours, that Fishman had never seen a single mouse in her life, having been born up there under the chimney pots, and lived all her life—kitten and cat—without once being allowed out of the front door of her owner's flat.

Yet she was forced to obey the ancient laws that none can counter, and hunt mice. And so she did. She hunted them in the broom cupboard, under the wardrobe in the bedroom, under stacked canvasses. But especially in our bathroom. She simply took what she could get—in this case potential mice—Rodent Presences—and became engrossed by them to the point of addiction. She spent hours with these latent spectres every day.

I was warmly attached to Fishman, and for all of this I had especial sympathy. I knew well the panic of feeling the phenomenal world bonded on to myself, and I sympathised with the cat for being adrift in the wrong frame of reference as it were, a creature inscribed, stamped and posted to the wrong address.

"I have to hop off now or I shall be late," croaked Lawrence, getting up from the table and making for the door. Breakfast was over.

Chapter Seventeen

A COUNTRY LIFE

Including Julia's *SNOW IN LAMBOURN*

[Soon after the Gowings' return from Italy, Lawrence was appointed Principal of Chelsea Art School. This necessitated yet another change of habitat. The Newcastle house was given up; the Percy Street flat, small as it was, became their working base in London, and they hunted for a country house in the Southern counties for weekends and vacations: this was something Julia had never owned, and she pinned many day-dreams on the prospect.

A house was soon found in Lambourn, Berkshire, not far from their wartime retreat at Chilton and within easy reach of Ham Spray. The move took place in December 1958. Lambourn was, and still is, a centre of horse racing, and something between a village and a small town. Several famous stables lie among the sweeping curves of the surrounding downs, along whose ridges run broad grass gallops. Weedy-looking stableboys slouch along its pavements, and a visitor in the front bedroom of Gordon House, which overlooks the street, will generally be woken at about 6 a.m. by the clip-clop of hooves passing the front door, and probably tumble out of bed for the pleasure of seeing the elegant animals go by, jockeys crouched on their backs and clouds of breath sprouting from their nostrils. These horses are the Royal Family of Lambourn; all cars draw in to the side of the road and wait respectfully as they cavort past.

Gordon House fronted the street a little soberly with pargetting and dark paint, but at the back it looked on to a largish, informal garden. True to type, in her first letter to me Julia regretted "our extremely comfortable, utterly warm Newcastle house." She soon began to take a passionate interest in birds and plants, tables of crumbs, weeding and watering, but the effect on her writing was curiously unstimulating and her imagination took time off. A daily help fortunately presented herself. Mrs. Rose was small and neat, white-haired and old-fashioned, and soon became a devoted retainer. The sessions Julia spent with her in the kitchen were largely for the pleasure of her company: she observed Mrs. Rose as delightedly as she did the garden thrushes, and noticed that when working she kept up a birdlike sound known as 'Mrs. Rose's tuneless whistle'.

Later on, when the death intestate of Julia's Aunt Dorothy Bussy resulted in many legal complications, the Strachey family asked Lawrence to go out to Roquebrune and value Simon Bussy's paintings, in his studio there. They were to set out in December, 1960.]

(Julia to F.P.)

February 5th, 1959. Lambourn. All our little doings at Lambourn bulk so large that they obscure the outer view. Nevertheless you will want to hear something of them, I dare say. The change from our extremely comfortable, utterly warm Newcastle house was devastating indeed. Lawrence's doctor says the shock of breaking off his life up there has lowered his resistance psycho-somatic-wise, and it is certainly true that he has been deeply upset, unhappy and worried about leaving the old life and parachuting into the blue.

Here, *none* of the chimneys were functioning; there wasn't a single room one could be warm in, and I don't think I've ever seen anything so awful as our ruinous attics and roof. My first sight of them, when (alone here) I went up with a torch on a snowy night, was a great shock. Water and snow were dripping through as in a grotto, and loathly swollen-up woodlice were fumbling around in the crevices, annoyed at being awakened. When I thought of escaping to London for a breather in the civilised world Lawrence almost burst into tears, and said someone must stay in the house and cope, or the pipes would all freeze up. But I have felt rather dismally *solitary* in the whole affair. Having gruelled you with these horrors I will now tell you that things are already ever so much better. My daily, Mrs. Rose, is *awfully* nice, and is of course the great mainstay of my life.

(Julia to F.P.)

March 3rd, 1959. Your letter was very interesting. The main point that affected me being what you said about the saving curtain of unreality and remoteness, and the pain of it being lifted. You are going through a

JULIA

grim time I realise—I read between the lines as best I can: I have to with you!*

I am still finding it difficult to think of this strange house and garden as my home—I'm still the visitor from Mars. It has been a major transplantation, really. Four days of each week Lawrence is away, and then the eternal silence and frozen loneliness is somewhat numbing. I get a sensation that I have lost my identity; but Lawrence seems to adore it all, which is a marvellous relief. Otherwise the birds in our garden and the visiting cats are the most life-enhancing characters on the stage.

(F.P.'s Diary)

September 3rd, 1959. At the Gowings last night, Julia was in her relaxed, informal mood, with her Mrs. Rose cooking the dinner. Three hours' steady talk and then we took our leave. Only this morning did Ralph and I get down to discussing Julia's philosophy of life and character, which had been weaving their way to the surface of my dreams. I find it strange that though she takes such a high line about values in general, she often talks as if, to her, the most important thing abut a person is the façade with which they confront the world—dress, appearance, social manner. Discussing X, she made no bones about her view that the 'dowdiness' and choice of unbecoming spectacles was her gravest offence. How wonderfully Lawrence has adapted himself to Julia's point of view, with his own accent added. Last night he said, with a faint comical twist to his face: "Julia feels that *not* to make yourself as attractive as possible is one of the worst crimes—and she's particularly sensitive in the matter of spectacles, which she understands so fully herself." He is like some wonderful Diaghilev, with Julia as Nijinsky; he steers her away from dangerous topics, both,to support her and to give a special emphasis to her remarks—'produces' her, in fact.

The Gowings had dined at Stokke during the weekend, and when I asked Mary [Campbell] how it had gone she said: "Not well, really. I think Julia was *bored*. She was very tart, which I don't mind when we're alone, but I don't like with visitors." Julia's account, on the telephone, confirmed that she had been bored. Mary, she said, had "gone on as if

* Ralph's health was worrying me, and indeed soon after suffered a severe set-back.

she was Kenneth Clark, saying which pictures one ought to like in no uncertain voice."

"It's clear that she's in Julia's doghouse," I said to Ralph.

"Julia's got an outsize doghouse," was his comment, "it includes almost everybody from Great Danes to Pekingese!"

How can one convince her that it is a purely relative matter where one draws the plimsoll-line of condemnation, and that if you find the whole of humanity falls below it you have simply made a mistake and drawn it too high. And are probably below it yourself.

(F.P.'s Diary)

November 29th, 1959. Jolly evening at the Gowings last night. Julia is very set up because her *Animalia** has been enthusiastically accepted by the *New Yorker.* Lawrence just as delighted, and Julia's censoriousness was in abeyance.

SNOW IN LAMBOURN

During a snowy spell at Lambourn, I set out one Sunday morning to call upon the woman who supplies us with eggs.

The egg-woman, Miss Smith, lived on the far side of the village. Sunday was the only time to catch her, for on weekdays—although herself an old age pensioner—she 'took off' in her late father's plaid overcoat and old jockey-cap with the peak sticking far out over her nose, to work at the almshouses. She mended the old people's clothes and cleaned their rooms; did not return till after dark. Miss Smith as it happened had no roof to her mouth and was also deaf. I began to feel the lightly joking conversation I had planned, about the strange noises made by the local bell-ringers, might not go off too easily after all. But *some* pleasant and not too serious opening could surely be managed before I turned the talk around, to enquire casually why the whites of the eggs she had lately been sending to our house had all changed, when boiled, to a dark and stormy battleship grey? We could then discuss what could be done about it.

That January morning snow was everywhere. I put on my warmest

* This was a paper written for the Memoir Club, which I (then its secretary) had extracted from her by main force. The *New Yorker* printed it as *Can't You Get Me Out Of Here?*

outdoor clothes, piling on everything I found hanging on the pegs in the boot-room. Finally I pulled on my gum-boots, still wet from yesterday, and off I set, crunching my way along the road. The thought came to me that if I were to stick my head into the big refrigerator in my kitchen at home it would feel something like this. For there was no light out of doors this morning: an arctic fog hung in the air, hiding everything. It took a little time to recognise the silhouettes of the cottages looming through the turnip-soup fog. The new council house, for example, and the willow tree on the river bank, whose old arching trunk had died and tumbled over into the water—all were mere shadows. And there was the same acute numbness of my nose, forehead and cheeks as there would be were I being savaged by my large fridge at home.

Arrived at Miss Smith's gate, I found pinned to it a pencilled notice saying that she was up at the almshouses this Sunday morning. But I was much too cold to care where she was. I turned round and followed the path that circled the village, heading for home. Next door to the house of our daily help—the ancient and greatly beloved Mrs. Rose—stood the cottage belonging to her greatest friend, ginger-haired Mrs. MacDonald. And as I passed Mrs. MacDonald's garden, now white and formless under a blanket of snow, I caught sight of a being in the garden whom I had heard much about from Mrs. Rose, but had never yet met—Mrs. MacDonald's Abyssinian cat. Here she was at long last!

She was standing alone in the middle of the snow-humped garden, facing in my direction and with her tail held upright and stiff as a ramrod. I halted on the path opposite Mrs. MacDonald's garden. At once the cat came running towards me, total stranger that I was. There was an urgency in her manner that made plain she had something of great import to ask me. But she was suddenly brought up short by the wire fence at the end of the garden. She stood there nonplussed; then she tilted up her prim oriental face, with her eyes fixed urgently upon me in a round, electric goosegog stare. At the same time her mouth opened wide, but silently. Opened and shut once more, but with an emotion so violently passionate that, soundless though the phantom mewings were, each one shook the cat's body through and through. It was like watching a desperately-roaring tiger, caught behind sound-proof glass.

What *did* that cat want?

She was plainly calling for help, felt herself in some disastrous predicament or extremity. The garden door was open into Mrs. MacDonald's kitchen, so she had not been shut out. Just a step or two—and inside the cottage was warmth.

Strange!

It couldn't have been a protest then against icy, aching paws. So what could be the trouble? I waited a minute or so, but what could I possibly do? I walked off home.

Back in my house I went straight to the kitchen, and recited the whole incident to Mrs. Rose. "Mrs. MacDonald's cat looked *so* upset there in the snow!" I added.

The old lady, tiny as an elf but still very handsome, did not answer. She seldom did; she 'kept herself to herself', as was her habit. She pushed aside a colander full of sprouts on the kitchen table, evidently to make room for something else.

I chattered on: "I don't blame her, I must say. Going by the pain in my own nose and ears, her paws must have felt excruciatingly cold."

Mrs. Rose bent down, opened the oven door behind her; in complete silence she took out the baking-tin with its half-roasted chicken and set it on the table. Then, "It wasn't only *that*, you see," she said unexpectedly. The old lady reached for the hollow glass rod resembling a thermometer, dipped it in the steaming gravy and began to baste the bird.

"You know, madam," she continued after a moment, her handsome face grim as it looked down at the chicken: "when a cat is accustomed to Doing its Business out on the grass or flower-beds, or among the green leaves and all—you understand what I'm talking about, madam?"

"I do. I do. A cat accustomed to 'do it' on the grass?—"

"Yes. Well, when they are trained properly for *that*, they can't do it anywhere else. Must have the green to be right for it. But after this snow it's all white. And the *white* is *wrong* for it."

"The white is wrong for it," I repeated thoughtfully.

"Yes, madam. They don't know what to do with theirselves—every *blooming* thing is white! It's pitiful."

"Pitiful," I echoed. "It is," said Mrs. Rose as she went on basting the chicken.

(F.P.'s Diary)

January 1st, 1960. Julia has taken on a new lease of life from her success with the *New Yorker*, looks blooming, is alert and lively. We discussed the New Year Honours, and whether Lawrence would accept a knighthood if offered one. "No," he said, "why should people have to preface my name with a little sibilant purr?"* Mrs. Rose in the kitchen was excited at having a 'television personality' (Robert Kee) to dinner. "Did you recognise him?" Julia asked her afterwards. "I didn't dare look at him," she replied.

(Julia to F.P.)

January 19th, 1960. Lambourn. I am a brute not to have written before.† But I'm not exaggerating when I explain that I've really nothing to say, except about the snow (so dreary), because our life is designed very carefully on the cork-lined study and white-kid-glove model. Meanwhile, since first mentioning the snow in this letter, it has mostly thawed. However I've stayed here in the country quietly, and let Lawrence go up to Percy Street alone. The dirt of the London flat terrifies me, and I do find all the chores gruelling. Catharine Carrington kindly rang up and offered to take me with her and Noel to see E. M. Forster's *A Passage to India*, made into a play at Oxford, but I couldn't be buggered—just gave an outlandish croak from my hole in the rocks and begged to be left quite alone.

(Julia to F.P.)

March 1st, 1960. Lawrence is awfully well, though struggling mightily and manfully against the L.C.C., and passing sleepless nights wondering how to persuade them that the Staff at his art school are useless and must go. "It's high time we saw those Partridges again!" he announced at breakfast one day last week—and I seconded the motion heartily. Do let us know as soon as you are back, we long to see you.

Oliver is in frightful trouble, oh dear, oh dear—behaved abominably, then broke his poor old leg, and has spent the last two weeks screaming at the top of his lungs like a—well, I'll make no comparisons. Pippa now blind. Marjorie's legs gone. Dorothy alone rides over Janie triumphant. What a world.

* Lawrence Gowing accepted a knighthood in 1982.
† We were spending the winter months in Spain, for Ralph's health.

(F.P.'s Diary)

April 8th, 1960. For the last few days I have been preoccupied by the emotions I experienced when listening to Mozart's Requiem; as I listened the music conveyed to me not only the splendour and tragedy of the universe, but also its acceptability, in a way that no impurer art than music can. Is there perhaps some special significance in the fact that a Requiem refers to the major drama of death, and so to life in its most essential form—the whiteness that is to be cancelled-out by the dense blackness of death?

On a walk with Julia yesterday we went over this same ground, though at the moment she seems to be weighed down by the hatefulness of the 'Cosmos'. "I think I've got melancholia," she said. "I'm so dissatisfied with everything." The Lambourn house is all wrong, she doesn't feel at home there and never will. When I pointed at the glades, carpeted with broad garlic leaves, leading down to a stream with white ducks on it, and suggested that while sight remained to one the universe was recognisably glorious, she agreed with alacrity. Though 'melancholia' doesn't seem the right word, Julia's state of mind is of course neurotic in face of her really fortunate position. (This of course I didn't say.) "I sometimes feel I'm living in a nightmare," she said, and I did for a second wonder if her mind was becoming unhinged.

A good Juliaism: (I wanted to buy some fish in one of her local shops.) "Oh yes; they have nothing grand, you know—only cod fillets, haddock, bream, and—what's it called?—Wadsworth."

"*Wadsworth,* Julia, what can you mean?"

"Oh well, I expect I must be thinking of that old painter Wadsworth: he's always seemed to have rather a fishy look!"

(F.P.'s Diary)

August 18th, 1960. Drove to Lambourn for a walk with Julia. As usual contact with her on neutral ground was far easier and better than it is either at her house or ours, and I delighted in her stimulating conversation. She talked a lot about her Strachey aunts, and was so absorbed in what she was saying that she led me in a number of small circles round the village of Lambourn, and was amazed to find herself constantly confronted by the church tower. Poor Julia, she was bursting with things she wanted to get off her chest.

This Spring there have died—in the following order—Janie and
Dorothy Bussy, Oliver. Dorothy died intestate, but Oliver did not, and
therefore his share of the 'Bussy inheritance' goes, according to his Will,
to his son Christopher, but not a penny to Julia or Barbara.* I felt
indignant when I remembered Julia's dutiful behaviour to him and his
lack of any solicitude for her. It is thought that the Bussys' house, La
Souco, at Roquebrune, may be worth quite a lot. Oliver's disinheri-
tance has been a hard blow, almost as much for psychological as
practical reasons—he never felt any responsibility for Julia, paid for
anything for her, and has now in death virtually disowned her.

She then went on to describe how difficult she finds it (intensely
critical as she is, and always wanting to mould her surroundings to her
liking) to come to terms with Lawrence's happy acceptance of them.
Though I think this attitude of his may be partly strategic—a means of
discouraging Julia's boundless appetite for house-decoration, which he
doesn't feel he can afford—the difference is there all right, and if two
people want to make a joint life together they must do better than just
paper the cracks. To treat it philosophically, in my own view it's not so
much the perceptible world that is so wonderful and adorable, as the
activity of the perceiver. But I don't think that would comfort Julia even
if she believed it. When I said I thought one must fight back at one's
troubles, "one couldn't just sit and suck them through a straw", she
was in perfect agreement; yet the obstacles to her writing, like not
having more household help, took her into a world of chimera. ("I
could die with envy of Proust and Virginia, my dear. They never had to
do *anything*.")

[On November 30th Ralph had his final, and fatal, heart attack. The
Gowings were among many friends who were boundlessly kind. They
suggested that I came with them to Roquebrune, where they were to
catalogue Simon Bussy's paintings. Meanwhile I spent a few days with
them at Lambourn, on one of which I found the following touching little
note on my breakfast tray:]

---

* Christopher and Barbara were the children of Oliver and Ray. The 'Bussy
inheritance' had to be divided into eleven shares. It included La Souco, a valuable
property on the French Riviera.

FRANCES. You really mustn't think in terms of kindnesses done in connection with our friendship, ever again you know!

For one thing, if that were the line, thinking of all the past kindnesses you have done me down my desolate years I should be at my wits' end to even up the score. But the fact is that you are a vital part of our lives—not only Lawrence's and mine, but also those of other devoted friends, Janetta, Robert and many more. When something happens to you it *literally* happens to us all, as you are a part of us for good or ill. And so you see we are determined it shall *not* be for ill.

(F.P.'s Diary)

December 17th, 1960. Roquebrune. I cannot write about these last seventeen days. It's been all I could do to live them. Ungrateful, though, not to mention the fabulous kindness of friends, which has altered my view of human nature. The Gowings and I left England by the Blue Train yesterday morning. Julia, wearing a deep extinguisher of a straw hat, hissed into my ear as we got into the Golden Arrow: "I *must* fight against my terrible desire to be taken for a millionaire duchess. Too shaming!" The usual speechless exhaustion overcame me about nine, not improved by the infernal racket of the dining-car. I saw that this worried poor Julia, who tried to get me to talk about wild-flower collecting. Lawrence is anxious for her to stop being anxious about me, and I'm already beginning to be anxious about making her anxious!

(F.P.'s Diary)

December 19th, 1960. Roquebrune. A hard day's work in Simon Bussy's dank mouldering studio. Lawrence enjoys his role as general, ordering Julia and me kindly about, dictating names and measurements of the pictures while striding about with a stalking movement like a large bird that seemed to be going to lay him flat on his nose at any moment, and making a running commentary, something like this: "A *marvellous* painter, *what* a marvellous painter! . . . This is simply terrible . . . Simon's sense of humour! . . . Grisly! . . . Ah, I see what it is, every bird or fish is a self-portrait."

(F.P.'s Diary)

December 22nd, 1960. Roquebrune. This morning Julia came into my room and said she would stay on here after Lawrence left until Clive [Bell] and Barbara [Bagenal] arrive at Mentone. I tried to protest but in vain, especially as tears welled up to fight against my protests.

(F.P.'s Diary)

December 31st, 1960. Roquebrune. Natural History of the Gowings: So long as Lawrence can arrange his day to allow of work, painting and plenty of sleep, he is the happiest man alive, with no desire for any changes.

Julia is of course in a perpetual state of dissatisfaction with her environment, in spite of all the intense pleasure she gets in watching cats, or in the ambience of this place, which has always been of special importance to her since her childhood visits to La Souco. She never forgets that *Cheerful Weather* was written here—the one place where life was run on oiled wheels and there were no obstacles to her writing. The first few days here she was day-dreaming about renting a villa here. She and I even went to look at one—a couple of tiny cell-like rooms with no amenities. Soon afterwards she announced that she had no desire whatever to live here.

[On January 12th, 1961, Julia returned to London, and I moved to a hotel on the front at Mentone, where I stayed until March, working on a translation.

While we were together at Roquebrune it came naturally to me to talk a good deal about what filled my mind—Ralph, my loss of him, and the past—and I did so, but this was a terrain Julia never embarked upon of her own accord, and I am quite sure she gave much thought to the subject and decided it was for the best: I must be encouraged to talk only of the future, and particularly about flats and houses, bathrooms and kitchens, country *versus* town. I found this disquieting and rather eerie, though I was deeply grateful for the Gowings' kindness, and also aware of myself as something of a street accident in their path. Nevertheless I missed their company greatly at Mentone; for the first time my loneliness rushed in upon me like a great draught of air. So that the long, affectionate letters she wrote me every week were a life-line in every sense. As they were largely concerned with my 'plans' however, together with bulletins concerning mutual friends, I have not included many extracts.]

(Julia to F.P.)

January 21st, 1961. Lambourn. Horrible about getting grippe! At the moment Raymond [Mortimer] will be with you; but after he goes will you be able to stand it? Don't forget that any moment you should have the impulse to fly there's a room here *always ready to receive you* . . . You really will consider a long stay with us, won't you? Making it your base, at any rate, and leaving all your things here. What news can I give you? Robin and Susan Campbell* brought their fortnight-old son William to lunch one day. The baby, when he did wake up to yawn and grimace restlessly, was like some énervé old intellectual bachelor, bored by the human scene and marking time till he should get back to his library and be lost to the world again.

My Aunts have now completely lost all interest in the Affaire Souco; didn't want even to hear what was going on. Marjorie greeted me with baffled rage and disgust, but it wasn't meant for me really, but for their German girl, who had failed to make the tea before going out, although she had left everything ready. I said:

"It's all right, Marjorie, don't worry! I'll have tea made in a jiffy."

"NO! No! YOU CAN'T! You don't understand the position!", tearing her hair and shrieking. Meanwhile Pippa, like a little old doubled-up bear, was hobbling purposefully through to the kitchen. I turned to Marjorie.

"Now look here, Marjorie, why on earth won't you let me boil the kettle and make tea?"

"OH! OH! OH! It's *impossible.*"

"But why?"

"Oh, because there's a kind of nozzle on the kettle—it's a WHIST-LING kettle!!" (this with a wild, demented look). "It has to come off when it boils and there are all *sorts* of complications!" I made tea as easy as winking of course. Oh là là, as they say in Roquebrune.

---

* Robin's wife, after his divorce from Mary.

(Julia to F.P.)

January 31st, 1961. Lambourn. I must confess that your letter, although apparently full of sordid horrors (that you were afraid might make me sick)—false teeth, chamber pots, berets with 'obsessional tails' and all the rest—was a riot of joy in the reading, and made me laugh till I fell off my chair. So there you are, you see, the alchemy of ART! seeing life through someone else's eyes has a magic in it, and I felt twice the man—or hag—after hearing about it all.

I suppose it is really impertinent to want to say something to a friend in real sorrow. Yet one can't help the desire, so forgive me for sending you an age-old chestnut from time to time. Such as: that even in those hours when desire for life absolutely fails, one still remembers surely that there are, objectively, things that are truly valuable and worthwhile, and the great thing is to get through the chasms between as best as possible—with the help of Irish whiskey by the barrel, or whatever suits your book.

(F.P.'s Diary)

May 18th, 1961. Lambourn. In the Gowings' spare bedroom, most kindly proffered and very nice too, as was Janetta's, even though I long to have one that is really my own. Heavenly peace here, though the weather has turned bitter cold. A walk with Julia, who had come out bemused with work, after a good session at her writing, and with writers' problems hanging in clouds around her. So that was what we mainly talked of, walking through the woods beside clumps of white violets. In the evening, a burlesque conversation in which Julia 'wrote off' various old friends, some for failing to measure up in the 'language of clothes', others for 'lack of awareness', or 'fundamental seriousness'. She does indeed live in a world of her own.

(Julia to F.P.*)

July 4th, 1961. Percy Street. Has it seeped through to you yet about the Sahara-like weather in which we are being grilled? On Sunday we endeavoured to take a picnic to Regent's Park. Hardly had we taken our first mouthfuls when thunder crashed and rain bucketted down in torrents. Lawrence was incurably happy and optimistic throughout, of

* Staying abroad with friends.

course. As he sat on his bench, mouth full of pie, thunder and lightning crashing round him, I heard him murmur reflectively: "Extraordinary.—Nice, though." I meanwhile was standing under a tree having quite given up all thought of food, mackintosh over my head and eyes closed, moaning.

I'm really enjoying my life on a desert island, not seeing a soul and trying not even to walk the streets of Lambourn or London more than strictly necessary. I really hate the world and all its ways, and the only time I feel serene is when shut up at home with a book—either someone else's or my own, and one can forget it all.

(F.P.'s Diary)

September 4th, 1961. Lambourn. I'm glad to be here with Julia and Lawrence. With my new little white car (dumpy, virginal, comic, engaging), and letters, and sorting out my life, I'm fairly well occupied. I am worried by Julia's meticulous attempts to forestall my desires —otherwise it's entirely relaxing and soothing here. Yesterday, there being too little light for Lawrence to paint, he sat in the arbour thinking about painting. As he sat looking into the woods it struck him that what he was seeing was much like the hollow half of a sphere, and he became obsessed by trying to work out how various geometrical shapes could be fitted into it—hexagons, for instance. So he rushed to the village toy-shop and bought a large child's ball *on appro*. I saw him sitting trying to fit hexagons on to its surface with a ballpoint pen. *They wouldn't go.* This discovery delighted him, though I can't remember why. He rubbed off the ink marks and returned the ball to the shop! When he told Julia at dinner how he had spent his afternoon, she stared at him as if she had never seen him before in her life.

I have much talk with them both about how to decorate my new London flat. Julia is of course perfectionist to an impracticable degree. If the colour of a wall is to be a setting for pictures it must be considered in relation to *each* of them. F: "But the walls have to be painted before the pictures come out of store." J: (looking horrorstruck) "Oh, that's *very* serious. Couldn't you have them taken out and sent up to London first?"

(F.P.'s Diary)

February 11th, 1962. Sitting alone in the Gowings' 'oak room', church bells cascading outside; it's nearly six o'clock. I've enjoyed being here, though uneasily worrying whether I'm *de trop*—Lawrence being in bed, and Julia anxious about him. Following on the headlines 'TICKLE IN LAWRENCE'S THROAT', we now have 'LAWRENCE'S NOSE DEFINITELY RED AND SORE.' The fuss that arises from such slight malaise has clouded the air, as well as keeping Julia on the hop up and down stairs with trays and preoccupations. We scurry to bed like shot rabbits as the clock strikes ten each night. Conversation centred largely upon writing, and some about female grievances—arising from Julia's reading Simone de Beauvoir's *Second Sex*. Groans emitted by an unsatisfied Lesbian who wishes to be man as well as woman are music in her ears. She feels women have a raw deal, and feels it so burningly that one must go easy when arguing with her. Then on to Art. Julia volunteered her definition of the aesthetic impulse as coming from the desire to glorify and preserve experience, with which I don't quarrel at all. I have enjoyed the spare beauty of February (not seen for the last five years since Ralph and I started wintering abroad). Trundled in the bus to Newbury under a grey sky, between leafless trees gently cooked brown at their tips, clumps of snowdrops amongst dark ivy leaves, streams brushed white by the wind, and the velvet texture of everything from horses and donkeys to the 'short pale grass'.

(F.P.'s Diary)

March 14th, 1962. Julia on the telephone, talking about poor old Pippa, nearly ninety, having 'a leg swollen to the thigh with arthritis' and unable to fend for herself or be fended-for at home. Julia has had to arrange for her to go into hospital today, but Pippa is resentful and looks bitterly at her. "It's always the same—Tommy used to be like that—the dog bites you as you are letting it out of the trap," says Julia.

(F.P.'s Diary)

April 21st, 1962. I went to the Gowings for Easter. On the Sunday there was a sudden marvellous explosion into Spring—it was literally almost stunning. I have a confused memory of two long walks with Julia over the rolling hills just bloomed with green, a pale misty blue sky above us, and a little negress, with woolly hair, and her black hands eagerly thrust among the white violets on a bank.

I had driven Bill Coldstream and his pregnant wife down, and Julia dealt manfully with her weekend party, provided splendid meals, and even rose to the occasion when Monica Coldstream told her in a sudden flood of tears that she had been having internal pains, and the poor things had to return to London. Julia spoke of the possibility of staying down at Lambourn two weeks running so as to get on with her writing. "But that means Lawrence leading a bachelor life in London, not a married life at all, and I don't like it." Another topic—the horror that the signs of age in herself filled her with. In vain I argued that age, though sad, was not obscene; in vain I told her how extraordinarily young for her age she looked—everyone thought so. "Well, I work hard for it, I can tell you."

Julia has taken the physicist's Universe under her wing; one mustn't say a word against it. It is a miracle.

"May one not criticise it *at all?*" I cried. "Must it be perfect in every detail?" Truth to tell, there is something both endearing and comic in her adoption of the starry spheres—entropy, Brownian movement, etcetera—as her special protégés, and she is always ready to lecture one about them, something in the manner of her aunts, and reminding me somehow of a dog walking stiffly on its hind legs with a lump of sugar on its nose. But no, Julia, NO, the Universe doesn't meet with my whole-hearted approval, any more than it really does yours.

(Julia to F.P.)

April 27th, 1962. Lambourn. How much we enjoyed your Easter visit, and how nice for me were the walks we took.

Looking back on the rather macabre remarks I must have seemed to be making, about covering up all signs of old age, I realise that you could not have understood from the way I was talking that I absolutely never *worry* about losing looks and growing old. I just 'accept' the fading into old age without question, and at the same moment I know that I would like to keep physical signs of it covered up as much as possible, on principle, and having decided that I never ponder the subject again. The fact is I have gone over completely to living in the mind—in books, and writings, pictures, in the imagination that is, which seems to me eminently the place to be during one's declining years. Digging myself up to gallivant to Venice* is not really an attractive proposition, for it will mean grappling with hordes of strangers and the 'world'. I don't really want to take part any longer in that fearful rough and tumble. Packing, spending hours on trains and waiting at airports—what a wearisome way to spend the time. I tell you all this rigmarole as I don't want to leave you with a false impression of my 'tragic outlook' on things; it's just that I'm happy and contented in my hole, and want to stay put. Forgive all this. Love from Toad-in-the-Hole.

(Julia to F.P.)

August 21st, 1962. Great thrill at Gordon House at the moment is that Lawrence has started painting Lord Attlee's portrait. He is a very poor sitter, fidgets no end and keeps dropping off to sleep, poor invalid —which he really is. But when Lawrence repeats his rewarding conversation I feel I was not wrong to place him on a pedestal in my Hall of Heroes. Clem and his wife live in a small semi-detached house with no help and no gardener. Lawrence gave a most comic description of the day they gave him lunch—Lady Attlee quite unable to cope (much like me), shelling the beans in the car, then bumping around like a cockchafer in the kitchen—everything out of tins, yet she was unable to open them. Finally Lawrence had to take over the lunch altogether. Afterwards they were so miserable about having no-one to clip their hedges and plant a tree a friend had sent them, that Lawrence took over *that* also.

We have redecorated the small writing-room where you used to work (and still will, I hope) and pride ourselves on a more Mediterranean ambience there. To be exact Lawrence left the whole thing to me, covering his eyes with his hands and groaning metaphorically. When I had finished it he declared it the finest room in the world, and vowed he'd never sit anywhere else in the house.

[In October, 1962, the pattern of the Gowings' life completely changed. Lawrence told Julia that he had fallen in love with a young teacher at his school and she with him. There is no sign in her letters that she had guessed, though the possibility must have occurred to her. She had

* A project which didn't materialise.

great powers of meeting crisis with altruism and this at first she summoned to her aid, telling herself and me that she was glad Lawrence had found a mate and that she liked Jenny. Everyone tried to behave considerately and sensitively, but the stress was bound to grow, and in the long run it spelt disaster for Julia and for the Lambourn ménage. The process was slow and agonising, though in the second of her two letters to me she wrote: "After the explosion, so to speak, when all the dust from the rubble had cleared away, I saw the new landscape clearly and the horror has gone. *I do realise, down to my very bones, that I can only be happy through Lawrence's happiness; this is not a pious aspiration but a practical fact.*"

The question of divorce and remarriage was soon raised but left without a definite answer.]

(F.P.'s Diary)

October 12th, 1962. Two letters from Julia have crashed into my consciousness. It is too awful what has happened, perhaps worse even than Julia realises, and I can hardly think of anything else, nor forgive myself for critical thoughts of her. Lawrence's proposition is that, since he will be taking nothing from Julia that she had before, they should have a *ménage à trois.* Poor Julia—what a shattering blow and shock. Her first letter was written in utter desolation; the second pulling herself heroically together, and saying that what makes Lawrence happy will make her also. She has met and likes the girl.

(F.P.'s Diary)

October 19th, 1962. My evening with Julia didn't materially alter the picture of the agonising situation, though accenting it with a few little painful stabs. I gave her the advice she had already picked out for herself—namely to let Lawrence and Jenny have all possible freedom —short of trying a *ménage à trois.* Julia's present fear is that Lawrence may defer the whole matter till the Christmas holidays, when he plans that he and Jenny should go abroad. She has asked me to go somewhere with her for Christmas, and of course I shall.

(F.P.'s Diary)

December 14th, 1962. On the eve of setting out for three weeks' married life with Julia,* I'm very well aware of the difficulties and sadness that lie ahead, and also full of humility and uncertainty about my appointed task.

(F.P.'s Diary)

December 19th, 1962. I have for three days been soaking in Julia's country peace, leaving behind the gas-ring of London life, on which I have been a simmering, bubbling pot. So far the change has been purely restorative, and everything is—I believe—going well. Julia has arranged the house so that almost nothing has to be done in the way of cooking, shopping, etc. Dear little old Mrs. Rose, piping away like a blackbird in the kitchen, cooks our lunch and leaves dinner ready—so that it usually consists of warmed-up meat, with warmed-up brussels sprouts and warmed-up mashed potatoes, followed by warmed-up mince pies! By this method, both of us get long hours of work, and take long brisk walks, favoured by brilliant cold days and the sensational English gloss on leaves, red berries and twigs.

Julia's new 'Goblin Teas-Made' might have been something out of one of her stories. I brought it down in my Mini, done up in three large Christmas-wrapped parcels, which when undone revealed a device combining an alarm clock with a kettle and a hideous square tea-pot with the spout at one corner. Julia spent hours putting it together and brooding lovingly over the instructions:

"Depress platform—now, what on earth can that mean? Oh, I suppose this is it, but it seems to be permanently depressed already. I see it's going to be *me* that's depressed, not the platform." When it was finally put together with the help of a certain Maureen from the village, she exclaimed suprisingly: "But the worst of it is I simply *hate* tea!"

(F.P.'s Diary)

December 20th, 1962. There is one danger I have to keep watch for in conversation with Julia, and that is anything like a logical argument. This sounds more cramping than it is: there's a world of subjects left,

* We remained at Lambourn, while Lawrence and Jenny were in London, instead of going away.

exploring our way through regions of cobweblike delicacy concerned with human behaviour, books, aesthetics and lots of other things. But if some matter of general principle arises, and I start getting into my arguing boots—boots which I see look more aggressive and combative than they feel to me—a sharp note of fear comes into her voice and she begs for the subject to be changed.

It's probably impossible in this secluded life, so exactly organised by Julia in every material detail, with two prime egotists sitting in the middle of her carefully-constructed nest, for tiny incidents not to bulk large. Amused as I am by them, I come near irritation at times as a result of her obsessional pernicketiness. And I do hope we shan't have 'warmed-up Spam' again. I can hardly swallow it, and was staggered when she offered me some in my sandwich lunch today: "A Spam sandwich might be rather nice?" Might it indeed!! The exact ritual also has to be preserved concerning coffee-pot, stove, the amount of air let into the room and turning off electricity. The coffee, for instance, must be given *exactly* 105 revolutions in the grinder! I have struggled to master these rituals but this morning there came an Aunty-Loo-like cry from the galvanised iron ash-bucket: "AH! we don't ever put paper in the ash-bucket, in case it catches alight." But I really must add that amusement makes up for everything, and that irritation is only a minute seed.

(F.P.'s Diary)

December 26th, 1962. I realise that this is my first English winter for several years, and I had forgotten how the cold *squeezes* in from all sides as if to strangle one's poor little vital spark. I do feel as if Julia and I were serving a prison sentence. For what crime? Or to what end? We hardly live; we subsist. We talk, think and read as much as the pincers of the extreme cold, which fasten on mind as well as body, will allow. Julia has had a letter from Lawrence, thank goodness, in which he sounded "quite homesick".

(F.P.'s Diary)

December 27th, 1962. Claustrophobic, soft and white, the snow is falling steadily. Julia and I have been out for a walk along the slippery lanes, dressed more or less as scarecrows, Julia holding an umbrella only part of which would go up, and wearing an immense mac over a number of coats and jerseys. Twice she fell suddenly full length into the snow, without a sound or cry, looking, indeed, as if she had no desire to get up. She told me that she had awoken this morning with a deep sense of failure in her relation with Lawrence. My heart bleeds for her, and I'm aware that the exacerbation of her nerves is such that anything may grate on them, yet try as I will, it's like walking on a tightrope to avoid some of her corns.

And this evening a cross word shouted up from below suddenly let loose the indignation I am beginning to foster, at being spoken-to twenty times a day as if I were a half-witted kitchenmaid whom Julia was hoping to train but despairing of!

(F.P.'s Diary)

January 2nd, 1963. Snow hysteria. At lunch I said something about the importance of friends being brought home to one by the snow.

Julia: "I have no time for friends in my life."

F.: "If I didn't value friends I should shoot myself."

Julia: "A creative writer with no servant has no time for anything else."

F.: "No servant? What about Mrs. Rose?"

Soon we were away among a lot of creative artists and writers and whether they had friends or not—none but the highest names were mentioned: Henry James, Turgenev, Flaubert and Charlie Chaplin (who only just squeaked in). What a mistake it all was! We are both scared of a Great Blizzard promised us by the wireless, and rather think of trying to get out of Lambourn before it strikes.

(F.P.'s Diary)

March 25th, 1963. On arriving in London after her first three-cornered weekend with Jenny and Lawrence at Lambourn, Julia rang me up and came to see me at tea-time. Her approach to the situation was modest and realistic, and she made not a single criticism of Jenny, while admitting that she would dearly have liked to find fault with her. She is mortified to feel that there is nothing left for her, no role to play in Lawrence's life which Jenny can't do better. What advice could one give her? I said: "You must try not to think in terms of wives, husbands and mistresses. As you're all three highly original and unconventional people, it's as an individual you must think of yourself—as Lawrence's

Julia." "Ah," said Julia, "now I'll tell you a funny thing. I told Lawrence that I felt Jenny was rather like me in some ways, and he said he'd always felt that, too. She even beat me at that. I must say I'm rather at a loss what to centre my life round."

(Julia to F.P.)

August 23rd, 1963. I have to tell you that we are in the middle of an earthquake down here. Yes—it's all over! He wants to marry her. Wants to shake me off in order to do it; and that's quite right and healthy. Everything is in the melting-pot about practical plans, but when we are in London I am to count him *out* of our life at no. 17 Percy Street. For the present, and maybe permanently, when in the country we shall all stay here. He likes this idea. But will she? And will I? And will *he* find it so jolly as he now thinks? (He has been wrong all along the line so far.) This all sounds more embittered than it actually is. Don't worry about my state of mind. I will always send you an S.O.S. if I am sinking, as you so very kindly made me promise to do. Jenny is away in Cornwall, and knows nothing of these definite marriage plans.

A lighter note: When I last visited Aunt Marjorie in her nursing-home she said to me, "Sometimes at nights I feel quite mad. But they don't manage these things well here. The other night I was so confused I thought I was Nelson at the Battle of Trafalgar—in fact, dying. So I rang the bell and the Nurse came and told me always to ring the bell if I felt worried. But if one's Nelson—and dying—how *can* one ring an electric bell?" Julia: "But how was she to know you were Nelson?" Marjorie: "She might at least have *asked*."

[On September 7th my son Burgo died of a totally unexpected heart attack. I went abroad and to stay with various friends, and Julia wrote me many kind letters, posting me with news.]

(Julia to F.P.)

September 25th, 1963. You've been on the go for five days—I meant to write before. It must surely be marvellous weather in the south of Italy. I *do* hope, dearest Frances, you are able to enjoy things out there, dear. I can't tell you what I feel about it all. I most anxiously await news of how you feel, you know. How lovely if it should happen you are cheering up a little bit. One's feelings are inexpressible and I am not going to try and express them.

(F.P.'s Diary)

December 26th, 1963. Lambourn, with Julia, Lawrence and Jenny. In the afternoon the rainclouds dispersed leaving a soft blue sky and quiet sunlight, and Julia and I had a long walk with rolling spaces all around us. Christmas day was mercifully ignored—except for the to-do about cooking yesterday's turkey. It must be roasted à la Gaylord Hauser, *exactly* 23 minutes to the pound, not a minute more or less; therefore it must go on soon after eight. I came down at nine however to find the oven not yet turned on, a mistake having been made in the sum. There followed a complicated scheme by which the egg-boiler was set to go off every quarter of an hour, and shifts were allocated to baste the bird. After quite a lot of this, Mrs. Rose appeared and took over the entire lunch.

So one more Christmas has blown over, almost unnoticed by me. The good manners preserved by the trio in this house are immaculate, but there are storms below the surface. I have started working hard on my translation, with tonic effect. I work in the Oak Room, Jenny sits in the Telly Room, Lawrence is in his studio and Julia upstairs. House Rules, almost Bedalian in character, are that drinks are served in the Telly Room, and conversation can be held there. The Oak Room, as well as my work-room, is for 'the silent reading of good books. Any conversation there disturbs Julia in the room above.' There's no denying there is a comic element in this agonising situation, but I'm rather shocked at my own interest. As the clock strikes ten we all go to bed, not sorry to end the day's tension.

[Julia had been enormously kind to me during my troubles. I very much wanted to do something for her. As she had always spoken of Rome as the city she had long 'idealised' above all others, I invited her to come out there with me. She needed no persuading, but it was not a success—indeed very much the reverse: the fact that she had last been there with Lawrence combined with some rather mysterious neurotic factors dating from her girlhood to bring on an attack of what she described as 'panic fear', and when in its grip everything unfamiliar—

such as the language, the streets, the name of our pensione, the routes of
the buses—all these filled her with acute and distressing bewilderment.
An undated note reveals that "at twenty-five I had been faced with a
really awful attack of panic of the Universe. It took me months, but I
got down to the roots of it and took it apart leaf by leaf." It seems
obvious that this was the 'nervous breakdown' of the winter of 1925,
referred-to on page 104.]

(F.P.'s Diary)

March 5th, 1964. A desperate call from Julia; we spent many hours
talking over the position. There is to be a divorce. To cheer her up I
have persuaded her to come to Italy with me, and written off to book
rooms in Rome. There is considerable fuss about our plans.

J: "I can't go by jet aeroplane."
F: "Why ever not?"
J: "I'm not sure why. Is it because it's too dangerous?"
F: "I've booked us on Alitalia."
J: "What's that? Not one of those charter planes?"
Later she rang up to ask whether we could find out the exact measure-
ment for baggage under the seat.

(F.P.'s Diary)

April 9th, 1964. Rome. Here we are, in a delightful pensione on the
Aventine, found for us by Joan Cochemé.* I lie on my bed, drinking a
swig of aeroplane whiskey and *thinking of Julia.* The journey went
without a hitch, though to catch the one o'clock plane she got up at *6.30*
a.m. I have three resolves; to remember she is desperately unhappy; to
treat her fuss as *farce* (which it is) and try to enjoy it as such; to be as
adaptable as I can. The limpid pure blue sky of Rome greeted us in full
glory, and so did the regal personality of this noble town. The Aventine
is charmingly beautiful and tranquil, with judas trees in flower, drifting
clerics. Julia does appreciate its beauty and its architecture, but I am
beginning to realise she is possessed with fear. What must it be like to be
encompassed by such strange dreads? "Are you sure this is the way?
How do you *know*? Are you sure this is the Corso? Do you remember the
number of our bus? Do you think we shall be poisoned by the water?"

* A friend who was living in the Traventine.

She is terrified of going up in Joan's lift, and would rather walk up five floors; refuses (like a horse) when about to cross the road.

6.20 p.m. I don't know how I could have written so heartlessly about trying to enjoy Julia's eccentricities. They are a great deal more than a joke—a desperate tragedy, which bids fair to sink me too with its leaden weight.

(F.P.'s Diary)

April 11th, 1964. Rome. We spent the morning in the Farnesina, Julia's choice (and no other soul in the place); then on to the island. ("Are you sure this is the *right* island?") Then over lunch in a good, cheap trattoria, poor Julia told me almost in tears that she might have to go home; the impact of Rome was too much for her; she was literally terrified all the time. I told her she must of course go at once if she wanted to, and talking about it seemed to relieve her. But I am worried to death about her. She seems to be in a state of perpetual confusion, and takes no joy in her surroundings whatever.

(F.P.'s Diary)

April 12th, 1964. Rome. This morning Julia is in a mood of valiant realism; she now feels Rome was the best place for her to come. But I cannot sleep for thinking about her; such an apathetic, inturned travelling companion is quite outside my experience. Today being sunny Joan Cochemé invited us to lunch on her terrace above the Tiber.

Julia: "Oh, on the *terrace?*—I don't think I want to sit in the sun. Well, I must think what clothes to put on for the *smuts*—must keep something for best."

I try to get her to say what she'd like to do, because I know anything I suggest will be found fault with. So desperately I bring out guide-books and lay Rome's wares before her. (Today she was 'too weary' to come to the Janiculum with Joan and me.) Selfish feelings well up in me, telling me I need some sort of holiday myself, and this is not much like one.

(F.P.'s Diary)

April 14th, 1964. Rome. Julia has by some sort of conjuring trick pulled herself together. She told me she had lain awake until one o'clock thinking out her problems, and staring into the blackness of her conclusions—that she must face the fact that Lawrence would never go abroad with her again, and that she couldn't rely on him for emotional sustenance. She must make a life for herself; focus it round some purpose or other. F: "When you can get back to it, there's your writing." J: (in a voice of real agony) "It has never been my real purpose in life." But she began yesterday as a new woman, wanted to go sight-seeing, braved St. Peter's, and even took a bus to the Capitol by herself. I'm full of admiration for the strenuous efforts she has made, and magnificently sustained. In her epic wrestling with her devil in the watches of the night she did achieve a real victory. Two nights ago we made our way through the dark streets to the Piazza Navona and dined in a restaurant there. Julia inspected Bernini's fountains from every angle: it's particularly the animals she likes: "Do look at that dear old lion—he's got such a *scholarly* expression."

(F.P.'s Diary)

April 17th, 1964. Rome. Since Julia took the plunge, I have been rejoiced to hear her laugh heartily and with abandon. She has made a stupendous effort and succeeded in quelling or controlling her fears in such a way that I find it hard to believe them deep-rooted. Her passage through life is a triumph of equilibrium, for I think she's well aware of the dark streaks in her character—vanity, and pleasure in censoriousness. Outside the Farnese Palace today a woman was sitting waiting. "Just *look* at her," said Julia. "Did you ever see anything so Kensington and tatty? How CAN she do it?" Her indignation was *moral*. She can't get over the fact that people are different from herself. What's more she thinks they ought not to be.

(F.P.'s Diary)

April 25th, 1964. Awoke early to a fine cold morning, and also to anxious thoughts about Julia. How can I get her to enjoy her last few days, and not feel the whole thing was a big mistake? We have had some very successful sight-seeing and she has asked me dozens of questions about what we look at, and always forgotten the answers the next instant. In fact I'm well aware that to me as a person she has not given a single thought, other than conceiving me as a banister to hold on to. I wish I'd been a better one. Today has passed in perfect serenity and amity, and she almost seemed to have read my thoughts and be making obvious efforts to remember that I too am a human being.

Today we had a good morning at the Thermae, and I suggested Julia choosing what she would like best this afternoon. She "would like to see the Bramante *tempietto* on the Janiculum, but the effort to get there would be too great." The Colosseum and its purlieus were "too like Bournemouth"! We chose three delightful little churches in the 'bulge' of the Tiber.

Our last evening at the Pensione. We shall never again see the old Riccis (who live here), fat little Robertina the spoiled house baby, nor the sallow Pakistani from FAO who has left two wives and eight children behind in his native land. An odd bit of life, like a roll or a sandwich, has come to an end.

(Julia to F.P.)

May 3rd, 1964. Lambourn. I have no doubt that my visit to Rome with you was exactly what I needed, and I do feel I have broken with my old attitude to a marked degree. All this I owe to you; your insistence on my getting away, and your infinite generosity in taking me there and looking after me during the three weeks. There is no way I can show my gratefulness. My 'panic fear' dropped to the ground on my return like a rough wind suddenly dying out and leaving calmness. I am more sorry than I can say that it should have gripped me in Rome, it must have been too harassing and distressing for words for you. Especially my not being able to keep in my head anything you said to me for two seconds, oh dear, oh dear. It was all part of the shock of my private situation.

(F.P.'s Diary)

May 21st, 1964. After two very warm letters Julia invited me to dinner—but it was as if she had been bewitched by some extraordinary spell, and she gave me a quite unexpectedly frosty reception, the note of which was distance and extreme formality. She had even dressed the part and was standing posed at the top of her rickety stairs, with conventional phrases issuing from her lips. If I hadn't felt so taken aback, so ready to burst into tears, the effect would have been absurd; but all my attempts at restoring some kind of human contact were futile, and I have always been a bad actress. The truth is that I simply have no idea what is the explanation, what my crime. I don't think she can really hold me responsible for the 'panic fear' in Rome, and she knows that I understood what a nightmare that was for her.

(F.P.'s Diary)

October 3rd, 1964. A letter from Julia two days ago, as friendly, even affectionate, as though no cloud had passed between us, and yesterday she came to dinner. The trio had spent three weeks together at Lambourn, after which Julia had a fortnight alone in London. She seldom goes to the London Library now, but stays at home 'sorting her notes' and depending more than ever on her 'wonderful purple heart pills' (amphetamines). I can't say I feel at all happy about her.

(Julia to Dorothy, Dowager Countess of Cranbrook*)

November 10th, 1964. Percy Street. It was a great pleasure indeed making your acquaintance. I felt so much at home in your house, if you will forgive my suddenly becoming rather personal. And to go one step further—I have never seen such a beautiful pair of blue eyes in my life as yours, or heard such a nice voice! So now you will consider me very *mauvais style*. And to go even *further* again—amongst other things, your distinguished and electrifying calls for 'Salt! *Salt*! SALT!' down the dinner-table still ring in my ears, bringing a joyful animation to my soul. For goodness' sake don't let Eddie† read this letter. Also forgive me yourself if you can.

(Julia to Anne and Heywood Hill)

November 13th, 1964. Percy Street. Your taking me away with you for last weekend was a tremendously kind thought, and I do assure you that it came at a time when I badly needed lifting by main force out of the pit, and this is just what your intervention did for me *miraculously*. I returned with my morale enormously better, you know. To be in the company of people one truly likes deeply is the best therapy in the world.

(Julia's Diary)

November 20th, 1964. I write letters to Lawrence telling him I much prefer honest loneliness to the artificially cheery friendship he offers me now. But in fact I never post these letters—he hasn't seen them. This is because, after writing them, from somewhere deeper still comes the realisation that I desire to steer clear of all destructive death-instincts

---

* Anne Hill's mother, who lived with her at Snape Priory.
† Gathorne-Hardy, Anne's brother.

and emtombments. I prefer to go on living; in the offered relationship there is still some of the respectable material of reality—*something* of the mysterious and divine machinery of human life—and this I revere and prefer to accept.

(Julia's Diary)

August, 1966. I wrote to Lawrence saying I didn't feel married to him any more, that I wanted to sell Lambourn. We met as usual and drove down there—but I hadn't realised what a stranger I should feel when I got there; the garden I had loved so much and found so thrilling was a dead world. On leaving, Lawrence was kind and assiduous about cleaning my shoes and insisting on picking me flowers.

Since then I have felt all the time a sense of disaster and catastrophe.

(F.P.'s Diary)

October 4th, 1966. Julia told me she had 'touched bottom' soon after I went to Spain, and could only lie on her bed feeling ill. She realised it was partly the 'purple hearts', now up to four or five a day, and has reduced them to one or even none by sheer will-power. "The thing is I was really frightened." Her present modus vivendi is the wildly impractical one of spending more than her entire income on having a typist to dictate to. "I can't write myself any more; yet as I lay on my bed I felt it was the one thing I must do, the one thing of importance before I die."

(F.P.'s Diary)

March 6th, 1967. Lawrence has told Julia that Jenny is having a child, and that he wants a divorce so as to marry her. He is extremely fatherly by nature, I believe. I have had long telephone conversations, and an evening alone here with Julia. With the help of the dreaded 'purple hearts' she is facing the new crisis bravely—but resentfully. It is going to be a very anxious time for all her friends, however. She depends very much on their rallying round, and they do; but she runs through them rather fast. I have been canvassing invitations for her shamelessly. Her comments aren't always enthusiastic. "Are all parents and their children so inharmonious? Do they all look so cross all the time? . . . Of course they had no time or energy to spare for me . . . no conversation, no . . . Well, there was all this washing-up, of course, but I was thankful to have it, as it prevented my brooding . . . Ben Nicolson has asked me to stay in Italy in August, with the Toynbees and Kees. I shall go and stick it out as long as I can, but I dread it really. I simply hate Italy in August." She talked about her writing, and wondered if anyone will ever want to read it. "After all, I'm not Proust, you know. And some of it is so corrected and scrawled over that no typist could read it." My practical suggestions were like planks thrown to a drowning woman— every one rejected, sometimes almost angrily. I felt she didn't really *want* her problems solved, but (as with the drowning woman) I couldn't give up trying.

Chapter Eighteen

LAMENTATIONS

Including Julia's *DOCTOR'S SURGERY* and
THE SUICIDE DRIVE TO KEW

[It is painful to linger over the last ten years of Julia's life, as she declined gradually towards her death in 1978. Her solitary existence in the small Percy Street flat was broken only by weekend visits, mainly to Lawrence and his family, who gave her all the support they could, but were unable to prevent her feeling that she had suffered a third and last rejection. Her outlook became more and more solipsistic; she was indifferent to the sorrows and anxieties of others, and she devoted most of her remaining energy to going over her recollections of the past with patient secretaries who were called-upon to type and re-type them, making tiny alterations.

She still wrote letters and saw friends. With me, her relations grew ever more erratic, and though we met often during most of this time, I might be greeted as a dear friend on Monday and an enemy on Tuesday. It was much the same with her letters, and some contained accusations over which I would like to draw a veil. I am quoting only from one of the last, received when we were both in our seventies.]

(Julia to F.P.)

[Undated] How *delighted* I was, dear girl, to receive your letter. I really felt great joy. I think I have learnt to be a little less touchy and quarrelsome. Let us put that to the test!

[The friend with whom she seems to have been most herself, and who gave her most support at this time was probably Robert Kee.]

(Julia to Robert Kee)

July 21st, 1973. I felt very much happier the next day after our lunch. I *did* unload a lot of bitter stuff about my own troubles on you—I'm sure it was that. Also of course, so nice to have your offer to help in the way of thinking up a psychologist for me, and the general feeling of comrades in distress together.

(Julia to Robert Kee)

October 17th, 1973. Percy Street. It *was* kind of you to invite me down to see you on the very day I was feeling so particularly blue—to have been left all alone that day would have been, I'm sure you realised, something of a nightmare. I think it only right and suitable that I (as an ancient old bag) who is yet quite a *cognoscente* in the male sex through years of looking around at them with considerable interest, and with whom you will know that I am not being 'Personal' to coin a phrase—no!! it's no good! I've lost hold of my sentence and will have to start again. In three words then: I have never seen you looking more *beautiful*, Robert, than you did the other night, and being at the very peak of your powers in every direction a success in everything. So let us strike a bargain: *I* will believe what *you* say in *your* sermons if you will believe what I say in *mine*—namely that the world is now your oyster—order a dozen, turn to and enjoy them. "See you!" as they all seem to say these days; or, even worse: "*Take Care!*"

[Julia's two last sketches give a picture of the nightmare feelings that now sometimes invaded her consciousness.]

DOCTOR'S SURGERY

The man I had been talking to got up and left me alone in the middle of my last sentence; simply got up and walked out of the surgery. I heard him conversing with an assistant in the passage outside the door: "A G.P. in Surgery Hour—especially a busy surgery so close to the Marble Arch—has a lot to put up with." I knew that. Obviously this doctor had not been listening.

Neither had *I* been listening to him.

I had been explaining to him why it was impossible to build my future, and quoting Paul Valéry, whose words seemed to fit the case. I had just been about to embark on a more personal note, if only he had waited. But the doctor on his side had been trying to persuade me to cut down on the anti-depressant pills on his prescriptions. Or 'tablets', as he preferred to call them.

Naturally, I told myself, somewhat hurt by his snub, I wouldn't have tried on this sort of thing in the surgery if I had not had specific instructions from my own doctor to describe my exact psychological state next time I came. My own doctor was interested in what went on in my soul. So today I had intended to tell his partner all.

I waited for several minutes alone in the consulting room; then took the hint—got up from my chair facing the doctor's desk, gathered up my possessions and walked across the passage into the waiting-room again. It was the only way to the street. The waiting-room benches were filled with patients. Suddenly a great fright, the oncoming of panic, attacked me. What if, after leaving me, this new strange doctor had gone straight to the secretary at her desk in the vestibule, and had cancelled my usual dose of anti-depressant pills?

What a fool I had made of myself! I should have cried out: "Doctor! I feel *awful*! Terrible! For God's sake increase my dose," as any ordinary female would do. Instead he had been well and truly crowned with the ideas of Paul Valéry, on top of which I had added some of my own stuff. The man had no doubt concluded that I must at least have gone off my head, and was wondering what sanatorium to send me to. In the crowded waiting-room I caught sight of myself in the looking-glass. I saw a monkey with a haunted expression, wearing a red jacket and cap, obsessionally gripping its parcels and umbrella, nervously overexerting the muscles of arms and stomach, holding everything aloft much too high, as if they were all bombs which might explode if allowed to slip to the floor. The hanging light-bulb shone on my smooth hair cut into a fringe, and on the little-girl style of my jacket. And on the pink and white, young-looking face, which nevertheless clearly showed up the ferociously scored violet circles under the eyes as well as the ugly puffiness beneath, criss-crossed with fine lines, and on the fever-bright, over-wide eyes themselves. I winced away from the mirror. In the doctor's hallway I found the secretary sitting at her fumed oak desk; she delivered over to me the usual quantity of the vital medicine without demur.

So the doctor had evidently decided after all to keep me from going under for a little while longer yet.

In the Edgware Road it was now dark. Six o'clock on a November evening: rush hour. Everybody was streaming towards Marble Arch. I walked fast because of the cold wind, and finally planted myself in the queue for the number 73 bus. Now it was war with the clatter, violence and chaos of the crowded city night. Everyone in the queue was shoving, tottering, brandishing. With all the others I was kept sawing backwards and forwards along the pavement edge and in the gutter. As the differently-numbered buses came swooping alongside, each gobbled up its prey and went roaring off again, leaving whirlpools of disintegration in its wake, and the hard-won pecking order of the moment before totally reversed.

A 73 bus of all things came gliding in to the kerbside. A renewal of life ran through our queue. From the step a female 'clippie' leant out and addressed the surging crowd: "Hoold Tate! Police! Maind har U goo." Then holding out her arm, she commanded "Pearson jars off the bus fast, police! Jahst warn minit police! Hoolt Tate. Fooah. Faif. Six. Syeven then kew!" As I jumped on the step and passed her she cried: "Thets enif then kew! Maind har U goo, hoold tate police," and away we went down Oxford Street, bounce, brake, bounce again.

Three elderly women sitting together took up a conversation they had evidently been engaged on before:

First E.W. "Yes, Annie's *mar*vellous, seventy-five now and going strong! Her hands have gone on her now of course. That was about a year ago. But she keeps going along."

Second E.W. "Well, Tim's the same—simply marvellous, considering. His legs have gone on him of course. His left knee went on him two years ago. Then last year his right foot went on him. He's all right if he's *with* someone. Marvellous really. Considering."

Third E.W. "Yes, well Walter's something of a miracle really! Trouble is he's got this bulge in the Alphabet. His ears have gone on him of course, and it's a bit awkward with this bulge. But *fine* really! Considering."

First E.W. (In a slightly lowered voice) "We had to send Ethel away. Couldn't manage her. Not alone. Much too heavy to lift On and Off. Oh no, couldn't possibly. And Doctor said: 'It's Her or You'. So I had to let her go."

So we whistled round the corner of Oxford Street into the Tottenham Court Road, where we stopped dead and everyone standing was thrown to the floor. I struggled through the tight packed interior to the door and leapt down from the bus to the ground. The night air had an immediate effect on me, for I remember nothing of my journey from 'our' bus stop to my bed on the top floor of Percy Street.

THE SUICIDE DRIVE TO KEW

"As for *Love*," I said to my companion at the wheel as we drove along the motor-way, "the whole thing is a HALLUCINATION—a great bundle of hallucinations, rather."

Robert [Kee] turned his face towards me for a brief second, questioningly. I tried to elucidate. "Both parties are trying so hard to fulfil their own phantasy roles, and also the other person's, that not a single word of truth is ever uttered, from beginning to end."

"Not one single word," Robert agreed heartily.

"Until of course the thing *has* actually ended," I added; "when all the truths that have been kept dammed up for so long come pouring out together."

"Yes," he said, "when it's too late."

"Perfectly."

An hour earlier on that same Sunday afternoon, I had been seized by an overpowering impulse to throw myself out of my top floor window at the back of the building, which looks out on a courtyard, so there would have been no danger of my landing on another human being. I hoped I would in this one smashing fall blot out my life and the world together.

Of all the suicide impulses I have been seized by (and for the last few years they have seldom been far from my mind) the one I had experienced that particular Sunday afternoon, as I stood alone in my flat listening to the silent emptiness of London, seemed more urgently pressing, a nearer presence than I had ever felt before. If I were to try to stave it off I must act at once and speedily, for my sense of desperation was such that I could not endure it for even another hour in my flat alone.

Robert is remarkably quick and deft at catching the feelings and ideas one so fumblingly throws at him. So quick in the uptake was he that he finished some of my sentences for me. Perhaps he happened to have the same reactions himself in the course of his life. It is the very heart of comforting companionship to make one find one's perceptions shared.

"What is the nature of these mysterious and oppressive laws, working away merrily inside and out, that solder one to the very substance of the Universe?" I asked. It was at this moment that I brought up the subject of love-affairs and hallucinations.

When we arrived at his house at Kew, Robert parked the car and opened the front gate for me. I immediately spied the children's kitten, standing in the long grasses in the windy May sunshine. It was a miniature cat—unbelievably tiny, with a miniature face, miniature nose, wide open staring eyes, the whole framed in a sickle-shaped spray of miniature whiskers. It was watching the Sunday crowds sweeping past the gate on their way to or from Kew Gardens.

"It's only just got to know 'out-of-doors' and can't decide what to make of it," Robert said.

"Well, what a surprise," I said, as we stood looking down at the kitten. "One moment we are talking about the foulness of the world and its inhabitants, and the next we catch sight of something like *this*, and immediately one's mood changes."

"Innocence," pronounced Robert, instantly putting his finger on the quality that had attracted us in the kitten. I nodded. I looked down at the spotlessly-groomed whiteness of the fluffy chest, and the tiny ignorant face peering inquisitively over the tops of the grasses.

I said, "Very young creatures have had no time to realise what a vile place they have been landed in, and where they must live out the rest of their lives."

[Among Julia's papers I found a tall grey notebook labelled LA-MENTATIONS, containing odd notes and diary entries, mostly dateless and often illegible, written during her sad last years. The need to express herself in writing was still strong, but there is little to be gained by dwelling on this melancholy coda, in which the sound of her voice is muffled and monotonous.

I have therefore extracted from many pages a few notes that show
flashes of her individual way of thought—her sharp mind and searing
wit, the flavour she gave even to sadness.]

There can be no separation of oneself from the rest of the whirlwind
universe—it has control of one's puppet strings and is engaged in
shaking them violently. Though I can still remember my former
wholeness of mind, I shrink from thinking of it, for now the world (for
me) has broken up into hundreds of unconnected fragments, and I feel
too alienated to fit them together, as before I rejoiced in trying to do. I
am left in a desert of unrecognizable pieces, like the newspaper photo of
the child sitting in the aftermath of the Japanese earthquake.

My link with life was Lawrence. Now this link is broken. I can't look
for more than a startled, horrified second at what was in fact my life. I
can think of the coffee I'm going to make and then drink. But I can't let
myself 'think' of anything with large connections attached. So I can't
write stories any more, or use my brain to put two and two together.
Lawrence suggests that it is not necessary to be a slave—to accept one's
surroundings as a basis for art. My answer is 'Not so.' I still believe that
though it is nightmarish, cruel and wicked, the cosmos is richer and
more interesting than any wishful thinking created by man, and that
though he may be able to exist in the company of Cézanne and
Masaccio, I have to think and talk about real life and real people.

*

Not until marriage with Lawrence did I have any escape or rest from
the sense of loss, of Chaos, which stayed with me all through my life.
What was it about Lawrence that I found so particularly sympathetic?
His seriousness in working, and thinking about art. His imagination,
which has wings—his obsession with the Artist's parallels and symbols
—hence his psychological interpretation of an artist's world.

*

Why has the story of Orpheus and Eurydice always had such a special
meaning for me? I was four years old and sitting on my father's knee
when I first heard how Orpheus journeyed down to the underworld,
and—with Pluto's permission—endeavoured to bring back Eurydice

and restore her as his companion and lover. I was immediately and profoundly smitten by it. I cannot understand by what mechanism, when only four and completely innocent of life, I at once comprehended this notion of a secret underworld, where life that was strangely and magically different from our daylight life went on; it instantly struck an answering chord in me, even though only as a three-week-old kitten finds its eyes opening to revelations partly known.

After the break-up of my marriage to Tommy, Lawrence was the only companion I ever had with whom I could share all my experience of this hidden, deeper world. He was the first who made the crowded, prosaic life of surface happenings acceptable to me, by sharing also what I think of as Pluto's underworld—that profound region of basic truth and poetry which underlies our normal 'public' activities.

For the first time in my long life I am experiencing the sensation that although not being physically dead, I am in fact a corpse in the sense that my former life—the only life I know—is OVER.

*

It is chiefly for me the body's various sensations as it goes through the daily round that trigger off the sudden, unexpected turning of the keys in the lock inside the brain, where memories are stored. Shelf upon shelf of small memories.

I am always amazed, *dumbfounded* I may truly say, at the instant transformation I undergo when I smell certain kinds of freshness and the fragrance of outdoor air. If a puff of it enters my small London window into my stuffy sitting-room, my personality changes, and I am the person who was experiencing that same smell with the downs ahead of me, the tangled hedgerows each side of my heavily-tramping gumboots, as I slither down the country lane.

*

Sunshine streams through the window curtains. After the long weeks of sitting still all day in the London Library and then again alone in my sitting-room, drinking first a double whiskey, then glass after glass of wine, to dull my consciousness of being alive and tortured—yet nine-tenths of my being passionately longs to get out and feel the sun on my face. Instead I take a lot of extra purple hearts, and sit alone on my bed, trying to forget the world which I loathe so much. These spasms of suicidal desolation occur all day long at intervals, and very suddenly, like missing one's step on a staircase.

*

I feel as I did at four years old, when an Indian conjuror held out to me a charming, plump, twittering baby sparrow, and then—as he put it into my eagerly outstretched hand—to my intense horror I saw a cherry-stone drop out from between my fingers. I wept in bewilderment and sense of betrayal. I think the incident is a symbol of life, and I have thought of calling my story *The Conjuror's Sparrow.*

*

Lying in bed after Asian flu, feeling too ill to be enthusiastic about anything. There is no hope for me anywhere, this I know. My fear is that I shall lose the only interest I still have in staying alive—namely the desire to get some of my past life materialised in my writing. But my memories—even the most vital and precious—seem to be fading also, like the daylight.

[To further this aim of Julia's, and at the same time show her quality as a writer and a human being, has been the purpose of this book.]

INDEX

INDEX